D1565452

Homelessness in America

Books in the **Contemporary World Issues** series address vital issues in today's society such as genetic engineering, pollution, and biodiversity. Written by professional writers, scholars, and nonacademic experts, these books are authoritative, clearly written, up-to-date, and objective. They provide a good starting point for research by high school and college students, scholars, and general readers as well as by legislators, businesspeople, activists, and others.

Each book, carefully organized and easy to use, contains an overview of the subject, a detailed chronology, biographical sketches, facts and data and/or documents and other primary source material, a forum of authoritative perspective essays, annotated lists of print and nonprint resources, and an index.

Readers of books in the Contemporary World Issues series will find the information they need in order to have a better understanding of the social, political, environmental, and economic issues facing the world today.

Homelessness in America

A REFERENCE HANDBOOK

Michele Wakin

ABC-CLIO®

An Imprint of ABC-CLIO, LLC
Santa Barbara, California • Denver, Colorado

Copyright © 2022 by ABC-CLIO, LLC

All rights reserved. No part of this publication may be reproduced, stored in a retrieval system, or transmitted, in any form or by any means, electronic, mechanical, photocopying, recording, or otherwise, except for the inclusion of brief quotations in a review, without prior permission in writing from the publisher.

Library of Congress Cataloging-in-Publication Data
Names: Wakin, Michele, author.
Title: Homelessness in America: a reference handbook / Michele Wakin.
Description: Santa Barbara, California: ABC-CLIO, [2022] |
Series: Contemporary world issues | Includes bibliographical references and index.
Identifiers: LCCN 2021040475 (print) | LCCN 2021040476 (ebook) | ISBN 9781440874857 (hardcover ; alk. paper) | ISBN 9781440874864 (ebook)
Subjects: LCSH: Homelessness—United States—History.
Classification: LCC HV4504 .W3244 2022 (print) | LCC HV4504 (ebook) | DDC 362.8/920973—dc23
LC record available at https://lccn.loc.gov/2021040475
LC ebook record available at https://lccn.loc.gov/2021040476

ISBN: 978-1-4408-7485-7 (print)
      978-1-4408-7486-4 (ebook)

26 25 24 23 22   1 2 3 4 5

This book is also available as an eBook.

ABC-CLIO
An Imprint of ABC-CLIO, LLC

ABC-CLIO, LLC
147 Castilian Drive
Santa Barbara, California 93117
www.abc-clio.com

This book is printed on acid-free paper ∞

Manufactured in the United States of America

Mom and Dad—This one is for you!

Bridgewater Scholars: Sefora Alcindor, Nelly Enongenepie Mbulle, Lorenz Marcellus, Rubie Marcellus, Anne Maxime, Nayara Semedo, Cincere Tarkpor, and Zachary Wright.

Thank you for being a source of grace and inspiration.

Homelessness in the United States is surprising because it is a country of great wealth. It is also surprising because the United States is viewed as a land of opportunity. When people are homeless, we don't often question how our society and economy have failed them. Instead, we wonder what is wrong with homeless people themselves. The American Dream is based on the idea that anyone can become rich and successful with enough hard work and dedication. Perhaps this leads us to think that homeless people are not working hard enough or that they are not dedicated enough. Systemic racism and cyclical poverty show us that this is not the case. Ongoing structural barriers prevent equal access to housing, education, and employment, excluding people from these basic resources and then blaming them for their own poverty and homelessness.

This book examines individual and societal risk factors that make people vulnerable to homelessness and poverty. It documents the nation's effort to understand and serve a growing, diverse population. It also shows that throughout the nation's history, access to housing is structured by race as a social category. This means that unequal access to housing has left people of color, and African Americans in particular, overrepresented in marginal, urban spaces and within the homeless population. As sociologists and race theorists point out, urban neighborhoods bereft of opportunity also become targets for law enforcement. This targeting is another shocking feature of U.S. society, world leader in class and race-based policing and incarceration.

In addition to housing, exploring access to education and employment shows that these resources are also identity based. Women and people of color have always been paid less in the U.S. labor market, excluded from training and educational opportunities, and shut out of certain professions entirely. Research shows that discrimination is not based on performance or ability but on stereotypical ideas of capability. Over time, being unable to accumulate wealth affects generations, not merely individuals. This means that it takes at least twice as long to purchase a home and to afford an education or quality health care, depending on who you are. Single mothers, for example, must work four times as hard at low-wage jobs to afford basic needs goods for their children. When they seek welfare assistance, they face strict eligibility rules, racism, time limits, and a punitive approach to poverty. Increasingly, welfare assistance and emergency services offer only temporary relief from homelessness and a life trapped in underfunded schools, low-wage employment, and substandard housing.

The effects of experiencing homelessness are traumatic for both adults and children. Children who experience chronic homelessness often face instability later in life. Even mere housing insecurity can have detrimental effects. The toll that homelessness takes on children affects their personal, social, and academic development, putting them further behind their housed peers. In addition, unaccompanied homeless youth are a growing portion of those experiencing homelessness. Factors that lead to youth homelessness include LGBTQ status, criminal justice involvement, foster care, physical and sexual abuse, and mental health and substance use issues. All of these are risk factors that can precipitate homelessness, lead to trauma, and make exit more difficult.

Understanding homelessness means seeing it as the dehumanizing experience that it is. It means examining the policies that created and perpetuate it. It means critiquing federal policies while pointing out the importance of supporting the national push to end homelessness by providing affordable, basic housing. This book examines homelessness among specific social categories including race, gender, and youth. It also examines individual risk factors like disability and mental illness. While some identity- and risk-based approaches to homelessness have been successful, this book focuses most importantly on overall homelessness as the experience of poverty, lack of housing, and frequently trauma. These are not seen as identity-based issues but human and civil rights issues. They apply to the entire U.S. population and not only those experiencing homelessness.

The first chapter of this book examines homelessness in the United States, using three crisis points: the Great Depression, the 1980s, and the Great Recession of 2007–2009. It examines how these crisis points lead to new ideas, approaches, funding, and legislation for homeless people. Crisis points are times of economic or social upheaval, during which housing and homeless policy take center stage. This chapter focuses on how the nation understands poverty and homelessness during these crisis points. It examines early efforts to count and track the homeless population and specific subpopulations. As the nation inevitably continues to face crises associated with advanced inequality, considering approaches that end homelessness permanently is of particular interest.

The second chapter examines three current problems and controversies about homelessness in the United States. The first is criminalization as a strategy for removing homeless people from public places or punishing their appearance or behavior. It examines the risks that criminalization poses for people who are unsheltered and potential violations of their constitutional rights. The second issue this chapter examines is housing. It offers a comprehensive overview of subsidized and homeless housing in the United States and weighs the risks and benefits of each type. It also examines the controversial use of motels as housing for homeless people. The third controversy this chapter examines is the change in welfare policy from AFDC to TANF, twenty-five years after its revision. This chapter evaluates whether or not this change was successful in reducing poverty and homelessness. Finally, because of the recent COVID-19 pandemic, this chapter briefly explores emergency housing for homeless people developed in response to this crisis.

Following current controversies, Chapter 3 offers perspectives from experts in the field of homelessness. It begins by examining education among homeless children and youth. It focuses on access to K–12 and higher education as well as the unique barriers and challenges that homeless students face. This chapter also focuses on the overlapping issues of legality, urban space, and criminalization. It examines how the flavor or character of urban space can inform policies that marginalize homeless people and how legal protections and provisions can be used to safeguard their rights. The third issue this chapter focuses on is the provision of housing. It describes the Housing First approach as an alternative to the ladder-like model of service provision, which emphasizes behavioral compliance as a condition of service. Finally, this chapter explores unique housing solutions developed during the COVID-19 pandemic and examines how local communities marshal federal support to save lives.

Chapter 4 offers profiles of government organizations that serve homeless people. These are ordered according to importance and scope, with those serving the overall population first and subpopulations second. This chapter examines the history and function of each organization. It reviews the central focus areas and publications for each and outlines future directions. In addition to government organizations, this chapter provides a summary of national, nonpartisan, and nonprofit organizations. These are included as they offer research and innovative approaches and ideas that have influenced homeless services and federal policy for generations. Finally, this chapter includes individual profiles of people centrally involved in developing research and policy to reduce and end homelessness.

Chapter 5 offers a review of the data and documents central to understanding homelessness in the United States today. It examines the current point-in-time count of homeless people as reported in the Annual Homeless Assessment Report (AHAR) to Congress. It documents important changes in the homeless population over time as well as changes in the provision of shelter and housing. It also offers an overview of the communities with the greatest numbers of homeless people. Following the AHAR, this chapter includes a summary of the most recent federal plan to end homelessness. This plan represents a departure from previous plans and is important to examine, as it charts the nation's current course toward ending homelessness and outlines funding and policy priorities. Other reports by national advocacy organizations examine housing affordability rates, the rising criminalization of homeless people, and federal provisions under the recent COVID-19 pandemic.

The resources provided in Chapter 6 offer avenues for further research. This chapter is organized to correspond with the crisis points discussed in the first chapter and throughout the book. Thematically, these sources offer an overview of hobo and tramp life in the early 1900s. Following this, the 1980s sources track the emergence of homelessness as a new social problem. While homelessness was definitely not a new problem, the characteristics and causes of homelessness in the 1980s seemed a departure from earlier decades. The references included in this section examine the unique features of 1980s homelessness. The third time period this chapter details is homelessness after 2000, with a focus on 2007–2009. This section examines the risk factors and policy solutions used to address the nation's homeless crisis. To compliment information in earlier chapters, a list of government and policy websites is included for further research.

Chapter 7 offers a chronology of important events in homeless history. It corresponds roughly with the crisis points outlined in the first chapter and focuses on legislation that upholds the rights and provisions of people experiencing homelessness and poverty. The glossary that follows offers a guide to the many acronyms and terms used to discuss homelessness.

Many of these are insider's terms, familiar to the advocacy and research worlds, but needing further explanation for readers.

Writing this book during the COVID-19 pandemic has been challenging. This public health crisis has caused the nation to rethink its approach to homelessness. This is particularly true in areas with high concentrations of homeless people. Emergency assistance in these areas, bolstered by federal and state support, has shown that it is possible to develop new and innovative housing solutions. It also shows that crisis points are catalysts for rethinking shelter and service provision and resource allocation. Yet, given the emergency nature of crisis points, long-term housing solutions often take a back seat to more immediate concerns, in this case isolation over congregate shelter.

In our nation's recent history, the arguments that have worked to support permanent housing for people experiencing homelessness are (1) that it saves money and (2) that homelessness presents a public health risk. This does not demonstrate the will to end homelessness but to protect "us" from "them." Underlying this book is the question of what it will take to create the will and way to end homelessness and to understand us as them.

Homelessness in America

Homelessness and poverty are shocking yet constant features of U.S. society. They are shocking because the United States is a wealthy nation, yet its rates of poverty and homelessness exceed many countries that are far less affluent. They are constant because, in some form, poverty and homelessness have been part of the nation's fabric since its very beginning. This chapter examines homelessness in the United States during three main crisis points: the Great Depression in the 1930s, the rise of "new" homelessness in the 1980s, and the Great Recession of 2007–2009. Solutions to homelessness that emerge during these crisis points illustrate the nation's struggle to assist an ever-changing and growing population.

How the United States understands homelessness affects its service and housing solutions. Populations seen as sympathetic or deserving can receive greater funding and better and more tailored services. Those seen as flawed because of personal weaknesses or failures often face punitive rules and restrictions and low-cost, temporary assistance. Each of the crisis points included in this chapter offers a summary of the causes of homelessness during that era and federal policy solutions. The latter typically begin by establishing a definition and estimating the size and demographics of the population. The size and

---

A migrant laborer travels through Napa Valley, California, in 1938, during the waning years of the Great Depression. This national crisis dramatically increased the population of hobos riding the rails in search of work. (Dorothea Lange/Library of Congress)

diversity of people experiencing homelessness in the United States make these efforts challenging. As a result, the focus is often on specific subpopulations, localities, or programs of interest. This strategy alleviates the burden of designing solutions that fit multiple, complex needs or that are too big or too expensive to implement.

It is also the case that addressing the underlying causes of homelessness, like a lack of affordable housing or an inaccessible job market, are seen as federal-level concerns, which everyday Americans are increasingly less able to influence (Miller 2018). Federal legislation to address homelessness and its root causes has most often emerged during times of crisis. While laws and policies designed to combat poverty date back to the Great Depression, the first legislation specifically focusing on homelessness was not passed until the 1980s, and an annual count of the homeless population in America only began in 2005. As a result, the nation is still in the early stages of providing an accurate count and offering long-term solutions. Even service providers and advocates, usually first in line to fight for the rights of homeless people, must often prioritize immediate, emergency needs over structural solutions. Some population-specific approaches, like ending veteran homelessness, have shown great success. Yet, these are always limited in scope, because even if homelessness is ended for one segment of the population, another always springs up in its place.

This chapter explores how crisis points stimulate emergency solutions—but often at the expense of more coordinated, long-term planning. Of course, in all of the crisis points described, innovative efforts to assist homeless people emerge and endure. Some of these focus on specific populations, and others change the way we think about homeless housing and other forms of assistance. Over time, the least controversial federal proposals to reduce homelessness and poverty are those that the entire population is entitled to, like Social Security, or those that serve populations viewed as sympathetic or deserving. The most contested solutions are those that earmark federal funding for populations seen as "dishonest," "lazy," or "flawed," like welfare. This fundamental split between "deserving" and "undeserving" Americans is part of what determines who gets assistance, how much they get, and what they must do to get it. As this book demonstrates, the nation's approach to homelessness reflects its prevailing concepts of community, social responsibility, and inclusion. How the United States understands and manages its most vulnerable populations is, after all, an important test of its national character.

This book understands homelessness through a sociological lens. It examines how historical and structural forces combine with individual circumstances to shape the experience of homelessness. It also acknowledges that access to opportunity in U.S. society is fundamentally structured by race, class, and gender, among other social categories. Over time, the uneven distribution of opportunity along these lines creates and perpetuates social inequality. This means that women, people of color, and poor people all face greater challenges when it comes to accessing affordable housing, quality education, living-wage employment, and accumulating enough wealth to weather crisis points. How people are perceived in society and where they live also impact their self-esteem and their ability, confidence, and readiness to enter or re-enter the mainstream.

For these reasons, examining how overlapping forms of inequality persist and deepen over time is an important part of understanding U.S. homelessness. Sociologists document how immigrants, racial minorities, women, and other groups experience forms of workplace discrimination that have nothing to do with their intelligence or work ethic but are informed by stereotypes that limit opportunity (Bertrand and Mullainathan 2011; Pager 2011). These limitations also exist in the housing market, where systemic racism and inequality keep low-income urban communities of color trapped in a cycle of poverty. For these populations, higher education—the main pathway to a well-paying job—either is inaccessible from the beginning or offers staggering debt as a prerequisite (Goldrick-Rab 2016).

These growing structural inequalities inform the size and composition of the population experiencing homelessness and affect their chances for exit. They also inform the nation's cultural and political response to providing housing, education, employment, health care, and welfare assistance.

Overview of Crisis Points

Formerly known as hobos, bums, tramps, and "knights of the road," homeless people have been a part of American society since its beginning, but only during certain points do they become a national focus. It is during these crisis points that our ideas about poverty and homelessness are tested and the nation struggles to establish definitions, identify causes and effects, and set social policy to offer solutions. Crisis points are times when our nation experiences an increase in various kinds of homelessness and poverty that raise questions about our national character.

This chapter examines the economic, social, and political trends that characterized and drove the rise of homelessness during the Great Depression, the 1980s, and the Great Recession of 2007–2009. These crisis points address two basic questions that inform solutions to end homelessness: (1) Is homelessness viewed as a result of individual actions, structural forces, or a combination of the two? and (2) Are we as a nation adequately addressing both systemic inequality and individual risk factors through social policy?

Income and wealth, housing, employment, and education are structural forces that affect overall life chances and access to opportunity. While these structural forces are larger than individual characteristics, the two always intersect, so it is difficult to tell which comes first. The loss of a job or welfare benefits can cause homelessness and can lead to addiction and depression—two negative consequences that can themselves also cause joblessness and eventually homelessness. Women and people of color have always been at a societal disadvantage when it comes to accumulating wealth. This means that they have a more difficult time weathering economic crises. Although larger patterns of inequality in U.S. society contribute to the makeup of the poor and homeless population, individual factors are often used to justify restrictive policies and decreased social welfare spending (Center for Social Innovation 2018).

This exploration of crisis points examines the role of the government, big business, and public opinion in defining homelessness and setting social policy to direct its future course. It details the development of service and shelter organizations and the rise of social movement activities offering solutions to the crisis. It also examines their successes, failures, and ongoing challenges. Homelessness in each era is understood in the context of poverty, inequality, housing, home ownership, and identity.

What home means to us, as a society, has changed from the early 1930s, when it was associated with family, community, and stability, to the 1980s, when a greater percentage of people rented rather than owned, lived in sprawling metropolitan population centers, and were less likely to know their neighbors. By the 1980s, alleged domestic threats, including an epidemic of illegal drug use, overshadowed the fight for social equity in housing and other areas of American life, and street homelessness became commonplace in cities across the nation. By the time of the Great Recession in 2007–2009, the face of poverty and inequality had changed again. In this era, predatory lending led to an increase in family homelessness, particularly for nonwhite families, and a further push into cyclical poverty. This discussion of crisis points will examine evolving efforts to assist the homeless population, depending on how they are defined, characterized, and prioritized during each era.

Crisis Point #1: The Great Depression

Prior to 1929, income inequality was at its highest point in the nation's history, with the richest top 0.1 percent of the people controlling 25 percent of the nation's total household wealth (Zucman 2019). The decade known as the "roaring twenties" saw technological innovation, the rise of consumerism, increased leisure time, and urbanization. The economy thrived, a reflection of the feelings of hope, progress, and excitement that ran through many communities in the post–World War I era. Accessing living-wage employment and aspiring to a settled life of family and home ownership were within reach of the average, blue-collar worker. Propelled by a sense of hope for the future, people invested in the stock market and deposited their savings in banks across the country. With the onset of the Great Depression, however, banks closed and the stock market crashed, wiping out one quarter of all national wealth and billions in savings. Millions of people plunged into poverty, and they blamed the greed of Wall Street for their plight. The most resounding critique was about the irony of overabundance in the midst of abject poverty.

While the public blamed big business, Republican president Herbert Hoover (who served from 1929 to 1933) insisted that there was no crisis. In a November 1929 speech, just weeks after the stock market crash that tipped the nation into economic decline, he insisted that its effects were isolated and that the economy remained sound. He sought to "disabuse the public mind of the notion that there has been any serious or vital interruption in our economic system" (Hoover 1929). In Hoover's estimation, people's fears about the future were unjustified and the economy would right itself in due time. He sang the tune of Irving Berlin's "Let's Have Another Cup of Coffee," comparing the economic crisis to a passing storm. At the same time, shanty towns of recently unemployed individuals and families known as "Hoovervilles" began to proliferate on the outskirts of cities nationwide. The increased number, size, and visibility of these encampments became a grim rebuke to Hoover's assertion that all was well (Gravelle 2015).

In addition to Hoovervilles and rising unemployment, the stock market crash set off a prolonged period of corporate failures and industry struggles. The precipitant losses were staggering. As McElvaine illustrates, "From the top of prosperity in 1929 to the bottom of depression in 1933, GNP [Gross National Product] dropped by a total of 29 percent, consumption expenditures by 18 percent, construction by 78 percent, and investment by an incredible 98 percent. Unemployment rose from 3.2 to 24.9 percent" (1984, 75). In the housing market alone, in 1932, a quarter of a million families lost their homes. In the first half of 1933, foreclosures reached over 1,000 homes per day, and 40 percent of the nation's home mortgages were in default (Leuchtenburg 1963, 53, 218).

Contributing factors that led to this crisis included income inequality, corporate corruption, an unstable banking structure, declines in U.S. exports, and an overall lack of economic intelligence (Galbraith 1954, 181). More than literal homelessness, this tumultuousness led to widespread poverty and a mounting sense of panic. Losses disproportionately affected the middle class, who allied themselves with the needs and concerns of the poor over big business.

Americans in the 1930s were not yet in the full embrace of the consumerism that would take hold by the 1980s and advance up to the Great Recession. Instead, greed itself was blamed for the crisis, and many people expressed fear about its grip on the American people. Instead of ushering in a wave of new spending, the rapid change and instability that characterized the Depression caused a beleaguered public to close their wallets and withdraw their savings. This "run" on banks, however, triggered thousands of bank failures, as people withdrew their money from banks that did not belong to the Federal Reserve System and were thus unable to fund withdrawals on such a scale. As a result, 9,000 banks failed in the 1930s, causing 9 million people to lose their savings (Egan 2006, 77), and the losses continued.

Many Americans protested these conditions, wrote to the government, and felt entitled to some answers. In 1932, a group of veterans organized a Bonus March on the capital to demand early pension payments due in 1945. The march was symbolic of the frustration and desperation that pervaded the country. It was also a reminder of the government's responsibility to provide for its veterans. The leaders of the Bonus March and their supporters, which popular sources estimated at over 40,000, eventually set up camp on the White House lawn, drawing national attention to this larger, more threatening Hooverville. The intention of this protest was, in part, to soil the nation's image by creating a visible symbol of poverty and need among its servicemen. Instead of paying the bonuses early, Hoover reacted to this makeshift tent city by calling in the U.S. military in July 1932. The subsequent violent, forcible removal of the protestors shocked many people and cost Hoover needed supporters.

In addition to visible symbols of poverty and unrest in urban environments, the 1930s brought an agricultural catastrophe that affected farms throughout the Great Plains and was particularly devastating in Kansas, Oklahoma, and northern Texas. Originally, the Homesteading Act of 1862 encouraged farmers, ranchers, and other settlers to populate these areas. It offered land for those willing to settle in parts of the country that were not yet developed, including the Great Plains area that in the 1930s would come to be known by another name—the Dust Bowl. Despite its rugged terrain and unpredictable climate, the homesteading impulse was strong—and given further momentum by predatory lenders eager to sell "the last frontier" of American agriculture (Egan 2006). To do so, they glossed over any challenges or dangers that might exist, including periodic, seasonal droughts, and in this sense at least partially caused the eventual crisis.

Homesteading was difficult, but it seemed the price of wheat would rise indefinitely, as it did so precipitously during the 1920s. With such plenty and the promise that it would be ever-increasing, farmers continued to plow, loosening the soil that held together millions of acres of native grasslands. Prior to this massive destruction, grasslands covered 21 percent of the United States and Canada and comprised "the largest single ecosystem on the continent outside the boreal forest" (Egan 2006, 19). Years of overplanting, combined with the postwar revival of agriculture in Europe, produced so much excess wheat that prices fell dramatically. Instead of rotating crops or letting the land rest and replenish, farmers responded to falling prices by plundering the grasslands even more furiously, ripping up the natural carpet of grass in a profit-driven feeding frenzy. These practices, combined with the onset of years of prolonged drought, produced the worst dust storms in U.S. history.

Without native grasses to hold the soil in place, massive storms blacked out the sky with frightening regularity, giving the entire decade the nickname, "the Dirty Thirties." The severity and duration of these storms were unprecedented. Journalist Timothy Egan described one such dust storm as "a cloud ten thousand feet high from ground to top . . . people close to it described a feeling of being in a blizzard—a black blizzard, they called it—with an edge like steel wool" (2006, 113). Many people felt that the storms were payback for conquering the land and its native people, and the arrival of new and distressing illnesses appeared to corroborate this theory. Choked by the dust that found its way into every home, people suffered from maladies including "dust pneumonia," which affected livestock as well. Dust, depleted soil, and continued lack of rain also made it impossible to grow crops, and many farmers packed up and moved west, as popularized in the literature of the time (Steinbeck 1939). During this period, the linkages among poverty and unstable living conditions, heightened health risks, and a threadbare social safety net became ever clearer. This instability became a regular feature of urban and rural environments, affecting families as well as individuals.

While hobos had been riding the rails since the turn of the century, many new Depression-era singles and families who had lost their livelihoods and homes in the Dust Bowl joined them on the nation's railroads and highways. Like the veterans who had joined the Bonus Army, people were searching for the promise of something—a payout, a chance to settle, to establish roots, to make a home. Many of them were destitute, victims of empty promises, shortsighted farming practices, failed policies, and bad luck. Some managed to survive the Dust Bowl without having to abandon their farms and dreams, but years of poverty and dust storms nonetheless forced a mass exodus from the Dust Bowl states.

The government intervened in the late 1930s, in an attempt to reseed the soil and make the land livable again. But the regulation of agricultural products and prices remained unstable, as there was too much of one thing and not enough of another. Overproduction, in the case of livestock or crops, was feared because it would ultimately lower prices, so the government sponsored crop burnings and cattle killings to offset the effects of the surplus (Egan 2006). Many people condemned this practice, as it symbolized the irony of pursuing programs to cut overabundance and waste at a time when America was facing widespread hunger and housing uncertainty. The calamities that occurred in the 1930s—bank closings, the stock market crash, unemployment, and the Dust Bowl—left a widespread feeling of instability, that poverty "could happen to anyone" and that it might never end.

The most visible symbols of hunger, homelessness, and poverty during the Great Depression reflected the new urban rural split that characterized the United States in this era. It was the first time in the nation's history that the urban population surpassed the rural. Soup kitchens and bread lines were common. The urban legend of stockbrokers leaping to their deaths on Wall Street symbolized the sudden, shocking loss of corporate wealth. At the same time, there was an ever-increasing tide of immigrants and people needing assistance in urban centers. Their struggles bore many similarities to those of migrant mothers and emaciated farm families, all of their worldly belongings packed on top of old trucks and automobiles as they wandered America's roadways in search of shelter and work (Lange and

Taylor 1939). The pervasive images of poverty in this era show the importance of visibility in signaling a crisis. During the Great Depression, unemployment, poverty, and homelessness are so widespread as to be disassociated from a specific group of people or geographic area. They are seen instead as problems caused by government policies, and thus the responsibility of government to address.

The New Deal and the Common Man

Franklin Delano Roosevelt was elected president in 1933, after overcoming an unusual, crippling case of polio at age 39. He was popular in part because he understood the underlying fear that permeated the mood of the American public—fear about where the next meal was coming from, fear that they would never be able to count on steady employment, and fear that the nation was going perpetually in the wrong direction. Rather than dismiss or allay the public's fear, Roosevelt confronted it head on, telling people in his inaugural address that "the only thing we have to fear is fear itself . . . which paralyzes needed efforts to convert retreat into advance" (Roosevelt 1933). This sense of advancement would be used to justify policies to restore a sense of community and to fight poverty. In the same address, Roosevelt decried "the rules of a generation of self-seekers" and suggested a return to "social values more noble than mere monetary profit." He understood the government's role as speaking to and for those at the bottom of the economic pyramid and fighting for equality over consumerism.

Part of the appeal that characterized Roosevelt's presidency was the feeling of mobility and hope he inspired. Millions of Americans took comfort in his expressions of confidence that he could reinvigorate the economy and get the battered nation back on track. Roosevelt also infused a sense of morality and community values into economic practices, criticizing the "money changers" for playing fast and loose with the nation's prosperity. His view, which was controversial at the time, was that the government was responsible for policies that led to poverty and that it was the responsibility of the government to ensure a basic standard of living for all citizens and to lift those at the bottom out of poverty.

Arguing for greater centralization and control of economic practices, Roosevelt inspired confidence that the government could succeed where the free market had failed (Bordo et al. 1998). The far-ranging programs developed under his administration showed a penchant for building infrastructure and fostering community values and faith in government. Part of Roosevelt's appeal was also his personal charm and the "fireside chats"—regular national radio broadcasts—that brought him into living rooms across the nation. These intimate messages gained people's trust and justified major changes in the nation's social insurance, welfare, labor, and economic policies. These changes would affect the percentage of people who remained in poverty and establish a minimum standard for the provision and distribution of government resources.

After being elected president an unprecedented four times and serving twelve years in office, Roosevelt's implementation of the New Deal has two distinct phases. During his first term, signature programs rolled out by the Roosevelt administration included the Works Progress Administration (WPA), the Wagner Act, the Social Security Act, the Federal Emergency Relief Administration (FERA), the Agricultural Adjustment Act (AAA), and the National Industrial Recovery Act (NIRA). These federal programs made an explicit commitment to putting people back to work and saving them the shame of going "on the dole." They were also an attempt to reconcile the government's role in creating the farming and industrial crises with its duty to provide for its most vulnerable citizens.

Perhaps the most important gain from Roosevelt's presidency was a change in mindset about the government's responsibility in providing a social safety net. Those with a history of employment, the aged, and those unable to take care of themselves were a focus of New Deal programs. These forms of support recognized that the tradition of relying on families, private charities, or local or state authorities for assistance had reached a breaking point (Leuchtenburg 1963, 248). Initially, one of the most controversial pieces of legislation relating to the government's treatment of welfare and relief concerned the provision of Social Security. At the heart of this legislation, the Social Security Act of 1935 resembles the spirit of federal work programs implemented under the New Deal. They convey the feeling that work can help people regain the independence and self-esteem that unemployment takes away.

The Social Security Act ushered in a system of federal financial assistance to retired workers, as well as some groups recognized as particularly vulnerable to poverty, such as people with disabilities, widows and orphans, and workers injured on the job. Through Social Security, we see the distinction between benefits people are entitled to because of prior employment and programs specifically targeted to serve poor people. Making Social Security an entitlement program for workers distinguished it from the often-stigmatized means-tested welfare "dole."

While the Social Security Act provided peace of mind to wage-earning workers that they would not live their retirement years in poverty, another New Deal law, the Fair Labor Standards Act, ensured rights to collective bargaining and workday standards, as well as unemployment insurance. These important protections prevented poverty on a massive scale for workers and the elderly for years to come.

Not all Americans were eligible for these programs, however. The Social Security Act's provisions excluded those who do agricultural and domestic work from benefits. This type of work, often with seasonal or flexible hours and often nonexistent benefits, was common among hobos, people of color, who often needed to work "under the table," and women doing domestic labor with variable hours or "off the books" work.

During the course of the 1930s, Roosevelt and his Democratic allies in Congress shepherded numerous major laws into existence to combat poverty, homelessness, and economic paralysis. These laws and the programs and initiatives they created have been credited with saving the American farmer, using WPA art projects to transform urban areas, bringing electricity to rural areas, employing tens of thousands in construction projects that modernized America's infrastructure, and regulating Wall Street and the banking system.

Although Roosevelt gave people faith that the federal government was behind them, full economic recovery from the Great Depression was not realized until the nation entered World War II (WWII). As historian Robert S. McElvaine notes, "The military buildup of 1940–41 did more to revive American industry and reduce unemployment than had any New Deal program" (1984, 320). Nevertheless, actions taken during Roosevelt's presidency reflected his conviction that traditional family and community order was the backbone of the nation's stability and prosperity. It was this sense of community responsibility that Roosevelt supported through governmental programs focusing on rebuilding traditional family and community roles that included work, welfare, and social insurance. He also regulated the national means of production in agriculture, industry, banking, and employment.

A Period of Transition

While the Roosevelt administration supported expanding the federal government's role as protector, some people worried that embracing "big government" would mean a compromise of democratic values. In fact, the idea of reigning in large federal programs to allow for the expansion of the free market became a signature feature of the government's approach to homelessness and welfare in the 1980s, the next crisis point. The free market approach also bolstered the United States' position as a global leader of capitalism, a role that President Ronald Reagan would embrace through federal policy. Although the 1980s led to a massive increase in homelessness, the decades leading up to it set the stage for this crisis.

The post–WWII era saw the fight for racial justice culminating in the civil rights movement. Civil rights legislation in the

1960s made sweeping advances in barring legal discrimination on the basis of race, sex, or nationality. During this decade, President Lyndon B. Johnson declared both a war on poverty and a war on crime. The first created and strengthened programs focusing on equal access to quality housing, education, nutrition, and welfare to lift people out of poverty. The second, however, resulted in what has been described as "the making of mass incarceration in America" (Hinton 2016). This refers not only to the rise of incarceration, or the "carceral state," but also the targeting of black Americans for increased regulation and harsher sentencing (Alexander 2010; Waquant 2009). This so-called war on crime was justified as a reaction to sweeping urban unrest that occurred during the tumultuous 1960s, when struggles for civil rights and against the war in Vietnam sometimes turned violent.

In the 1960s and 1970s, poor urban communities were also targeted for redevelopment because the inner-city housing projects that had been created in the 1950s became increasingly run-down, dangerous, and crime infested. Instead of empowering these communities to keep order and enforce laws themselves through resident organizations and coalitions, the federal government spent more on policing. This change in emphasis fell most heavily on black male youth who came under heightened police attention and scrutiny. White flight out of cities combined with an exodus of middle-class black people and ongoing systemic racism turned some neighborhoods into ghettos bereft of jobs or opportunities for social mobility. Despite this, people blamed ghetto pathology on residents themselves (Wilson 1987). In fact, the very word "ghetto" became a signifier for dangerous areas and an insult to people of color (Jones and Jackson 2018). This is important, as race-based targeting also helped fuel the proliferation of jails and prisons known as the prison industrial complex. This became a primary mechanism for controlling the black, urban, homeless population. Prisons also became default housing for people experiencing mental illness and homelessness, who are often lost in the system. At the same time, the nation as a whole was buffeted by economic forces during the 1970s that increased unemployment, homelessness, and financial vulnerability in communities all across the country. By the 1980s, the rising number and diversity of homeless people on the street caused the nation to rethink its approach to homelessness, poverty, and inequality.

Crisis Point #2: The 1980s

By the time Ronald Reagan ran for governor of California, he was familiar to the nation as a Hollywood film actor and as a television spokesperson for General Electric. He appeared on the company's weekly television show from 1954 to 1962, making him a familiar living-room presence, just as Roosevelt's radio fireside chats had done for him during the Great Depression. Popularly known as the "Great Communicator," Reagan's training as an actor meant that he was comfortable in the spotlight and spoke clearly and passionately about his favorite subjects. These included reigning in big government, reducing taxes, and containing the communist threat. In fact, well before he assumed the presidency, Reagan advocated for dismantling "big government." This would eventually translate to drastic cuts in federal spending on urban infrastructure, education, and social welfare programs. He also rolled out a "war on drugs" that included aggressive new federal law enforcement initiatives and more severe criminal penalties for individuals at all levels of the illegal drug trade. By contrast, the Reagan administration initially took little action to address the rising problem of homelessness.

In the 1980s, poverty and homelessness were not seen as governmental responsibilities, especially in conservative political circles. These issues, it was argued, should be left to the will of the free market. Poor people were increasingly categorized as burdens to middle-class consumers, and literal street homelessness became a nationwide social problem for the first time since the Great Depression. Reagan's understanding of social welfare programs, though, was that they were too costly and under-mined the ideals of freedom, independence, and democracy. In an early 1964 speech endorsing presidential candidate Barry Goldwater, Reagan warned that "those who would sacrifice freedom for security have embarked on a downward path. . . . Those who ask us to trade our freedom for the soup kitchen of the welfare state are architects of a policy of accommodation" (Reagan 2016). Throughout his political career, Reagan viewed the expansion of governmental programs as a means of social control.

The federal government's response to homelessness in the 1980s offers an interesting contrast with the first crisis point, the Great Depression. During the Great Depression, the government provided basic needs or the tools to access them. From education and employment to housing and electricity, the New Deal greatly expanded federal social welfare programs. Reagan explicitly touted the progress of the New Deal, but his administration focused more on cost. While it is true that federal welfare spending ballooned in the 1970s, reasons for that growth included streamlined welfare application procedures, increased eligibility, and measures to expose racial bias in these programs. These changes resulted in more people receiving welfare benefits, and costs skyrocketed. In contrast, Reagan's view was that the key to prosperity was cutting social spending while building wealth at the top with the belief that those economic benefits and rewards would eventually trickle down to the "bottom"— poor and working-class Americans. This economic strategy, called "Reaganomics," came to be regarded by many critics as a key factor in the rising crisis of homelessness.

Negative views of impoverished people were evident in Reagan's speeches well before he became president. As governor of California, a position he assumed for two terms beginning in 1967, he referred to people in poverty as "welfare bums." He also favored reducing the state's budget deficit by making steep cuts to social welfare programs. Reagan was also a pro-life advocate who made racist remarks about diplomats from

African nations, calling them "monkeys" in an October 1971 phone conversation with President Richard Nixon. Reagan also denigrated labor unions and called on police and the California National Guard to subdue protestors at the University of California, Berkeley's People's Park. Critics claimed that the policies Reagan enacted as governor clearly indicated his lack of sympathy with the struggles of marginalized people, as well as his belief that the government, state or federal, was not responsible for helping them.

When Reagan became president in 1981, his priorities were informed by the domestic unrest that characterized the 1960s and 1970s. Urban riots in the 1960s were caused by a mix of "relative deprivation" and mounting disillusionment among African Americans (Abeles 1976). The promise of socioeconomic equality contained within the civil rights movement proved to be elusive, and African Americans were justifiably frustrated. Increased policing of urban areas, surveillance of black youth, and crackdowns on street crime followed in the wake of the riots (Bellisfield 1972). Despite this massive urban unrest, Reagan's domestic policy vision included decreased spending on programs he saw as ineffective. As a result, African Americans living in urban areas saw increased policing and decreased spending on housing, education, and infrastructure. Massive rollbacks in social welfare spending, the loss of industrial jobs, rising rates of substance abuse, and a war on drugs all contributed to the rise in homelessness.

Targeting poor families and people of color was not the explicit goal of 1980s criminalization and drug policy, but its effects are unequivocal. The Reagan administration characterized drug use as an epidemic that required both punishment and treatment (Hawdon 2001). Punishment, however, was the primary focus. In fact, the war on drugs, which included mandatory minimum sentencing and measures to lengthen sentences for drug-related offenses, produced a rapid expansion in the nation's prison population (Gotsch and Basti 2018). Meanwhile, privatizing government services emerged as a major policy initiative for the Reagan administration. This push opened the door to the eventual privatization of many of America's prisons. The first private prison companies, which by 2016 were housing one out of twelve Americans in the prison population, were established in the early 1980s. Some critics contended that the Reagan administration's "war on drugs" was responsible for creating a moral panic and an industry to answer for it (Hawdon 2001).

Homeless people also faced criminalization, as they were described as a danger to their communities and were subject to laws that disproportionately targeted them for occupying public space or committing nuisance crimes. In this sense, said some observers, the government's treatment of homelessness and poverty focused on punishing its effects rather than addressing its causes. In addition to this punitive response, however, some communities took action to provide better services to hungry and homeless people. It is both the critical mass of homeless people and the diligence of advocates who call attention to homelessness as a social problem and act to remedy it.

New Homelessness

In the same way that Hoovervilles came to be seen by many Americans as a symbol of the government's indifference to widespread poverty in the early 1930s, street homelessness signaled a crisis during Ronald Reagan's presidency. Across the nation, and particularly in urban areas, street homelessness emerged as a highly visible and much maligned reality. It inspired various forms of fear, hate, and criminalization (Mitchell 2001), as well as sympathy, protest, and advocacy. One thing was clear: homelessness in the 1980s became a more visible problem, and, for the first time in larger numbers, women and children were among the people sleeping on city streets. The street population was highly visible in most major cities, reinforcing the outcry for service and shelter. Reactions to this "new" form of homelessness were split. Some people without homes, like the

blind and the aged, were more likely to be treated sympatheti-
cally, as victims of forces beyond their control. Others, like single men and addicts, were seen as causing their own condition
(Hoch and Slayton 1989; Rosenthal 1994). In this good/bad
juxtaposition, victims deserve assistance and the guilty deserve
punishment.

In response to the increases in street living, particularly in
urban areas, cities attempted to "clean up" public spaces. These
efforts, though, were sometimes driven less by altruistic concern for the homeless than by a desire to attract tourist dollars. First initiated in New York City, some police departments
embraced the "broken windows" theory of policing, which
held that by focusing on stopping and punishing petty street
crimes, like scrawling graffiti or breaking windows, more serious crimes were less likely to occur (Wilson and Kelling 1982).
Many cities subsequently relegated poor and homeless people
to marginal spaces (Wolch and Dear 1993)—and punished
them for conducting life-sustaining activities, like sleeping
(Mitchell 2001; National Law Center on Homelessness and
Poverty 2019). Shelters also became a grassroots-inspired, federally supported solution to homelessness in the 1980s. These
two solutions went hand in hand as both criminalization and
shelters work to contain an unruly population (Wright 1997).
The spatial control of homeless people in the 1980s was a one-
size-fits-all strategy for managing the emergency nature of the
problem.

The question of what to do with so many people sleeping outside became a rallying cry for advocates, news media,
citizens, and homeless people themselves. All of these groups
focused on the need for shelter. Although Reagan was reluctant
to assume federal responsibility for this crisis, widespread grassroots action and the support of government officials helped
change his mind. The first federal task force on homelessness was formed in 1983 to allocate surplus federal property
to house homeless people in temporary shelters. Indicative of
the immediate, emergency nature of the problem, these were

bare-bones accommodations, not designed for human habitation. Many of them lacked sanitary facilities, heat, or other basic services. Although temporary shelters served an immediate need, they did not provide long-term assistance, and they never became numerous enough to serve a majority of the homeless population.

Part of the reason for this is that federal efforts to assist poor people were controversial in the 1980s. Reagan and many other conservative Americans repeatedly characterized welfare as a threat to democratic values and capitalist advancement. Solving the overall problem of poverty and inequality was seriously in question because of rising costs and skepticism about the service population. This was a dramatic shift in outlook from the New Deal era, in which the government understood its role in causing economic and social crisis and felt an obligation to enact programs and policies to provide basic needs, employment possibilities, and rebuild family and community stability. Under Roosevelt, these were seen as public goods for the common man, to be provided by the federal government. Under Reagan, they were unnecessary expenditures that would increase taxes on hardworking people. Reagan suggested that most people did not really need welfare and that they were taking advantage of the system. In his view, they were morally suspect and not worth the expense.

Reagan blamed expensive welfare programs for a depressed economy. Part of his solution to the growing budget deficit was to reduce welfare expenditures and stimulate economic growth and consumption at the top. This economic policy meant reducing taxes, cutting social welfare spending, and encouraging monetary restraint (Jenkins and Eckert 1989, 129). Rather than cut spending overall, though, Reagan increased military spending and cut social programs. Under Reagan, the nation's defense budget skyrocketed. To protect the nation from nuclear missiles, Reagan proposed a strategic defense initiative, popularly known as "Star Wars," which included an invisible barrier to shield the United States from nuclear attack from the

Soviet Union and other countries. While the initiative was shut down in 1985, Reagan's military strategy included a buildup of troops and improved weapons and intelligence to ensure the nation's position as a global power.

Because of the country's economic woes, including inflation rates that were the highest in decades, some people saw programs like Star Wars as superfluous. Corporate greed was at least partially to blame. Reagan himself was a proud advocate of big business and technology as keys to a better future, and he suggested that conditions for workers in the 1980s were better than in prior years. He argued that modern workers enjoy leisure time and "freedom from backbreaking and mind-dulling drudgery that man had known for centuries past" (Reagan 2016, 27). This assertion, though, did little to reassure unskilled workers in the 1980s, confronting increased job insecurity and diminished purchasing power. Service economy jobs replaced working-class industrial ones, union membership plummeted, and wages stagnated. Nevertheless, Reagan remained a dogged advocate of the idea that building U.S. wealth and power at the top would eventually lift the common man out of poverty.

During Reagan's presidency, government support for the poor was called into question. Reagan and his allies justified cuts to welfare benefits as a means of social progress, as a way to protect the public's freedom from governmental meddling, and as a vehicle for saving middle-class consumers from unnecessary taxation. Positioning people on welfare as the enemy of the middle-class consumer provided the Reagan administration with justification for social welfare cuts in the 1980s. Partly as a result of these cuts, wealth became more concentrated, with higher gains for the top 1 percent and for a select few of the middle class. Instead of wealth "trickling down" from the top to the bottom, as Reagan's economic strategy had promised, the number of Americans living below the poverty line doubled from the beginning to the end of the 1980s (Young 1988, 69).

Scholars have pointed out, however, that the nation was not suffering from a lack of prosperity during this time but rather a problem with the unequal distribution of prosperity. Even in the midst of the 1980s homeless crisis, middle-class Americans enjoyed unprecedented rewards in the areas of accumulated wealth, educational opportunities, and employment. Income growth for those at the top also widened, a trend that continues to the present (Stone et al. 2020). Rewards in the 1980s clustered at the top of the income scale and were primarily felt by white Americans. The pervasive fear during the 1980s was that a domestic or foreign enemy would threaten capitalist advancement and emasculate the American people. Reagan's response to this fear was a military buildup that he insisted would protect the United States and democracy abroad. At home, the result included minimal antipoverty measures and a war on drugs to curb addiction and unrest in low-income communities of color.

Trends in Social Welfare Investment

A child of poor parents, Reagan's own survival story made him a proud defender of "do it yourself" democracy and the reign of the free market. Reagan was reluctant to address unemployment, failing school systems, blighted housing conditions, racism, and other historical inequalities throughout his presidency (Hinton 2016, 307). Instead, he redefined government accountability from the New Deal model, which saw a responsibility for addressing the needs of the common man, to a model that saw government's role as protecting free market consumerism and reserving assistance for those Americans who were seen as unable to care for themselves. The working poor, for example, became ineligible for Aid to Families with Dependent Children (AFDC) and were no longer trained under the public service employment program or the Work Incentive Program. As America's social safety net shrank, growing numbers of poor people found themselves unemployed, ineligible for food stamps or Medicaid, and homeless.

In contrast with Roosevelt's strategy of developing federal agencies, policies, and programs to address social welfare issues,

Reagan saw the provision of social welfare as best governed by states and private and faith-based organizations. In this sense, he reprivatized social problems that were formerly government responsibilities (Young 1988). Unfortunately, the dramatic increase in poverty and homelessness that accompanied these cuts overwhelmed existing organizations. States scrambled for resources and often increased the stringency of requirements for receiving public assistance. This tightening of qualifying criteria did produce cuts in the number of Americans on welfare—but did not bring about reductions in homelessness or poverty. In fact, "the average AFDC family had only $385 a month in 1984 with which to purchase housing and all other necessities, compared with $568 a month in 1970" (Burt 1992, 84).

During the 1980s, the Reagan administration cut $25 billion from the federal budget, 70 percent of which came from programs for poor people. In fact, the budget for federal housing subsidies alone was cut in half. By 1985, recipients lucky enough to qualify for housing assistance faced a shortfall of over 3 million units. The single rent occupancy (SRO) hotels that served as cheap lodging in skid row areas also suffered massive reductions due to redevelopment and gentrification, particularly in the mid- to late 1980s (Hoch and Slayton 1989). This resulted in fewer affordable housing options for poor people to escape homelessness in urban areas. In addition, the Reagan administration cut spending on libraries, schools, municipal hospitals, clinics, sanitation, police, and fire departments. In 1980, the federal government accounted for 22 percent of funding for big city budgets. After Reagan's second term, it dropped to 6 percent (Dreier 2004).

For people living in the nation's inner cities, these cuts reduced access to basic needs including housing, education, health, and safety. At the same time, benefits for middle-class and wealthy Americans increased. The practical implications of cutting welfare programs and reducing investment in urban infrastructure were disproportionately felt by black people, as over half lived in central cities in 1979. Many African American families had little financial margin for error during this period. The median income for black families in 1984 was 44.3 percent less than it was for white families (St. Pierre 1991, 331), and 51.7 percent of all black female-headed households lived below the poverty line. When the social safety net shrank during the 1980s, black women and children fell through the cracks, and black men were incarcerated more than any other group in the nation's history, both in terms of sheer numbers and as a percentage of the overall population (Western 2006).

Part of the justification for spending on or cutting social welfare programs involves who the programs and policies are designed to serve. If people receiving welfare are seen as innocent victims of economic downturn, as otherwise enterprising young people, families, and workers, or as contributors to the nation's defense (such as soldiers), greater support exists for providing public assistance. Yet there is always the fear that if assistance becomes too generous or too easy to get, people will be uninterested in working and will live life "on the dole." Reagan perpetuated this fear in his efforts to drum up public support for his social welfare cuts. Using stereotypes about people buying "T-bone steaks with food stamps," Reagan invoked the image of the "welfare queen," a black woman defrauding the welfare system, making $150,000 a year, and driving a Cadillac. These images offered up the offensive, racist idea of black women living "high on the hog," as a way of confirming their presupposed guilt and dishonesty. It was also a way to justify additional cuts to social welfare and assistance programs.

While at least one actual case of a woman defrauding the welfare system in the manner described by Reagan has been documented (Levin 2019), the idea that all welfare recipients were gaming the system was tremendously damaging for everyday people in genuine need of assistance. The caricature of the welfare queen informed the redefinition of welfare policy and empowered social welfare agencies to disqualify recipients for minor rule violations. Making application procedures and eligibility requirements daunting is a way of cutting expenses and overall numbers enrolled. The problem is that it reinforces cultural and behavioral norms about the importance of wealth, marriage, and home ownership. Despite these negative effects, however, cutting welfare expenses was touted as a win for the federal government and American taxpayers.

Reagan also made the unpopular argument that Social Security should be seen as a welfare program rather than a social insurance program and that it should be limited or eliminated entirely. In his view, government-sponsored welfare compromised the nation's values of independence and self-sufficiency. Using the example of "a young man, twenty-one years of age, working at an average salary," Reagan argued, "that would guarantee $220 a month at age sixty-five. The government promises $127" (Mann 2019, 184). This example championed the free market but did not take into consideration cases of sporadic employment, disability, injury, and other circumstances that show the need for a safety net. In addition to arguing against Social Security, Reagan also criticized Medicaid, saying that the federal health care program for eligible poor Americans provided a lower standard of care and cost too much.

Federal Homeless Legislation

In 1986, the Urgent Relief for the Homeless Act was introduced in Congress to address emergency needs as well as preventative measures and long-term solutions for homelessness. Instead of treating homeless people as deviants, the act characterized them as "the nameless, placeless people we pass everyday living on the grates or panhandling on the streets of our cities" (P.L. 100–77). It also noted that they are a hidden population that includes youth, victims of domestic violence, people struggling with mental illness, and veterans, "all struggling to survive in a system which offers pitifully little help." The crafting of the legislation reflected a belief among some members of Congress that the federal government did need to play a role in combating homelessness, despite Reagan's contrary beliefs.

Later renamed the Stewart B. McKinney Homeless Assistance Act, this legislation was passed by Congress in 1987 and reluctantly signed into law by Reagan. In 2000, the legislation was renamed the McKinney-Vento Homeless Assistance Act by President Bill Clinton after the death of Bruce Vento, a member of congress who had been a longtime advocate for the homeless. It required the federal government to disburse funds to states to provide homeless shelters and services. Although it was amended several times subsequently, the original text focused on ensuring basic, emergency services for adults and access to a public education for young children. The rest of the population experiencing homelessness, including those with histories of mental illness and criminal justice involvement, were not specifically included in this legislation and its protections. It also excluded prisoners, people living doubled up with other people or in other institutions. Critics asserted that the legislation's focus on only some sectors of the overall homeless population was a grave mistake, given the criminalized and hidden nature of homelessness and its concomitant issues and challenges. This response highlighted the emergency nature of homelessness in the 1980s, characterized by the sheer visibility and diversity of homeless people in public. The need for an immediate solution meant making decisions quickly, and long-term remedies remained elusive.

The Stewart B. McKinney Homeless Assistance Act of 1987 was an important first step in developing federal provisions of assistance for homeless people, but its immediate impact did little to quell the growing tides of those without shelter. McKinney consolidated responsibilities that were previously scattered among governmental organizations under the U.S. Interagency Council on Homelessness (USICH). The USICH was created to coordinate federal assistance among public and private sector organizations and state and local governments. Its stated goal was to maximize the federal government's efficacy in contributing to the end of homelessness through resources, organization, and planning.

Because of the challenges involved in beginning such a massive effort, early years were primarily spent developing a course of action to guide future directions. Distributing McKinney Act funding and establishing reliable, national, ongoing estimates of the homeless population were key objectives that would shape policy for years to come. Yet, a coordinated point-in-time (PIT) count of the homeless was not developed until 2005, well after these early stages of development. As a result of this slow start, people active in homeless advocacy circles were frustrated with their inability to offer support or engage in long-term planning. Nevertheless, grassroots activism was ignited in the 1980s and encouraged the above legislation and protest activities that drew attention to the federal government's responsibility for the deepening crisis of "new" homelessness.

In direct contrast with Reagan's suggestion that homeless people were more comfortable sleeping outside than in shelters, advocates for the homeless organized protest activities like the Housing Now! March on Washington in 1989. This event drew over 200 organizations and thousands of individuals arguing for housing and shelter. Like other protests about homelessness throughout the 1980s, the Housing Now! event focused on basic rights and the government's essential role in providing them (Snow et al. 2005). National homeless advocate Mitch Snyder, a member of the Committee for Creative Non-Violence, was instrumental in bringing the struggles of homeless people to the forefront of American consciousness in this era. An outspoken and aggressive advocate for homeless people, Snyder ran Washington, DC's first, largest shelter on federal property. He also challenged the idea, popularized by Reagan, that homeless people choose to sleep outside, noting that local shelters were full beyond capacity.

Despite growing activism and increased government awareness of the problem, Reagan persisted in suggesting that homeless people walk away from available shelters and mental health facilities in the name of freedom over care. In reality, the closure of mental health facilities in the 1960s and 1970s forced many people onto the streets and greatly added to the numbers of people experiencing homelessness. The community care facilities that were supposed to replace hospitals in treating mental illness never fully materialized (Wagner 2005). As a result, prisons and streets became the default housing for this population.

Counting the Homeless Population

In the decades immediately prior to the 1980s, homelessness was not seen as a pressing concern for the nation. Many precipitating forces led to a rise in homelessness in the 1980s, however, including federal housing policy and housing shortages, a rising unemployment rate, the economy's shift from manufacturing jobs to lower-paying service jobs, inadequate public benefits, rising numbers of single-parent families, an increased cost of living, and the policies of deinstitutionalization that began in the 1960s (Burt 1992). Mental illness, alcoholism, and drug abuse also made people more vulnerable to homelessness.

To get a handle on the crisis, several studies offered estimates of the number and demographics of people experiencing homelessness. This exercise, which would become central to efforts to secure federal funding to combat the problem, was fraught with difficulties. Early counts struggled to produce comparative, generalizable estimates and to sample both sheltered and unsheltered populations. In addition, experts argued about whether to conduct a one-night PIT count or to assess numbers and demographics on a regular basis throughout the year. Part of the issue with a one-night count is that weather may affect the whereabouts of the local homeless population. Communities may also lack the funding or volunteers needed to conduct a representative count. In addition, because homelessness is often hidden and episodic, even with adequate resources, it may be difficult to find people living in street or makeshift locations. As a result of these challenges, early count methodology and results varied widely.

The first estimate, produced in 1983–1984 by the U.S. Department of Housing and Urban Development (HUD), sampled sixty metropolitan areas with over 50,000 people. It included estimates from shelter directors about both street and shelter populations. This strategy would later be called into question, specifically regarding people living unsheltered. The street portion of this count was combined with a 1980 Census "casual count" of homeless people in public locations in large cities. HUD also attempted to estimate the street population by conducting local studies in Phoenix, Pittsburgh, and Boston, taking an average street-to-shelter ratio from counts in these cities. The early estimates described here (Table 1.1) indicated that the unsheltered population far exceeded the number of people in shelter.

The second attempt to enumerate the homeless population was conducted in 1987 by Martha Burt and Barbara Cohen for the Urban Institute (Burt and Cohen 1989). For this count, the definition of homelessness included people who slept in a shelter, in other nonconventional housing, or in an institution (including hospitals, jails, and mental health facilities) or stayed with friends or relatives during the week prior to the count. They used a sample of 1,704 shelter users in 453 soup kitchens in 20 cities with populations over 100,000. They also sampled 999 people in homeless hangout locations. The study estimated that the number of people experiencing homelessness in 1987 was more than double that found with earlier counts, and Burt and Cohen also concluded that a majority

Table 1.1 Early Counts of Homeless People

	1980, 1983–1984	1987	1989
Shelter	69,000 (15,000 families)	194,000	180,000
Street	123,000	306,000	N/A
TOTAL	192,000–267,000	500,000–600,000	

Sources: Burt, M. R., and B. E. Cohen. 1989. *America's Homeless: Numbers, Characteristics, and the Programs That Serve Them*. Washington, DC: Urban Institute Press; U.S. Department of Housing and Urban Development. 1984. "Report to the Secretary on the Homeless and Emergency Shelters." Washington, DC: Office of Policy Development and Research.

of America's homeless were unsheltered. The inconsistencies between these counts are pronounced, particularly for the street or unsheltered population, always the most difficult to enumerate (Garfinkel and Piliavin 1995).

How do we interpret these results? Do numerical differences reflect actual population changes or merely a different count methodology? Part of the answer has to do with how each study defined homelessness. The Urban Institute used a more flexible, expansive definition than the first HUD count, which focused on literal homelessness—people sleeping on the street or in shelter on the night of the count. This definition is important because it questions our understanding of homelessness as a one-night crisis or a sporadic condition. Episodic homelessness is more common overall and for people experiencing long-term poverty. Counts that are limited to a single night are, therefore, often viewed as inadequate in measuring rates of homelessness. Early counts showed that more single homeless adults slept in shelter over street locations from 1984 to 1987, yet these were the primary years of shelter construction. This suggested that changes in rates of homelessness and shelter may simply have been due to a shift in population location rather than a change in overall numbers.

In 1989, HUD conducted a second shelter study, which looked more like the current housing inventory counts conducted in cities nationwide as part of the federal funding process. It focused primarily on the availability of shelter beds and the number of people using them. The survey took place over almost a year, from 1987 to 1988, and did not include estimates of the unsheltered population or direct contact with people in shelters, so it was easier information to gather than earlier counts. For this count, a stratified random sample of shelter managers provided information on people in their programs. There were several additional efforts to enumerate the national homeless population in the 1990s, including a one-night count by the U.S. Census Bureau in 1990 and a more comprehensive survey conducted by the Urban Institute in

1996. Annual national estimates of the homeless population would not be available until the mid-2000s and still face methodological inconsistencies and challenges.

Crisis Point #3: The Bush Economy and the Great Recession

President George W. Bush was elected in 2001 amid controversy. Former governor of Texas and son of George H. W. Bush, forty-first president of the United States, he faced democratic opponent Al Gore in his run for the presidency. At the same time, Bush's younger brother, Jeb, was serving as governor of Florida, a linchpin state in determining the winner of the election. Citing faulty ballot issues, Florida was almost forced to do a recount. In the end, though, after weeks of legal wrangling and a controversial Supreme Court ruling, Bush was awarded the state's electoral votes. The addition of Florida gave Bush the necessary electoral college vote count to claim the presidency, even though Gore narrowly won the popular vote. Bush was sworn in as the nation's forty-third president in 2001 and would go on to serve two terms in office. Under Bush, however, the United States would witness the largest financial downturn since the Great Depression. This "Great Recession," as it came to be known, led to increased housing insecurity, inequality, and poverty, which in turn generated higher levels of homelessness.

A recession is less serious than a depression, although neither is a prerequisite for increased homelessness. It is an economic downturn characterized by a high unemployment rate, stock market decline, and a decline in overall consumption and production. Although there were multiple mini recessions throughout the 1970s and in 2001, the Great Recession widened inequality and saw more people enter poverty than in the previous decade. One of the most contentious aspects of this recession is that it was caused by corruption in the banking and securities markets. But instead of criminal prosecution as punishment, corporations received federal assistance as lawmakers scrambled to lift the economy out of recession (Brown 2015).

The Bush administration ended in 2009 and Barack Obama, the nation's first African American president was elected. Under Obama's leadership, the nation wrote its first strategic plan to end homelessness and launched a plan to end veteran homelessness. Because of the Obama administration's support of people in poverty in these and other policy areas, critics found it ironic that the government appeared to be prioritizing bailing out corporations over homeowners in danger of losing their homes and people who had already been pushed into homelessness. This is almost the direct opposite of the government's approach to the Great Depression in the 1930s.

Part of what facilitated the predatory lending practices that caused the Great Recession was the repeal of the Glass-Steagall Act in 1999. This legislation, originally passed under Franklin D. Roosevelt as part of his administration's New Deal, was intended to protect consumers from the evils of speculation in banking. When it was repealed, these protections were lost and several banks merged their securities and banking operations. This made them more competitive on a global scale but led to increased risks for homebuyers, who were approved for mortgages with variable interest rates and balloon payments. When the economy faltered, many mortgage holders defaulted, and foreclosures skyrocketed. The overall loss of household wealth was staggering. Popular news reports estimated that $8 trillion in household stock market wealth and $6 trillion in home value were lost. People lost their personal residences at a rate not seen since the Great Depression (Muolo 2009).

Banks exploited the dream of home ownership by preying on would-be buyers who either did not understand or were not prepared to negotiate the terms. Many of those who bore the brunt of the crisis were first-time homebuyers, disproportionately women and people of color. Both groups historically lacked access to loans and mortgages that would allow them to buy in the first place, making this a double betrayal (Modi and Sewell 2015). Those who were able to afford homes lost equity when housing prices fell below the amount still owed. Many people defaulted, losing the initial outlay for the purchase and the chance to accumulate wealth. Many never recovered. In fact, the gap between black and white home ownership remains below 1968 levels, when housing discrimination was legal (Young 1988).

The loss of a home causes many people to slip into poverty. When this happens, their entire families follow and may stay there for generations. People living in poor neighborhoods in the United States face consistent barriers to upward social mobility, including higher crime rates, inferior schools, and poorer physical and mental health outcomes. As one analysis summarizes, "They tend to go to poor-performing neighborhood schools with higher dropout rates. Their job-seeking networks tend to be weaker and they face higher levels of financial insecurity" (Kneebone and Holmes 2016, 1). Urban sociologists have examined the impact of substandard housing on civic participation, overall health, and access to health care (Fitzpatrick and LaGory 2000; O'Connell et al. 2010; Scott 2011). They found that poverty and housing instability lead to higher levels of stress and depression and greater exposure to violence and trauma. Low-income black families living in poor neighborhoods, without the accumulated wealth that white and middle-class families rely on, were slower to recover in the postrecession period (Conley and Gifford 2006; Kneebone and Holmes 2016).

The recession brought national attention to the issue of housing discrimination and the evils of predatory lending as a matter of class, race, and gender. It also highlighted reasons why people of color are disproportionately represented within the homeless community over time. Sociologists and leading authors document ongoing racial discrimination in housing, known as "redlining," that has historically stopped African Americans from leaving inner cities for the suburbs and from moving into housing developments in urban areas (Austen 2019; Drake and Cayton 1945; Rothstein 2018). Because of ongoing discrimination in the housing market, black people have been left behind in terms of housing and accumulating wealth. This makes the impact of the Great Recession even more poignant, as it perpetuates cyclical poverty. This leads to stagnant growth and reduces a family's ability to weather a financial crisis.

The 2007–2009 recession also signaled a shift toward society that defined participation and satisfaction in terms of market relationships (Collins 2011). Our very understanding of the common man in this era is the assurance of prosperity and of the market itself as keys to a good life and a stable economy. Instead of focusing on the common man through large-scale work programs or an expansion of welfare and housing opportunities, the government bailed out big business to the tune of $700 billion (Muolo 2009). This was a glaring signal of the role of corporate wealth in shaping the nation's economy and political structure. In fact, "from 1979 to 2007, just before the financial crisis and Great Recession, average income after taxes for the top 1 percent of the distribution quadrupled" (Stone et al. 2020). This happened along with regulations that would ensure political power and influence for the nation's wealthy corporate elite. Similar to the "trickle down" strategy promoted under the Reagan administration, this bailout operated under the ideology that some firms had become "too big to fail." This meant that saving them would shore up jobs and industry, ideally preventing the U.S. economy from deeper recession.

Just as the lure of owning property brought many families to settle in the Dust Bowl, the lure of home ownership drew many families into subprime mortgages that they would eventually default on. One of the primary differences in these crisis points is that during the Great Depression, the government understood its own role in creating the crisis and acted to restore the public's faith. In the 1980s, the federal government denied that it had any culpability for that decade's homeless crisis; instead, it blamed poor people themselves for becoming homeless.

As these crisis points show, the government's support of big business and treatment of "the common man" greatly impacted the policies designed to manage homelessness, a well-worn feature of U.S. society by the 2000s. The irony of the 2007–2009 recession, despite growing housing insecurity, particularly among families, is that rates of homelessness saw a 30 percent reduction during the crisis years. Usually, in times of economic downturn, homelessness increases. Garfinkel and Piliavin (1995) suggest that, instead of an actual decrease in the number of homeless people overall, large shifts in numbers reflect a movement from street to shelter or to other types of housing. Inefficient count methodology, in other words, makes the reduction seem like a result of policy, when it may more accurately reflect a shift in location.

The Continuum of Care

The idea of a continuum of care (CoC) began in the 1990s as a way of streamlining applications for federal funding and encouraging cooperation across agencies. Along with the evolution of PIT counts, implementing the CoC as a planning approach is an important indicator of federal strategy. The idea is that people experiencing homelessness can be helped by a step-by-step process that begins with outreach, moves to temporary shelter, and then shifts to transitional housing before eventually reaching permanent housing. Only through surmounting the many barriers, rules, and regulations that go along with each step can people eventually attain housing (if it is available). Because of the rules that shelters often require residents to abide by, and the poor conditions that prevail in some shelters, many people opt out of the continuum somewhere along the way. The behavioral compliance that is a feature of most shelter settings is a barrier to seeking service, and avoiding them is considered a form of resistance (Wagner 1993).

Throughout the Great Recession, more and more people experienced a loss of housing or the inability to pay for both housing and basic needs. For this reason, the ideas of homeless prevention and rapid rehousing began to take center stage. The "Housing First" initiative, founded by Pathways to Housing NY, also earned nationwide attention during this era. This approach eliminates the linear step-by-step treatment model and de-emphasizes behavioral compliance as a condition for getting or maintaining stable, permanent housing. Although Housing First initially focused on people with mental illness, it gradually expanded as advocates came to see it as a more effective strategy for managing homelessness than homeless shelters. As its name implies, Housing First programs offer stable accommodations without treatment or case management beyond minimal check-ins and without the threat of eviction.

By 2010, CoC regions implementing the Housing First model could gain points that would prioritize their funding applications to HUD. This was enough to encourage many regions to claim that they were implementing this strategy, but they often did so with little oversight. The push for permanent housing is also buoyed by research that shows that emergency needs and shelter services are costlier for people experiencing chronic homelessness than permanent housing (Culhane et al. 2011). This is a winning argument to make in this era because it trades on how much capitalism has come to structure our relationships with one another and our understanding of our place in the world. As Robert S. McElvaine wrote,

> Most contemporary Americans have fully adopted the consumption ethic that was rising in the 1920s but was briefly reversed during the Great Depression. We have become accustomed to buying as a way of life and to living for the moment, even if that means incurring large debts that threaten our own and our descendents' future standards of living. (1984, xxv)

The ethic of consumption has far-reaching consequences that ripple out from incurring large debt to threatening the health of the planet (Klein 2014). Despite these risks, the possibilities for immediate gratification often outweigh thinking about long-term costs. Deferring responsibility, in fact, is a signature feature of how we explain ourselves as a society in the United States and how we develop policies to shun or reintegrate our homeless population (Wakin 2020).

Who Is Homeless in This Era?

Similar to the 1980s, the 2007–2009 recession was pivotal in defining homelessness, assessing the demographics of the homeless population, and offering assistance at the federal, state, and local levels. By 2005, PIT counts became the universal tool for all CoC regions applying for federal funding. The PIT count was used to estimate the number of shelter and transitional housing beds, the number of people occupying those beds, and the number of people who are unsheltered. It also offered some detail on the demographics and maladies of the overall population. As the name indicates, the PIT count was a snapshot count, on a single night in January.

From its inception, the count has included subpopulation estimates of the number of homeless people experiencing any of the following: chronic homelessness, severe mental illness, chronic substance abuse, domestic violence, HIV/AIDS, as well as counts of veterans, and youth under 18. All of these are focus populations for U.S. homeless policy. HUD offers data by state, CoC region, and for the nation. It also includes estimates of the number of families experiencing homelessness. In addition to these breakdowns, the national PIT count finally included a breakdown of homelessness by race and gender in 2015.

Much of the data collected for the PIT counts is obtained through the homeless management information system (HMIS), a software tool developed in the 1990s, to assist in tracking people served by homeless shelters. The collection of

HMIS data is done regularly, as a feature of the intake procedures in emergency and specialized shelters and transitional housing. It allows communities to track shelter use during a given time period, typically three to twelve months. It can, therefore, track homelessness more accurately than a single, snapshot count, which does not take into account sporadic homelessness, meaning that people may drift in and out of a shelter several times during the course of a year. Because shelters typically keep digital intake records, obtaining this information is easier and less time consuming than conducting a physical count or including a survey or interview component.

HUD distributes guidelines for conducting the unsheltered portion of the count. Its implementation reflects nonstandard methods of data collection across communities, and it remains the most costly and labor-intensive part of the PIT count. Although it is only required every other year, communities often elect to do street counts annually, with the goal of estimating needs and numbers, raising awareness about homelessness, and attracting support for local solutions. The many limitations of the PIT count include its timing in January, when cold weather areas see an increase in their sheltered populations and a corresponding decrease in the number of unsheltered, and the fact that it is conducted only once a year. Many communities also note that local counts can be affected by policing efforts before the count, ineffective publicity to raise awareness of the count, or specific weather events that occur during or prior to the count.

Even with its limitations, however, the PIT count is an important way of estimating changes in the nation's homeless population over time. Beginning in 2007, PIT and HMIS data has been used by HUD to write the Annual Homeless Assessment Report (AHAR), required by Congress. Because the PIT count is tied to federal funding and policy decisions, accuracy is important, yet comparisons of early counts show that many communities took several years to standardize the methods used to collect data.

Comparing results from the first two AHAR reports show different methodology and coverage areas, as well as new demographic data in the 2008 report, which was collected using HMIS. As a result, it is difficult to tell if population changes were because of actual reductions in numbers or shifting or uncertain count methodology, particularly for the unsheltered population. The 2008 AHAR estimated demographic changes, beyond what was included in 2007, to focus on subpopulations of interest, age, and family status. As baseline reports, the 2007 and 2008 AHARs are difficult to interpret. The first claims that there had been few changes in the homeless population over the past ten years. The second claims that lower numbers of people experiencing chronic homelessness are a result of government efforts targeted to this population.

In addition to developing an annual PIT count, the early 2000s were also important, as arguments for ending homelessness focused on it as a matter of economics. In 2002, Phil Mangano was appointed executive director of the USICH. Under his charismatic leadership, the USICH prioritized reducing homelessness. The organization emphasized that the cost to taxpayers of homeless programs could be reduced if they are placed in housing. This strategy takes morality out of the equation and makes sheer economic self-interest a reason to house people over leaving them on the streets. This money over morality approach to ending homelessness was an effective strategy that was eventually used to justify Housing First as a central part of the national approach.

This era, and the government's response to the Great Recession told us several things about the state of homelessness, more than three decades after the crisis that began in the 1980s. It told us that the distance between rich and poor had grown, that the goal of reaching the top of the economic pyramid is so compelling that many are willing to shut out the needs of the poor. This is in direct contrast with the 1930s, when easing the struggles of the common man was more central to governmental policy making. It also tells us that economic over moral concerns are at the forefront of the modern homeless service industry's decision-making processes. When solving chronic homelessness became a way of saving money, there was a momentary convergence of the needs of homeless people and advocates, policy makers, and service providers, as all were in agreement that permanent housing is a better, cheaper solution to shelter than shelters themselves. This is an important approach to pay attention to, as we move to examine current controversies about solutions to homelessness in the next chapter.

Conclusion

Focusing on specific crisis points shows how the nation has changed over time in how it regards homelessness and who the government chooses to assist. It also shows differences in prevailing solutions to homelessness in each time period and evolving public opinion about homelessness. During the Great Depression, the federal government aligned itself in word and deed with the needs of the "forgotten" or "common" man. This phrase was at the forefront of speeches, policies, and governmental organizations directed to provide employment, protection, and sustenance for people facing economic calamity. Restoring community and prosperity was seen as a common good that deserved governmental support. Many people who endured the Great Depression also explicitly blamed the unfettered growth of big business, along with wasteful, inefficient government programs, as causing the crisis.

In contrast, in both the 1980s and during the Great Recession, federal authorities prioritized protecting and reviving big business, which was seen as the backbone of the nation's economy. Instead of recognizing the responsibility of the government or big business in causing poverty and inequality, during these crisis points, poor and homeless people were more likely to be blamed for their own poverty. The idea that benefits should not encourage joblessness or laziness by being too generous was common to all three crisis points. This logic was used to justify spending on social insurance over welfare programs. The latter almost always relied on determining beneficiary eligibility and imposing restrictions targeting behavior and morality. In the 1980s, these restrictions reflected a growing emphasis on differentiating between sympathetic "deserving" people and "undeserving" people.

The 1980s was also pivotal in showing that grassroots activism could have a larger impact on the movement to end homelessness. In fact, advocates during this era formed a powerful, sustained protest movement that raised awareness about why street homelessness increased and what people sleeping on the streets really wanted. This movement was instrumental in creating the Stewart B. McKinney Homeless Assistance Act of 1987, the first and only federal legislation to provide for homeless people. It established an annual count and housing inventory and an agency to oversee these activities and dole out funding to states to help their homeless populations. One of the ironies of the provision of shelter in this decade was that it came with increased criminalization of people living on the street. This involved targeting them for nuisance offenses associated with homelessness, like violations of rules against sleeping, trespassing, or loitering in public areas. As a result, prisons became default warehousing facilities for people experiencing homelessness and mental illness, and they remain so to the present day (Greenberg and Rosenheck 2008; Robst et al. 2011).

During the Great Recession of 2007–2009, when corporate greed caused the subprime mortgage crisis, housing insecurity, rather than literal homelessness, became a top national issue. Predatory lending practices in the years leading up to this punishing economic downturn caused many people to lose their primary source of housing. Many moved in with friends and relatives, but others had little choice but to populate the nation's shelters, live in tent cities and encampments, or spend their nights on the streets. By 2019, forty-six of fifty states had tents or homeless encampments within their borders (National

Law Center on Homelessness and Poverty 2019). Affordability is also an issue, as the average homeowner now spends over 30 percent of their income on housing, a much higher percentage than in earlier decades. Understanding homelessness during this most recent crisis point means reckoning with the increasing distance between upper- and lower-income levels, which has made housing insecurity a far more widespread part of U.S. society than homelessness ever was.

Over time, approaches to welfare, housing, and social services created a growing homeless service industry (Gowan 2010; Willse 2015), or what one journalist refers to as the "homeless industrial complex" (Ring 2019). Although homelessness has long been a problem in the United States, the nation still struggles to identify its scope and characteristics and to create a viable plan to end it permanently. Experts agree that doing so will require increased and enduring government attention to the chronic homeless population. This focus was inspired by research showing that people who live on the streets for longer periods of time cost taxpayers more than those living in apartments (Culhane 2002; Culhane et al. 2011). Homeless advocates emphasize that focusing on the poorest of the poor is not only a moral imperative but also that it will save local, state, and federal governments' money in the long run.

The embrace of consumerism over community that occurs from the Great Depression to the 1980s is supported through economic and social policy. Reagan's economic strategy of supporting big business to strengthen those on the lower end of the income ladder became more entrenched by the Great Recession of 2007–2009, when the government bailed out the very banks and securities firms responsible for the crisis.

The next chapter examines three of the current controversial issues related to homelessness: criminalization, housing, and welfare. It explores the overall effect of these contemporary problems on the numbers and demographics of people experiencing homelessness. It also offers examples of policies that attempt to offer solutions and evaluates their efficacy.

References

Abeles, Ronald P. 1976. "Relative Deprivation, Rising Expectations, and Black Militancy." *Journal of Social Issues* 32(2): 119–137.

Alexander, Michelle. 2010. *The New Jim Crow: Mass Incarceration in the Age of Colorblindness*. New York: The New Press.

Austen, Ben. 2019. *High Risers: Cabrini Green and the Fate of American Public Housing*. New York: HarperCollins Publishers.

Bellisfield, Gwen. 1972. "White Attitudes toward Racial Integration and the Urban Riots of the 1960's." *Public Opinion Quarterly* 36(4): 579–585.

Bertrand, Marianne and Sendhil Mullainathan. 2011. "Are Emily and Greg More Employable Than Lakisha and Jamal? A Field Experiment on Labor Market Discrimination." In *The Inequality Reader: Contemporary and Foundational Readings in Race, Class, and Gender*, Second Edition, eds. David B. Grusky and Szonja Szelènyi, 254–259. Boulder, CO: Westview Press.

Bloss, William. 2007. "Escalating U.S. Police Surveillance after 9/11: An Examination of Causes and Effect." *Surveillance and Society* 4(3): 208–228.

Bordo, Michael D., Claudia Goldin, and Eugene N. White. 1998. *The Defining Moment: The Great Depression and the American Economy in the Twentieth Century*. Chicago: University of Chicago Press.

Brown, Tristan. 2015. "Nobody Goes to Jail: The Economics of Criminal Law, Securities Fraud, and the Great Recession of 2008." *Criminal and Civil Confinement* 41: 343–365.

Bullard, Robert D. and Beverly Wright. 2009. *Race, Place, and Environmental Justice after Hurricane Katrina: Struggles to Reclaim, Rebuild, and Revitalize New Orleans and the Gulf Coast*. Boulder, CO: Westview Press.

Burt, Martha. 1992. *Over the Edge: The Growth of Homelessness in the 1980s*. New York: Russell Sage Foundation.

Burt, M. R. and B. Cohen. 1989. *America's Homeless: Numbers, Characteristics, and Programs That Serve Them*. Washington, DC: Urban Institute Press.

Center for Social Innovation. 2018. "Supporting Partnerships for Anti-Racist Communities." Stage 1 study findings.

Collins, Jane. 2011. "Wal-Mart, American Consumer Citizenship, and the 2008 Recession." *Focaal* 61: 2–12.

Conley, Dalton and Brian Gifford. 2006. "Home Ownership, Social Insurance, and the Welfare State." *Sociological Forum* 21(1): 55–82.

Culhane, Dennis. 2002. "Public Service Reductions Associated with Placement of Homeless Persons with Severe Mental Illness in Supportive Housing." *Housing Policy Debate* 13(1): 107–163.

Culhane, Dennis, Jung Min Park, and Stephen Metraux. 2011. "The Patterns and Costs of Services Use among Homeless Families." *Journal of Community Psychology* 39(7): 815–825.

Drake, St. Claire and Horace R. Cayton. 1945. *Black Metropolis: A Study of Negro Life in a Northern City*. New York: Harcourt.

Dreier, Peter. 2004. "Reagan's Legacy: Homelessness in America." Shelterforce: The Original Voice of Community Development.

Dyson, M. E. 2005. *Come Hell or High Water: Hurricane Katrina and the Color of Disaster*. New York: Basic Civitas Books.

Egan, Timothy. 2006. *The Worst Hard Time*. Boston: Mariner Books.

Faber, Jacob W. 2018. "Cashing In on Distress: The Expansion of Fringe Financial Institutions during the Great Recession." *Urban Affairs Review* 54(4): 663–696.

Fitzpatrick, Kevin and Mark LaGory. 2000. *Unhealthy Places: The Ecology of Risk in the Urban Landscape*. New York: Routledge.

Galbraith, John Kenneth. 1954. *The Great Crash 1929*. Boston: Mariner Books.

Garfinkel, Irwin and Irving Piliavin. 1995. "Trends in the Size of the Nation's Homeless Population during the 1980s: A Surprising Result." Institute for Research on Poverty, Discussion Paper no. 1034–94.

Goffman, Erving. 1963. *Stigma: Notes on the Management of a Spoiled Identity*. New York: Simon & Schuster, Inc.

Goldrick-Rab, Sara. 2016. *Paying the Price: College Costs, Financial Aid, and the Betrayal of the American Dream*. Chicago: University of Chicago Press.

Gotsch, Kara and Vinay Basti. 2018. *Incarceration: US Growth in Private Prisons*. Washington, DC: The Sentencing Project.

Gowan, Teresa. 2010. *Hobos, Hustlers, and Backsliders: Homeless in San Francisco*. Minneapolis, MN: University of Minnesota Press.

Gravelle, Randal. 2015. *Hooverville and the Unemployed: Seattle during the Great Depression*. Middletown, DE: Randal Gravelle.

Greenberg, Greg A. and Robert A. Rosenheck. 2008. "Homelessness in the State and Federal Prison Population." *Criminal Behavior and Mental Health* 18: 88–103.

Hawdon, James E. 2001. "The Role of Presidential Rhetoric in the Creation of a Moral Panic." *Deviant Behavior: An Interdisciplinary Journal* 22: 419–445.

Hinton, Elizabeth. 2016. *From the War on Poverty to the War on Crime: The Making of Mass Incarceration in America*. Cambridge, MA: Harvard University Press.

Hoch, Charles and Robert Slayton. 1989. *New Homelessness and Old*. Philadelphia: Temple University Press.

Hoover, Herbert. 1929. *November 19, 1929: Statement on the Economy*. Washington, DC: National Archives and Records Administration, 1988.

Jenkins, J. Craig and Craig Eckert. 1989. "The Corporate Elite, the New Conservative Policy Network, and Reaganomics." *Critical Sociology* 16(2/3): 121–144.

Jones, Nikki and Christina Jackson. 2018. "You Just Don't Go Down There: Learning to Avoid the Ghetto in San Francisco." In *The Ghetto: Contemporary Global Issues and Controversies*, eds. Ray Hutcheson and Bruce Haynes, 83–110. New York: Routledge.

Klein, Naomi. 2014. *This Changes Everything: Capitalism vs. The Climate*. New York: Simon and Schuster.

Kneebone, Elizabeth and Natalie Holmes. 2016. "U.S. Concentrated Poverty in the Wake of the Great Recession." Brookings Institute Report. March 31. https://www.brookings.edu/research/u-s-concentrated-poverty-in-the-wake-of-the-great-recession/

Lange, Dorothea and Paul Schuster Taylor. 1939. *An American Exodus: A Record of Human Erosion*. New York: Reynal & Hitchcock.

Leuchtenburg, William E. 1963. *Franklin D. Roosevelt and the New Deal 1932–1940*. London: Harper Perennial.

Levin, Josh. 2019. *The Queen: The Forgotten Life behind an American Myth*. New York: Little, Brown, and Company.

Mann, Robert. 2019. *Becoming Ronald Reagan: The Rise of a Conservative Icon*. Lincoln, NE: Potomac Books.

McElvaine, Robert S. 1984. *The Great Depression: America, 1929–1941*. New York: Three Rivers Press.

Miller, Caleb R. 2018. "'What Is to Be Done' When There Is Nothing to Do? Realism and Political Inequality." *An International Journal of Critical & Democratic Theory* 25(4): 602–613.

Mitchell, D. 2001. "The Annihilation of Space by Law: The Roots and Implications of Anti-Homeless Laws in the United States." In *The Legal Geographies Reader*, eds. N. Blomley, D. Delaney, and R. T. Ford, 6–18. Oxford: Blackwell Publishers.

Modi, Radha and Abigail A. Sewell. 2015. "Wealth Inequality among Young Adults during the Great Recession of 2008." American Sociological Association.

Muolo, Paul. 2009. *$700 Billion Bailout: The Emergency Economic Stabilization Act and What It Means to You, Your Money, Your Mortgage, and Your Taxes*. Hoboken, NJ: John Wiley & Sons, Inc.

National Law Center on Homelessness and Poverty. 2019. *Housing, Not Handcuffs: The Criminalization of Homelessness in US Cities*. Washington, DC: National Law Center on Homelessness and Poverty.

O'Connell, James J., Sarah C. Oppenheimer, Christine M. Judge, Robert L. Taube, Bonnie B. Blanchfield, Stacy E. Swain, and Howard Koh. 2010. "The Boston Healthcare for the Homeless Program: A Public Health Framework." *Framing Health Matters* 100(8): 1400–1408.

Pager, Devah. 2011. "Marked: Race, Crime, and Finding Work in an Era of Mass Incarceration." In *The Inequality Reader: Contemporary and Foundational Readings in Race, Class, and Gender*, Second Edition, eds. David B. Grusky and Szonja Szelènyi, 260–268. Boulder, CO: Westview Press.

Reagan, Ronald. 2016. *The Last Best Hope: The Greatest Speeches of Ronald Reagan*. New York, NY: Humanix Books.

Ring, Edward. 2019. "The Homeless Industrial Complex." *The California Globe*, May 28. https://californiaglobe.com /fr/the-homeless-industrial-complex/

Robst, John, Robert Constantine, Ross Andel, Timothy Boaz, and Andrew Howe. 2011. "Factors Related to Criminal

Justice Expenditure Trajectories for Adults with Serious Mental Illness." *Criminal Behavior and Mental Health* 21: 350–362.

Roosevelt, Franklin D. (Franklin Delano). 1988. *Franklin D. Roosevelt's Inaugural Address of 1933*. Washington, DC: National Archives and Records Administration.

Rosenthal, R. 1994. *Homeless in Paradise: A Map of the Terrain*. Philadelphia: Temple University Press.

Rothstein, Richard. 2018. *The Color of Law: A Forgotten History of How Our Government Segregated America*. New York: W. W. Norton & Company.

Scott, Janny. 2011. "Life at the Top in America Isn't Just Better, It's Longer." In *The Inequality Reader: Contemporary and Foundational Readings in Race, Class, and Gender*, Second Edition, eds. David B. Grusky and Szonja Szelènyi, 614–621. Boulder, CO: Westview Press.

Seager, Stephen B. 1998. *Street Crazy: The Tragedy of the Homeless Mentally Ill*. Redondo Beach, CA: Westcom Press.

Shlaes, Amity. 2007. *The Forgotten Man: A New History of the Great Depression*. New York: Harper Perennial.

Snow, D., S. Soule, and D. Cress. 2005. "Identifying the Precipitants of Homeless Protest across 17 US Cities, 1980 to 1990." *Social Forces* 83(3): 1183–1210.

Steinbeck, John. 1939. *The Grapes of Wrath*. New York: Penguin Books.

Stone, Chad, Danilo Trisi, Arloc Sherman, and Jennifer Beltrán. 2020. *A Guide to Statistics on Historical Trends in Income Inequality*. Washington, DC: Center on Budget and Policy Priorities.

St. Pierre, Maurice. 1991. "Reaganomics and Its Implications for African-American Family Life." *Journal of Black Studies* 21(3): 325–340.

Urgent Relief for the Homeless Act. Public Law 100–77. *U.S. Statutes at Large* 100 (1987): 482–538.

Wagner, David. 1993. *Checkerboard Square: Culture and Resistance in a Homeless Community*. Boulder, CO: Westview Press.

Wagner, David. 2005. *The Poorhouse: America's Forgotten Institution*. Lanham, MD: Rowman & Littlefield Publishers, Inc.

Wakin, Michele. 2020. *Hobo Jungle: A Homeless Community in Paradise*. Boulder, CO: Lynne Rienner Publishers.

Waquant, Loïc. 2009. *Punishing the Poor: The Neoliberal Government of Social Insecurity*. London: Duke University Press.

Western, Bruce. 2006. *Punishment and Inequality in America*. New York: Russell Sage Foundation.

Willse, Craig. 2015. *The Value of Homelessness: Managing Surplus Life in the United States*. Minneapolis: University of Minnesota Press.

Wilson, James Q. and George L. Kelling. 1982. *Broken Windows: The Police and Neighborhood Safety. Atlantic Monthly*, March.

Wilson, William Julius. 1987. *The Truly Disadvantaged: The Inner City, the Underclass, and Public Policy*. Chicago: University of Chicago Press.

Wolch, Jennifer and Michael Dear. 1993. *Malign Neglect*. San Francisco: Josey Bass.

Wright, Talmadge. 1997. *Out of Place: Homeless Mobilizations, Subcities, and Contested Landscapes*. Albany: State University of New York Press.

Young, T. R. 1988. "Class Warfare in the 80s and 90s: Reaganomics and Social Justice." *Wisconsin Sociologist* 25(2–3): 68–75.

Zucman, Gabriel. 2019. "Global Wealth Inequality." *Annual Review of Economics* 11: 109–138.

The previous chapter examined how society responds to homelessness during crisis points, when the nation's core political and economic beliefs are challenged. It examined the development of federal policies to count the homeless population and to develop housing and service solutions. It looked at possible ways of mitigating the effects of homelessness on individuals and communities or ending it completely. It also explored demographic changes in the homeless population and evolving social and cultural views on homelessness. Although innovative policies and approaches have emerged, the controversies presented in this chapter prove that we are still a long way from solving the problem.

This chapter discusses criminalization, housing, and welfare as three of the central issues that characterize the nation's response to homelessness. All three have long histories, yet they remain contemporary social problems. These controversies relate to the crisis points discussed in the first chapter because of their emergency nature, resource focus, and emphasis on stigma as it informs public policy. Each debate has two sides that remain relatively consistent over time and across issues. On one side, homeless people and advocates argue for additional services, rights, and provisions. They work to raise awareness about causes of and solutions to homelessness. On the other

_____

A homeless child looks away from the camera. Without stable housing and welfare assistance, children experiencing homelessness face multiple, ongoing challenges that place them at risk. (Ekaterina Naumenko/Dreamstime.com)

side, citizens, business owners, and city officials argue for limits to these provisions that ensure their temporary, low-cost status. In some cases, the interests of both sides converge, as in the case of tent cities used as temporary accommodations for homeless people (Heben 2014). More frequently, they remain divided on the best ways to address homelessness as a societal ill and to help specific homeless populations (Burt 2016).

The first controversy this chapter examines is the criminalization of homelessness. Criminalization includes strategies that target homeless people for legal action based on who they are, where they are, or what they are doing. Criminalization focuses on homelessness in urban, public spaces as a problem to be addressed through enforcement. Unsheltered homeless people often receive repeat citations for offenses they are routinely guilty of, like sleeping in public. Known as "anti-homeless" ordinances, many cities adopt these measures to control, hide, disperse, or eliminate their homeless populations. This chapter explores criminalization by examining a 2019 court decision to allow street sleeping in cities without adequate shelter, known as the *Boise* decision (*Martin v. City of Boise* 2019). This case provides an avenue to challenge the notion that criminalization is an effective solution to the problem of homeless people sleeping in public. It demonstrates that targeting homeless people violates their civil and human rights and prolongs homelessness. It also shows that criminalization and housing are overlapping concerns, as without housing, homeless people are at heightened risk of receiving citations for life-sustaining activities.

Housing is the second controversy this chapter focuses on, as access to housing shapes opportunities in such vital areas as health care and education. It is also the only resource that can unequivocally end homelessness. In U.S. society, the home is a combination of its physical space and the emotional value we attach to it. One's home is also symbolic of one's role or place in the world. As a society, the United States generally views the home as a source of comfort, but this meaning is not locked or fixed. Whether one lives in an apartment or a house, the home can be a place of safety or a place of trauma. Many people experiencing homelessness are searching to reconnect the ideas of safety and acceptance with physical space and the idea of home. Place-based solutions to homelessness focus on developing a positive relationship between self and dwelling and emphasizing safety and community. These solutions are at the heart of advancing placemaking activities and identity work (Snow and Anderson 1993; Wright 1997). These are strategies used by homeless people to develop a sense of self-worth and a semblance of home and to combat social stigma.

This section reviews the kinds of housing available to different segments of the homeless population. It examines the services and amenities and rights and entitlements that go with each kind of shelter, subsidy, or program. It also reviews how the right to shelter and the provision of emergency shelters for people experiencing homelessness have evolved over time. Finally, it explores current, innovative housing solutions. Although the "right to shelter" and housing are not universal in the United States, some states are less punitive than others. This section provides a case study of Massachusetts, one of the few "right to shelter" states, and reviews the efficacy of its use of motels as housing for homeless families. It explores how being a "right to shelter" state affects the prevalence of family homelessness and creates or exacerbates the cycle of poverty.

The third controversy this chapter examines is welfare policy, including the change from Aid to Families with Dependent Children (AFDC) to Temporary Assistance for Needy Families (TANF), as a tool to end homelessness. Ideally, welfare payments are combined with other resources that assist people in securing and maintaining housing, purchasing food, accessing training, employment, education, and medical care. In reality, accessing welfare benefits is a complicated process that depends on specific eligibility criteria and offers limited provisions. Concerns about identity and who qualifies for assistance have always been central to the issue of welfare assistance. Cost savings and administering program rules and eligibility requirements are also key concerns. Calls to reduce spending on welfare have been popular in American politics since well before the 1980s and extend across party lines. Many of these calls focus on alleged links between moral culpability, race, sex, and poverty and the overall impression of welfare as a symbol of self-induced failure. Research shows that rigid rules and restrictions are used to reduce the number of women on welfare and cut expenses and that these policies often have a disproportionately severe impact on women of color. This section examines welfare's overall efficacy in offering education, employment, and assistance to lift families out of poverty and prevent or end homelessness.

In addition to these three controversies, the emerging COVID-19 pandemic presents an opportunity to explore a current crisis as it unfolds. This chapter presents a brief overview of how the pandemic affects homeless people, people of color, and frontline workers as overlapping categories. It uses the case of Project Roomkey in Los Angeles to examine emergency measures to provide housing and slow the spread of the virus. It examines the rapid mobilization of government resources to provide permanent housing for the most vulnerable. It also explores the likelihood that long-term housing will be a part of the national conversation and examines whether or not California can end its homelessness crisis.

All of the controversies discussed in this chapter pose challenges for homeless people, the communities they live in, and the nation as a whole. Occupying public space presents a challenge for people experiencing homelessness because of criminalization. The inadequacy of public shelters, public housing, and welfare benefits only makes criminalization worse, as it punishes people without alternatives. The controversies in this chapter critique approaches to homelessness. They raise the basic question: Do these approaches reduce or end homelessness or make the problem worse? Housed communities, federal and local governments, and service providers spend time and money moving and removing homeless people, offering services, shelter, and housing. They must simultaneously minimize cost, loss of revenue, or risk to the general population. Researchers have long been making the case that housing homeless people is less expensive and more effective in returning people to "normal," community life. Yet, punitive, temporary solutions still dominate the field of homeless service and delivery. The positive and negative solutions to homelessness that are outlined in this chapter demonstrate conflicting approaches about how to treat, manage, or end it.

The Stigma of Homelessness

Attaching meaning to homelessness, or any other feature of identity, is part of how we construct social reality. Views of a stranger as good or bad, deserving or undeserving, are social constructions informed by appearance and the meaning attached to it and by the economic, social, and political context. Of course, people do differ in terms of intelligence, strength, and aptitude. Stereotypes unfairly attribute these differences broadly to social categories like poor and rich, black and white, female and male. These associations are so strong in U.S. society that they create an implicit bias against stigmatized groups (Melamed et al. 2019). Of course, overt discrimination is also a part of U.S. society. Implicit bias is a subconscious belief in the inferiority of one group over another, often informed by years of exposure to social stereotypes and their infusion in societal institutions and culture.

Sociologists writing about these issues are interested in the effects that society's ideas about race, sex, poverty, and other social categories have on whether we see people as good or bad, dangerous or kind, smart or unintelligent. They also focus on how people internalize stereotypes, which in turn can create self-doubt. People are aware of the traditional associations between women and caretaking of children and households and pernicious stereotypes of black people as physically gifted but lacking in academic or intellectual capacity. These stereotypes can be so deeply internalized that women discount their own ability to achieve professional success and black people come to doubt their own academic ability, particularly when put under pressure. People fear, in other words, confirming societal stereotypes, and it inhibits performance, a process known as stereotype threat (Steele 2011). The ideas of stereotype threat and implicit bias are important because they show how strongly our understandings of others and of ourselves are shaped by identity and inequality in society. They also show how damaging stereotypes can be as they limit opportunity and cause stress and trauma.

In 1963, Erving Goffman published *Stigma: Notes on the Management of Spoiled Identity*, in which he described the various ways people are viewed as tainted or discounted in social situations based on appearance and information about personal history. In simplest terms, we assign value to other people based on how they look, how they act, information we find out about them, stereotypes, or a combination of these. We also attribute meaning to individual actions based on who we think that individual is. This is often measured at first glance, as an appearance-based assessment. Homeless people are stigmatized along the lines of some of U.S. society's most intractable forms of stigma, including the overlapping categories of race, class, gender, and mental and physical ability status, among others. In this sense, the actions of the homeless, even in pursuit of their own survival, are seen as illogical, illegal, degraded, or as a sign of questionable moral worth. Instead of understanding how poverty and homelessness are caused by structural inequality, society often blames individual homeless people for their present condition.

As the first chapter's discussion of crisis points showed, the United States has become an increasingly unequal society since the 1980s. This reality shapes our understanding of homelessness as clashing with the values of consumerism and financial success as measures of self-worth and social value. Homeless people in the United States are seen as "no longer 'useful' and/or 'functional' members of capitalism, since they do not actively work and support the system" (Belcher and DeForge 2012, 929). For this reason, policies to assist people experiencing homelessness often focus on cost reduction and on forcing participation through work. Along with criminalization, this is a way of reducing money spent on a population seen by some Americans as useless or helpless. For this reason, and to better understand how the stigma of homelessness works in modern America, the concepts of stigma and inequality are briefly discussed. Exploring these concepts can provide a greater understanding of the current composition of the homeless population, the provision of services to the homeless, and the shape of social policy for each of the three controversies presented in this chapter.

For people experiencing chronic homelessness, the effects of multiple forms of stigma intersect with personal biographies that often feature poverty, violence, addiction, and trauma. For many people, these are co-occurring and can make it very difficult to exit homelessness. These barriers also affect the demographics of the homeless population. They impact the ability to construct a positive sense of self or social worth, which can in turn inhibit progress in securing work, food, service, and shelter. The effects of these forms of stigma are also cumulative, reflective of ongoing inequality and generational poverty.

The ability to access welfare assistance varies depending on individual and group membership, with certain populations favored over others. Ending veteran homelessness, reducing the cost of chronic homelessness, and ensuring access to K–12 education are examples of identity-based solutions to poverty and homelessness. They focus on sympathetic individuals and groups or those seen as too costly to leave on the street because of their frequent use of emergency services. Traditionally, in the United States, the amount and direction of assistance are based on the prevailing political climate and cultural norms and preferences. Approaches to homeless assistance have historically focused on who people are or what they cost society, and provisions often come with stringent rules and requirements and a backlash of punishment. Shelters, for example, are a provision that reinforces criminalization because, when shelters are available, homeless people can be cited for not using them, or policed as guests. These laws and regulations often serve to force homeless people into what society views as their proper place—the shelter, jail, or prison.

It is important to combine our understanding of the stigma of homelessness with attempts to assist and house homeless people. These efforts have evolved considerably since the crisis points outlined in the first chapter. One of the most significant accomplishments in the field of homeless assistance since the 1980s is the attempt to produce data-driven social policy through careful assessments of population demographics and specific needs for assistance. First initiated by the federal government, production of a national, annual assessment of the U.S. homeless population has become a cornerstone of planning and funding efforts.

Current Homeless Population Trends

The Annual Homeless Assessment Report (AHAR) to Congress has tracked national trends in the homeless population through the point-in-time (PIT) count since the first report was released in 2007, reporting on the 2005 count. All planning bodies that coordinate homeless housing and services within a continuum of care (CoC) region are required to conduct an annual count of people living in shelters, transitional housing, and safe havens. They are also required to submit a biannual count of the number of unsheltered homeless people in the same area, although CoCs may elect to do so annually. The U.S. Department of Housing and Urban Development (HUD) provides guidance for both types of counts, but the rules for counting are lengthy, confusing, and often difficult to implement because of local limitations including funding, volunteer shortages, weather, and other logistics (see Burt 2016). For these reasons, both the methodology guiding early counts and the data included in corresponding reports fluctuate wildly, particularly for the unsheltered count.

Los Angeles is known for its large unsheltered homeless population. The second homeless count for the Los Angeles CoC region, in 2009, includes data compiled over three days. It attempts to count "hot spots," or areas known to have large homeless populations. It also offers a stratified random sample of census tracts within the region, beyond the initial "hot spot" areas. This was done instead of the labor-intensive, street-by-street count conducted in 2007. It was intended to produce more credible population estimates. With this change in methodology, results showed a startling 28,000 person drop in the number of unsheltered homeless people. This number was roughly half of the original 2007 estimate of 57,166 homeless people (AHAR 2009), and without a massive influx of housing, jobs, or other conditions that would warrant the decrease. Eventually, in 2014, the AHAR was corrected for the Los Angeles CoC region and showed a drop in the homeless count of between 9,000 and 20,000 people per year from 2007 to 2013. Particularly in the Los Angeles area, where unsheltered homelessness remains a proportionately large segment of the homeless population, obtaining an accurate count is instrumental to developing solutions.

The Detroit CoC also saw a large decrease in its unsheltered population from 2008 to 2009. The reason for this is that the count in 2008 did not proceed street by street. Instead, an extrapolation factor was used to estimate the number of homeless people in areas throughout the region. When this approach was dropped in 2009, the area's homeless population estimates also dropped by over 15,000. Similarly, New Orleans' first count was conducted in 2007 but because the city was still regrouping after Hurricane Katrina, those numbers were widely regarded as unreliable. The New Orleans CoC region conducted a new count two years later that showed an increase in its homeless population of over 7,000 people (AHAR 2009), apart from Katrina victims.

These results are not indicative of policy or population changes, or even the result of natural disaster or wider economic expansion or contraction. They are the result of differing, inconsistent PIT count methodology. This makes funding and planning particularly difficult for people living unsheltered, who remain the most challenging to count and serve. Despite the PIT count's limitations, however, it can be useful in showing general trends in overall numbers and demographics, particularly for those living in shelters. It also allows the nation to track changes in specific regions and subpopulations of interest and to make more informed decisions regarding federal funding and policies related to reducing homelessness.

In addition to the PIT, the housing inventory count (HIC) is used to track the number and types of beds available in a given CoC region, including emergency and transitional shelters, rapid rehousing, safe haven, and permanent supportive housing. It is submitted annually with the AHAR as a separate Part II, beginning in 2012. It uses data from the homeless management information system (HMIS), a database management system used to better track shelter usage. Its strengths are that it includes data collected over the course of a year instead of a one-night count. It also eliminates duplicate counts and allows for more coordinated, comprehensive service provision. Its primary weakness is that its focus on shelter bed availability and usage makes it of limited usefulness in addressing the unsheltered homeless population.

Beginning in 2009, HUD also released a quarterly PULSE Report to examine the effects of the Great Recession on people experiencing homelessness. The first PULSE Report was substantially shorter than the AHAR. It covered the last quarter of 2009 through the first quarter of 2011 and was designed to offer more detailed, specific information than the annual PIT count. It examined the effects of the economic recession, rising foreclosures, and increased unemployment on sheltered homelessness. Only a small number of CoC regions, eight to start, participated in the ongoing data collection required for the PULSE Report. While several regions, including New York City, experienced substantial growth in newly homeless individuals and families, results were not conclusive or representative. Data suggests that people who have recently lost formerly stable housing often transition to another temporary location rather than immediately seeking emergency shelter. In addition, the uneven housing inventory across the sampled CoC regions may account for the percentages of individuals and families in each housing or shelter type instead of offering accurate information on service needs. Because of this limited methodology and scope, new homelessness appeared to be declining for families, so the report was discontinued.

Despite its shortcomings, however, the PULSE Report offers important conclusions. The first is that a focus on special populations may require specific methodology changes. This is because, as the Great Recession demonstrates, people experiencing homelessness may endure various episodes over the course of one or several years. They may also move between various forms of precarious housing, juggling several options at the same time. This fluidity makes accurate data collection particularly challenging, as not all kinds of housing require the inventory of HMIS. Many units are in the private housing market, as people often double up with family or friends or couch surf as a temporary but viable housing option.

Along with retooling data collection efforts and focusing on families, this era also brought about various forms of federal assistance designed to counter the effects of the Great Recession.

Combating Homelessness in a Recession

In 2009, President Obama signed the American Recovery and Reinvestment Act, a set of measures designed to jump-start the nation's economy. This act included investments in technological infrastructure, energy independence, the expansion of educational and employment opportunities, and new tax relief and health care initiatives. The Homeless Prevention and Rapid Re-Housing Program (HPRP) was part of this act, designed to offer short-term limited subsidies geared toward keeping families and individuals housed so as to prevent a new influx of homeless people as a result of the housing and foreclosure crisis. Both the Bush and Obama administrations feared an upsurge in recession-related homelessness, as research had already shown a 40 percent increase in family homelessness from 2005 to 2007, before the Great Recession even hit (Burt 2016). Housing stabilization and financial assistance under HPRP provided rental assistance to qualified enrollees for a maximum of eighteen months. Although HPRP helped produce a short-term decrease in the number of homeless families, many beneficiaries were not able to keep their housing over the long term. As a result, this particular prevention measure was eventually called into question for its long-term efficacy.

A separate annual report on veteran homelessness was also released in 2009, as part of a partnership between HUD and Veterans Affairs (VA) to create supportive housing vouchers. This program, known as HUD-VASH, began in the 1990s but ramped up with the return of soldiers from the Iraq War in 2007. Under President Obama, the initiative became an integral part of the official planning and reporting process. This included the federal government's plan to end homelessness, released in 2010. Titled *Opening Doors: Federal Strategic Plan to Prevent and End Homelessness*, the plan was a directive from Congress to the U.S. Interagency Council on Homelessness (USICH). Its goal was to create a comprehensive plan for ending homelessness in the United States through the Homeless Emergency Assistance and Rapid Transition to Housing (HEARTH) Act. The plan's four key goals included timelines associated with ending homelessness for chronically homeless people and veterans (in five years) and families, youth, and children (in ten years). HEARTH also charted a path for comprehensive planning for the overall population (USICH 2010).

Updates and amendments to the plan were released in 2012, 2015, 2018, and 2020.

The 2018 Federal Strategic Plan touted decreases in individual homeless people (by 13 percent since 2010) and corresponding decreases in people living unsheltered (17 percent), homeless veterans (46 percent), and homeless families (27 percent). In fact, since federal criteria and benchmarks to end veteran homelessness were released in 2015, over sixty communities representing thirty different states have met these criteria, and three communities have met the criteria for ending chronic homelessness (HUD 2018). In addition to these policy and data-driven successes, the 2018 plan offered a renewed emphasis on specific focus areas including affordable housing, prevention and diversion, unsheltered homelessness, rural communities, employment, and learning from those with lived experience. Yet areas of concern remained, in particular regional and population variations in homelessness and heavy concentrations of homeless people in urban areas. Addressing these regional and geographic disparities is difficult to do using annual data, and appealing for federal support for new programs is left up to individual CoC regions.

Interestingly enough, the brilliant but lofty goal of ending homelessness in a ten-year period originated ten years earlier, in 2000, with the National Alliance to End Homelessness (NAEH). Founded in 1983, this citizen-founded, nonpartisan, nonprofit organization released the first plan to end homelessness: *A Plan, Not a Dream.* This plan introduced the strategy of closing the "front door" by preventing people from becoming homeless and opening the "back door" by offering a way for people to find and keep shelter. The idea was to build the infrastructure necessary to end homelessness by creating sufficient inventories of affordable housing. The plan challenged communities to create their own ten-year plans to take into account the underlying causes of homelessness and put systems in place to make it a temporary instead of a chronic condition. By 2009, there were over 230 plans to end homelessness in communities across the nation. By 2015, there were over 1,000 such plans. This demonstrates the importance of national-level, nongovernmental leadership in offering data- and population-driven social policy. The alliance continues to organize to inform policy and work with federal agencies to end homelessness.

With all the local, regional, and federal money and coordination put into homeless services, housing, and assistance programs, and to developing a timeline to end homelessness, what is the upshot? Have these efforts been successful in reducing or ending homelessness, or are they an inefficient and poorly coordinated set of resources used to extract worth from a surplus population (Willse 2015)? Despite overall gains in reducing the number of homeless people, it is the more specific policy and data-driven targets that show the most significant improvement. More than a decade after the first AHAR in 2007, only fifteen states showed net increases in their overall homeless populations; only five states show increases of over 20 percent. On the face of it, this suggests that homelessness has decreased, although nationwide, over 560,000 people can still be counted on a single night in 2019 (HUD 2019). Using the ten-year period from 2009 to 2019, the AHAR estimated 62,512 fewer homeless people across the United States, a 10 percent decrease of 6,251 fewer homeless people per year. Most of this reduction is due to gains in housing security for specific populations, many of which were expressly targeted for new programs and policy innovations.

One of the things influencing PIT count estimates is that, as part of an application for federal funding, certain information is emphasized, like a CoC's record of reducing chronic homelessness or its wider population decreases or increases. Communities gain or lose points for meeting the goals prescribed by HUD, so it is in their best interest to report decreases. CoC regions that show 5 percent reductions for specific populations, like "first time" homeless, chronically homeless people, families, and veterans, receive incentive points. With this obvious impetus to reduce numbers and the time-consuming, frenetic scramble for scarce resources, how can we be sure that reductions represent true gains and do not simply encourage officials to cut assistance or move populations to meet funding and budget targets? As NAEH points out in a 2019 report, the funding process that CoC regions must undergo is extensive and competitive and leaves the populations it serves at risk. Given the fact that a majority of HUD support goes to renewal funds for shelters and other ongoing projects, innovation is limited, and assessing real gains in communities remains elusive.

Reducing homelessness for specific populations is difficult, even with generous funding and policy support. What about the general population experiencing homelessness? In 2019, 37 percent of the total homeless population was unsheltered or living in makeshift locations that the report describes as "not suitable for human habitation" (HUD 2019). This is the exact same percentage reported in 2009, suggesting that the unsheltered population is the most difficult to assist in exiting homelessness and that its size remains relatively consistent over time, despite policy changes. In addition, approximately half of the nation's unsheltered homeless people live in or close to larger urban areas and totals vary widely across states. Statewide increases in homelessness from 2018 to 2019 show that California's is the most dramatic. It reported a 16 percent increase, or 21,306 people, with approximately 18,000 of them living unsheltered (HUD 2019). In addition, trends show that African Americans and Latinos continue to be overrepresented in the overall homeless population versus the general population.

Certain groups, like homeless families, veterans, and unaccompanied youth, showed population decreases by 2019, although 50 percent of homeless youth (under 18) remained unsheltered. Targeted legislation and programming have resulted in fewer families living unsheltered and fewer homeless veterans overall, but it is important to proceed with caution when interpreting these results. They suggest that parts of the problem of homelessness have been effectively addressed through targeted funding and policy. If this is the case, then the goal must be to continue these initiatives and expand them to encompass all states and, eventually, the entire homeless population. Housing First is a strategy that does not differentiate between types of homeless people, aside from its initial and ongoing focus on chronic homelessness and mental illness. Yet despite the national endorsement of Housing First, the number of people in the chronic category, who are often unsheltered, continues to rise, offsetting gains for other populations. In addition, there is insufficient oversight of communities implementing a Housing First strategy, so it is difficult to measure its success in reducing homelessness overall or for specific populations.

Programs that work to reduce homelessness have received modest annual increases in the federal budget for a number of years, but in 2019, massive cuts to these programs were proposed by the Trump administration. Opponents said the proposed cuts would further depress housing markets, cut welfare spending, deepen societal inequality, and add to the large numbers of homeless people on the nation's streets. Officials in the Trump administration justified cuts by blaming homelessness on four factors: overregulation of housing markets, permissiveness about street sleeping, the prevalence of homeless shelters, and ineffective policies by prior administrations (Council of Economic Advisers 2019).

In a 2019 policy brief, the NAEH pointed out that these claims ignored or overlooked the disparity between housing costs and homeless incomes. It assumed that shelters themselves cause homelessness, unfairly critiqued Housing First, and minimized the importance of the 2010 federal plan. Critics of the Trump administration charged that the only "solutions" it proposed to reduce homelessness were punitive. Advocates for the homeless emphasized that increasing federal spending on housing and service solutions was the only way to address the problem. This understanding was also reflected in the original 2010 federal plan to end homelessness, which predicates budget approval for its recommendations as essential for fulfilling its goals.

The Trump administration argued that the federal government had little responsibility for either causing or reducing homelessness. Federal officials blamed state governors as well as homeless shelters and homeless people themselves for the nation's population of families and individuals living on the streets. National antipoverty organizations worried publicly that the effect of blaming the victim would reduce homeless people's overall life chances, deepen cyclical poverty, and disproportionately impact children and families and people of color. Using the case of California, which has a large number of homeless people as well as high percentages of homeless people living in unsheltered circumstances, the National Alliance showed that limited funding from HUD, relative to the state's housing market and expenditures on homeless assistance grants, contributed to California's large numbers of homeless and unsheltered people. In fact, although the Trump administration decried the amount spent on welfare, the vast majority of annual funding (91.3 percent) went to existing programs. This meant that there was little room for new policy innovations or expanding access to existing programs to serve additional populations.

Some of the proposed solutions for solving the problem of homelessness in U.S. society are provisional. On a structural level, these kinds of solutions suggest increasing the role of government in providing communities with a basic standard of housing, employment, and welfare assistance. On an individual level, provisional solutions suggest planning and policy that value homeless voices and citizen buy-in; Housing First and trauma informed care are notable examples of this approach.

Criminalization and Other Punitive "Solutions" for Homelessness

Other so-called solutions for homelessness are punitive. They involve correcting what are seen as social ills, like homeless people in public, by criminalizing their behavior. Punitive solutions are also those that force beneficiaries of federal assistance to obtain work without providing the training, education, access to transportation, and other resources needed to make sustainable employment feasible. Shelters with stringent rules and regulations, like curfew and work requirements, have been criticized as punitive as well because they require compliance as a condition of service. Supporters of these shelter rules, however, contend that rules that impose curfews or forbid the use of illicit drugs, for example, make shelters safer for other residents.

"Criminalizing" homeless people is a strategy designed to protect cities' and communities' ability to generate and accumulate wealth. Critics also say that such laws banish homelessness from public view, making it easier for lawmakers and ordinary citizens alike to forget that the problem exists. One of the ways that the criminalization of homelessness is accomplished is by enforcing public space norms and provisions that designate what kind of an area a place is and who belongs there. The visible presence of homeless people in a public park or on a main street is seen as a sign of disorder. Whether this is because of the health risks allegedly posed to the larger population or the unpleasant or intimidating sight of homeless people in public, excluding them from public places is frequently framed as a way of protecting the public interest. If people feel safer in a given area, they will be more inclined to spend time and money there and attract others to do the same.

This sense of ownership over public space reflects societal rules and norms of entitlement that drive homeless people and shelters away from communities and neighborhoods populated by residents who subscribe to what is sometimes called a "not in my back yard" attitude, or NIMBYism. Pointing this out is important, as structural solutions to the problem of place must often contend with antihomeless sentiment and ongoing, systemic prejudice and discrimination. Locating housing or shelter for homeless people in residential, mixed-use areas is a way of normalizing and mainstreaming the relationship between homeless people and their housed neighbors. It is an important corrective to being spatially segregated from the general population in prisons, shelters, or industrial or abandoned "throwaway" areas, as homeless people often are (Padgett et al. 2016).

Chronically homeless people spend a majority of their time in public places and often bear the brunt of criminalization measures, particularly in the nation's urban environments, where public space is at a premium. Instead of solving the problem of chronic homelessness, repeat ticketing and the incarceration of people deemed to be in violation of local ordinances make receiving welfare and housing benefits, accessing employment, and exiting homelessness far more difficult (National Law Center on Homelessness and Poverty 2019). National studies have bemoaned the cost that long-term homelessness causes the taxpayer in emergency services including, most notably, shelter, health care, and criminal justice (Culhane 2002; Culhane et al. 2011). Ironically, housing is less expensive to provide than all of these services combined.

Historians who have written about crime and policing in the United States also point out the tremendous cost of developing and expanding the carceral state and the racial disparities in policing and sentencing that still exist. The U.S. Department of Justice notes that racial disparities in rates of imprisonment have declined since the late 1980s. But even in the late 2010s, black and Hispanic people are still far more likely to be incarcerated than white people. They are also overrepresented in the homeless population, particularly among the unsheltered. People experiencing mental illness and homelessness are also overrepresented in the nation's prison population. Instead of being rehabilitative, incarceration often leads to recidivism and is a feeder into chronic homelessness and cyclical poverty.

Criminalization is one of the most hotly contested issues related to homelessness and public space (National Law Center on Homelessness and Poverty 2019). Criminalization measures have targeted the poor and indigent for generations (Cresswell 2001; Wagner 2005), and since the 1980s, they have grown increasingly punitive. Cities nationwide have implemented public space regulations that make outdoor areas less hospitable to people who want to sleep, sit, or otherwise spend time in these places (Mitchell 2020). These measures are typically not intended to hurt homeless people but to make city spaces safer and more accessible for other residents and visitors. However, for people living on the streets without adequate shelter or access to other basic needs, these measures make even simple comforts elusive and have been castigated as cruel and unusual punishment—especially for the many homeless people afflicted with physical, emotional, or mental challenges (National Law Center on Homelessness and Poverty 2019).

Constitutional Considerations

The National Law Center on Homelessness and Poverty (NLCHP), which was founded in 1987 and recently renamed the National Homelessness Law Center, focuses on legal advocacy for all people experiencing homelessness. This is a particularly important resource, as criminalization measures are prevalent in cities nationwide, even though they are in potential violation of several constitutional amendments. The Fourteenth Amendment to the Constitution, for example, was crafted to protect people from biased treatment at the hands of law enforcement and ensure equal opportunity before the law. But legislation targeting specific people or groups underlies most homeless criminalization. Criminalization of homelessness has also been condemned as a violation of the First Amendment, which provides broad free speech protections, and the Fourth Amendment, which protects from unreasonable search and seizure. Finally, legal advocates say that criminalization statutes violate the Eighth Amendment, which prohibits cruel and unusual punishment.

When homeless people are cited for "panhandling," or begging for money, but others can ask for donations at sporting events, for example, this calls the First and Fourteenth Amendments into question. This is because laws can only target offenses and not specific groups or individuals. If cheerleaders can ask strangers for money, so can homeless people. Similarly, when homeless camps are swept away and meager possessions are destroyed, the Fourth and Fourteenth Amendments are potentially being violated, as housed citizens would have their property tagged and returned. Advocates assert that this unequal treatment is at the heart of both racial profiling and antihomeless criminalization. These strategies, which include banning panhandling or breaking up homeless camps, are enforced in communities that struggle to keep public parks and business areas safe for the general population. The questions that it raises are as follows: Are these legal strategies that fix the problem or emergency measures that exacerbate it? Does criminalization lead to safer spaces or feed a prison industrial complex and prolong homelessness?

The Eighth Amendment focuses on punishments seen as "cruel or unusual." This is a good reminder that criminal enforcement is intended to focus on action, not identity or status. Punishing someone for visible poverty is not legal in the same way that police cannot arrest a pickpocket simply because they are known to be one or because they look like one. The person must be caught in the act of pickpocketing to justify citation and arrest. Similarly, homeless people must be caught in the act of sleeping in areas that have been classified as off-limits for

Table 2.1 Constitutional Amendments and Homeless Criminalization

	Constitutional Amendments and Criminalization
Amendment 1	Freedom of Religion, Speech, and the Press (free speech)—panhandling
Amendment 4	Protection from Unreasonable Searches and Seizures (seizure and destruction of property)—sweeps of homeless camps
Amendment 8	Excessive Bail, Fines, and Punishments Forbidden (punishing involuntary behavior)—sleeping/camping ordinances
Amendment 14	Rights of Citizenship (equal protection)—targeting homeless people

Source: The National Coalition for the Homeless and The National Law Center on Homelessness and Poverty. 2006. *A Dream Denied: The Criminalization of Homelessness in US Cities*. Washington, DC: The National Coalition for the Homeless and The National Law Center on Homelessness and Poverty.

such activities to justify ticketing. Homeless advocates contend that because sleep is a biological necessity, homeless criminalization that focuses on sleep violates the Eighth Amendment. "When cities prohibit life-sustaining conduct, they present homeless people with an unconstitutional mandate," said one activist "Follow the law and die or stay alive and risk arrest" (Walters 1995, 1620). In this sense, criminalization is a controversial strategy for managing the problem of homelessness because it does not focus on its underlying causes but instead punishes its effects. It also often does so repeatedly, creating additional barriers for people wishing to exit homelessness.

The other side of this debate is the perspective of the housed citizen, police officer, or business owner. Imagine walking down a city street and seeing homeless people sleeping on the sidewalks, or clustered in doorways, or in front of your place of business. Imagine how it feels to be aggressively asked for change on your way to work or in front of your children. Housed people are typically bothered by visible poverty and homelessness, particularly in public places that revolve around tourism and enjoyment. They avoid areas that show these signs of unrest and do not spend money there. Similarly, police are often confronted with a mandate to remove street sleepers, even when the city has no treatment or rehabilitation options to which they can be directed. This is understandable, as policework focuses on enforcement. But these practices present ongoing risks for people living unsheltered, particularly if they have repeated interactions with law enforcement. Over time, criminalization focuses more stringently on removing homeless people and their possessions from city spaces and leaves rehabilitation to social service agencies.

The Right to Sleep

Focusing on sleep as the first controversy shows that local communities struggle to manage the presence of chronically homeless people in public. Urban sociologists are particularly interested in issues of public space, identity, and entitlement because they show how cities are shaped by political, economic, structural, and cultural forces that determine what type of place an area is, who belongs there, and what behaviors or activities are permitted. Other researchers focus on the meaning of specific places for people without shelter, noting their importance in establishing a sense of belonging and identity, control, and comfort (Dordick 1997). When cities seek to maximize profit, what researchers refer to as the "exchangeability" of public spaces (Mitchell 2020), homeless people are often pushed to the margins (Dear and Wolch 1987). They are punished for conducting life-sustaining activities in public or for not adhering to behavioral norms. This has disastrous effects on an already stressed and traumatized population and makes exiting homelessness more difficult (Goffman 2014; Roschelle 2019).

Homeless people have consistently been characterized as a threat to public health, public access, or as an economic drag on cities that lose tourist revenue. This discussion of criminalization focuses on sleeping and camping in the context of homelessness, urban space, and social stigma. While there are national-level trends related to the criminalization of homeless people, local approaches use municipal codes to target activities like sleeping, camping, or sitting down in public, as well as more aggressive behaviors like panhandling or trespassing. Some of these activities are unavoidable for people without shelter, who may endure repeat citations for the same violation or be targeted for specific sanctions. Other actions, like threatening people, are avoidable and are a threat to public safety. Because unsheltered homeless people spend the majority of most days on the street, they are the most frequently targeted for antihomeless criminalization. This vast and hidden segment of the homeless population remains the most difficult to understand, quantify, and serve.

Since the implementation of a nationwide PIT count in 2005, challenges have included a complicated count methodology that has undergone significant changes; differing political, economic, and social conditions over time and geographic area; and issues unique to urban versus rural settings and warm versus cold weather areas. People living unsheltered are particularly difficult to count accurately for several reasons. The first is that they often hide to avoid criminalization or negative public attention, or double up with others in shared housing. The second is that a one-time snapshot count does not capture the number of people who cycle in and out of homelessness in a given year, particularly in cold-weather areas that force many people into shelters and other indoor locations during winter months.

Even despite these challenges and discrepancies, some overarching patterns emerge. The first is that homeless people who are unsheltered tend to cluster in one of three states: California, New York, and Texas. California alone saw a one-year increase of approximately 18,000 unsheltered people from 2018 to 2019. Unsheltered homeless people often congregate in urban areas and take longer to exit homelessness than other groups. Since the PIT count takes place in January, experts argue, it may produce an undercount of the unsheltered population, which often cycles between shelter and outdoor or makeshift settings, depending on weather. Shelter policies in warm weather areas also favor seasonal closings, which make year-round shelter difficult to come by, particularly for chronically homeless individuals and families. For this reason, the unsheltered homeless population is disproportionately affected by the criminalization of sleeping and camping in public areas.

Unsheltered homelessness and the problems associated with it appear most often in communities with high rental costs, an inadequate supply of affordable or subsidized housing, insufficient homeless shelter options, and a job market that does not pay a living wage. Unsheltered homelessness also poses several risks that communities act to protect themselves against. The first is related to public health and the second to public order. The health issues associated with chronic homelessness, now well documented because of the COVID-19 crisis, pose a threat not only to citizens in host communities but also to homeless people themselves. The USICH addressed this problem in 2018 by noting that the immediate safety of unsheltered people should be considered in tandem with the rest of the community rather than one over the other.

Despite the various risks that homeless people face, preserving city spaces for public use by all residents and visitors is a genuine concern. When homeless people sleep in parks or beaches, they can detract from the venue's sense of order and safety. Criminalization that focuses on sleep overlaps with housing and housing rights because people are frequently given citations for sleeping in public or in places not deemed suitable for habitation. Legally, it is difficult to prove that someone is sleeping, as people experiencing homelessness sleep in various hidden, makeshift locations. If police focus on the act of sleep and not the status of homelessness, then they must actually catch someone in the act of sleeping to issue a citation. As research on makeshift sleeping demonstrates, this is particularly difficult when people sleep in vehicles or other inaccessible locations (Wakin 2008). If the evidence of camping over sleeping is targeted, then a bedroll or other visible signs of homelessness can be enough to issue a citation. So in many ways, it behooves homeless people to have few possessions, to hide themselves well, and to try not to bring attention to themselves by looking and behaving in ways that reveal their homeless status.

To fight criminalization for sleeping, legal arguments focus on sleep as a necessity for human health and well-being. The necessity defense allows for criminal behavior if enacted under emergency conditions and to prevent greater harm (*Pottinger v. City of Miami*, 1989). Someone who pulls off the road to take a nap to prevent falling asleep at the wheel, for example, can have a sleeping citation overturned. If a person experiencing homelessness sleeps on a public street, they can be charged with trespassing and public sleeping. If shelter beds or affordable housing are available when the person is cited, then the citation is typically upheld, because there was an available, legal alternative to street sleeping. But if no shelter is available, then every time homeless people fall asleep outdoors, they can be cited. When this happens on city streets, where AHARs show homeless people disproportionately tend to cluster, multiple citations are often issued to the same groups and individuals. As early as the 1980s, researchers pointed out that issuing multiple citations about violations of public space rules in this manner has the effect of pushing homeless into the prison industrial complex (Aulette 1987).

The *Boise* Decision

In 2005, in *Jones v. City of Los Angeles*, six homeless appellants who had received multiple citations for violating the city's municipal code against sleeping on the street filed an appeal with the Ninth Circuit Court. They won a nightly injunction against enforcing the antisleeping ordinance in the city's impoverished "Skid Row" area, where many of the city's homeless congregated for safety, support, and a sense of community. The injunction meant that street sleeping became legal on Skid Row during certain hours. Three basic conditions made this ruling possible. The first relies on the Eighth Amendment, which views sleep as involuntary and limits state power to criminalize particular groups. This means that sleep is not a criminal activity and targeting homeless people or other specific groups is not legal. The second is the presence of other conditions seen as involuntary and often concomitant with chronic homelessness, like mental illness and addiction. The third is the inadequate number of shelter beds and lack of affordable or subsidized housing in Los Angeles. Armed with evidence that homeless appellants received multiple citations, that shelter was unavailable, and that homelessness is typically an involuntary and traumatic state, the case was won.

Unsheltered homelessness is particularly prevalent in Los Angeles, but other communities experience similar issues. In 2009, eleven homeless people filed an injunction against the city of Boise for citations that it gave out to homeless people for illegal sleeping, camping, sitting, and other nuisance offenses. One appellant, who had difficulty walking, received a citation for resting near a shelter and was ordered to pay a $150 fine. The *Martin v. Boise* decision, filed in the Ninth Circuit Court of Appeals, ruled that ordinances against people experiencing homelessness cannot be issued in cities without adequate housing or shelter (National Law Center on Homelessness and Poverty 2019). This ruling is controversial, as it takes away local power to enforce city ordinances.

In a 2019 decision, the Supreme Court refused a request to review the decision. Cases of cities trying to ban homeless encampments and homeless people in the process have appeared throughout the states that the Ninth Circuit Court presides over, which include California, Idaho, Oregon, Washington, Montana, Nevada, Alaska, Arizona, and Hawaii. In these states, criminalizing homeless people for sleeping in public is considered "cruel and unusual punishment" (National Law Center on Homelessness and Poverty 2019). The Supreme Court's decision not to review the case rests on its recognition of the biological necessity of sleep as an involuntary behavior, as well as an awareness that public sleeping is the only option for homeless people without shelter. For cities and states mired in problems associated with outdoor street sleeping, the dilemma they face is to provide adequate housing or shelter or manage the presence of outdoor sleeping.

Solutions to reduce street sleeping demonstrate that, although there is not an established national right to housing in the United States, as there is in some other nations, communities are moving toward an approach that either offers shelter or permits street sleeping. In this sense, the burden is on cities to offer shelter or clemency (Wakin 2008). This does not amount to a solution to homelessness or street sleeping as much as it signifies a legal compromise. The same kinds of compromises emerged in cities nationwide during the COVID-19 pandemic, when homeless encampments became a national symbol of inequality and job and income losses rendered many people "housing insecure." Many people found themselves newly homeless or doubled up in unstable, unpredictable living situations and without a safety net to weather the storm. Allowing tent cities was a temporary measure, enacted during a crisis because there was no other viable alternative.

Shortages of Affordable Housing

The second controversy this chapter examines is housing. Although the provision of affordable housing could single-handedly solve the problem of homelessness, in the United States, it is not a right or entitlement. With rising housing and rental costs nationwide, even people with stable jobs often struggle to afford housing costs and cover basic needs. However, providing public housing is controversial, with critics claiming that such programs encourage laziness or amount to "tricking the system." The two primary housing solutions created for homeless people are public, locally administered, federally funded housing and the housing choice voucher program known as "Section 8." These programs apply to low-income and homeless renters who find units in the private market, and public housing agencies (PHAs) administer the program locally.

Section 8 can also be associated with a specific program, so vouchers are either "tenant" or "project" based. The difference between a tenant- and a project-based voucher, in addition to whatever services or case management a program requires, is that tenant vouchers belong to the individual. If someone decides to leave an apartment and does so legally, without being evicted, they take their voucher with them. If the voucher is obtainable only through a program or project, however, then leaving the program typically means leaving the voucher behind as well. The problem with both public housing and Section 8 is that the number of units or vouchers is woefully inadequate when measured against overall need and as related to location and condition.

According to the HUD, in 2021, the federal government provided public housing for approximately 1.2 million households in housing managed by approximately 3,300 local housing authorities. Public housing units are given to people based on income; on elderly, disabled, or family status; and on citizenship or legal immigration status, and homeless people are not the only ones competing for units. The qualification procedure is often lengthy, requiring extensive, ongoing documentation and wait lists, and local housing authorities can close the list completely when the number of people waiting exceeds the available units. Local HAs manage and operate the housing choice voucher program. Units consist of both apartments and houses, where families pay an amount determined locally, based on annual income and allowable deductions. Determining the financial contributions of families for such units is fraught with loopholes that are difficult to understand and plan for, and units are often unavailable.

In 2019, the National Low-Income Housing Coalition estimated that over 50 percent of housing choice voucher lists were closed to new applicants, with 65 percent of lists closed for at least one year. This makes the mean wait time for housing assistance in 2019 approximately 1.5 years. Public housing is only marginally better, with a mean wait time of nine months. For would-be homeless renters, long waiting lists pose a significant problem, because notification is typically sent via mail or internet. Anyone who becomes eligible for either type of housing and who does not receive notification returns to the bottom of the wait list. Because reliable mail and internet service are often unavailable in shelter settings and because people drift in and out of homelessness without a stable residence, some homeless people never even learn when they become eligible for assistance. The inability to maintain a stable address or computer access shows how a lack of access to basic services perpetuates homelessness. When public or Section 8 housing does become available, renters must still adhere to the terms of the lease, managing neighbors, rules, and responsibilities that many have little experience with (Roschelle 2019). As a result—and because many units are in poor condition—these forms of housing have been described as substandard and precarious.

The other options typically available for homeless people are emergency and transitional shelters and permanent supportive housing. These forms of shelter typically begin as a way of managing an emergency and gradually transition to permanent housing as a safer, less expensive way to end homelessness. Transitional shelter is a midway point. It is intended to offer temporary housing and accompanying support services, with people contributing a portion of their income to receive these supports and ideally to move on to permanent housing. But the results from transitional shelter are mixed. Many transitional programs more closely resemble emergency shelter because they do not lead to permanent housing or because they include time restrictions that punish or evict people who do not move on quickly to other accommodations. The physical accommodations in transitional shelters are only slightly better than those found in emergency shelters, so they impose greater restrictions and offer fewer amenities. Part of the reason for including transitional or permanent housing is that communities gain valuable points on applications for federal funding. But with little to no federal oversight of these programs in moving people on and out of homelessness, the "transition" is often in name only.

In contrast with transitional shelter, permanent supportive housing has shown more success in reducing overall homeless numbers, particularly among the chronically homeless population. The NAEH estimates that the focus on permanent housing has led to a 26 percent reduction in chronic homelessness from 2007 to 2015. Some of this reduction is simply due to changing methodology, as the early count varied widely and the unsheltered count remains the most inconsistent. Nevertheless, this approach to permanent housing allows the portion of the homeless population seen as most difficult and costly to serve to enter low-barrier, permanent housing, with minimal ongoing case management. Instead of jumping through treatment hoops, this solution moves people directly into housing and saves money in emergency services and corrections. These are important components of the Housing First initiative (Padgett et al. 2016).

The focus on permanent housing and on rapid rehousing over emergency shelter began in the 1980s and was reinvigorated in the wake of the Great Recession. This economic crisis brought the focus on housing to families, who were the primary victims of pre-Recession predatory lending that caused them to lose their homes and equity when the economy faltered. This crisis brought about increased housing instability and called attention to the inadequacy of emergency shelter in serving all populations. Many emergency shelters remain ill-equipped to serve families, for example, because they do not allow couples or children or because they are not geared toward addressing the specific issues families face. In addition, the fact that many families in this era are newly homeless or housing insecure changes how service and shelter are understood. As a result, rapid rehousing and tenancy preservation become primary strategies for keeping people housed. More money is targeted for these initiatives and for the creation of transitional and permanent units than for emergency shelter.

Even when shelter beds are available, some homeless people avoid such accommodations because of dangerous or dirty conditions or stringent rules and regulations. In fact, researchers have documented the degradation that is often par for the course in both individual and family shelters (Crowley 2003), the segregation of shelters in marginal city areas (Dear and Wolch 1987), the hazardous conditions and health risks that sometimes can be found in such facilities, and the lack of housing for couples and pets (Irvine 2013). But what are the alternatives? Assuming that most people experiencing homelessness will not get into public housing and will not receive a Section 8 voucher, their other options are fitting into a permanent or transitional housing program, living in an emergency shelter, or being temporarily housed in prisons, jails, or other makeshift locations, like homeless street encampments. Make-shift living arrangements like these are developed on the fly, in opposition to shelter, as a result of its rules and risks, or because of its absence.

Motels as Shelter in Massachusetts

Massachusetts became a right to shelter state for families in 1983, and New York did so in 1979, amending coverage to include families with children. Washington, DC, also offers the right to shelter. Initially it did so only during extremely hot or extremely cold weather, but it expanded to year-round begin-ning in 2015. Being a right to shelter state or district means that on any given night, temporary emergency services must be offered to those who qualify. For this reason, and because of its unforgiving winter climate, Massachusetts has a relatively low percentage of families who go unsheltered, at only 4.5 per-cent of its total homeless population (HUD 2019). To qualify for shelter, families must fall below 115 percent of the pov-erty line, which, in 2020, means an annual income of approxi-mately $30,000 for a family of four, or $2,511 per month. In addition, their homeless status must be verified and caused by one of four conditions: domestic violence, eviction, disaster, or health and safety risk. If these conditions are met, families can access congregate or scattered site shelters with services, community apartments, or hotels/motels. Depending on their circumstances, homeless families may qualify for other forms of assistance, but emergency housing for homeless families is limited to these programs.

Massachusetts is a high shelter state, along with North Dakota, New York, Maine, and Nebraska. Collectively, these states house 95 percent of the sheltered population in the entire country. As housing prices in Massachusetts became increas-ingly out of reach, however, the need for emergency family units outpaced availability, and hotels and motels across the state were used as temporary housing. By 2014, bussing costs to bring homeless children back and forth from these facilities to their school of origin were estimated at over $14 million, provided through McKinney-Vento funding for transportation costs. By 2013, the cost of emergency shelter for over 2,000 families living in hotels and motels across the state was estimated to be $1.1 million per week. Local news stories decried the situation as an example of poorly coordinated services and a burden to taxpayers. Although the cost is significant, the services provided to families staying in motels were inconsistent at best and typically off-site. The motels themselves offered minimal privacy and lacked cooking and other facilities. In light of these various shortcomings, dismantling this part of the emergency shelter system became the order of the day.

Removing families from hotels and motels reduced the expense borne by taxpayers. But, without adequate replacement housing, does prohibiting hotel and motel use for homeless people actually decrease family homelessness? In addition to the emergency shelter options for families and to reduce the number living in motels and shelters, Massachusetts created the HomeBASE program in 2011. This program served approximately 5,000 families with two-year rental subsidies. When these ended in 2013–2014, families could access up to $8,000 in HomeBASE household assistance funding or residential assistance to families in transition (RAFT). Both HomeBASE and RAFT were designed to offer short-term assistance to keep families in current housing.

Although many of the 5,000 families who utilized Home-BASE resources remained in stable housing six months after the program ended, the 2014 PIT Count showed an increase of approximately 3,000 people in homeless families across Massachusetts. Despite the provisions of HomeBASE and RAFT, family income levels remained too low, and rental and home prices too high, to prevent numerous families from sliding back into homelessness or housing instability.

Like emergency housing for families, HomeBASE and RAFT initially showed success in temporarily housing families experiencing homelessness. Prior to their implementation, the state received federal stimulus money to offer short-term housing subsidies to offset the effects of the Great Recession. The South Shore Continuum of Care Region, one of ten state regional networks, reported that from April 2009 to September 2010, 319 newly homeless families moved into permanent housing, 266 of 385 homeless people in shelter were moved to housing, and 476 families on the verge of homelessness were able to remain housed (South Shore Network to End Homelessness: Regional Report Card for April 2009–September 2010). Like the temporary funding offered under HomeBASE and RAFT, these forms of assistance proved effective, but the results were short-lived, and when subsidies ran out, many families that had benefited returned to homelessness and poverty.

Predicting rates and fluctuations in family homelessness and meeting corresponding housing and shelter needs are challenging, as is developing programs that end homelessness permanently. Yet the persistently increasing rate of family homelessness in Massachusetts is alarming, as the state has the largest increase in people experiencing homelessness in families, which has grown by 78.7 percent from 2007 to 2019. The two measures used to estimate the homeless population and statewide shelter beds are the HIC, which provides an estimate of the number of beds available, typically separated into emergency, transitional, and permanent supportive housing. The second is the PIT count, used to estimate the number of individuals and families in emergency and transitional shelter and broken down by HUD-designated subpopulations.

These sources show that the number of emergency beds for families rose steadily from 2009 to 2019, with a total increase of just under 5,000 beds overall, or roughly 500 new beds per year for ten years. By 2019, the state of Massachusetts offered an overall total of 11,849 family emergency beds and 876 transitional beds. PIT count estimates for the same year reported 11,428 families in emergency shelter, 775 in transitional housing, and 9 unsheltered. So the population size and number of shelter beds aligned pretty closely, with what looks like a sur-plus of just over 500 beds. Unfortunately, since the PIT count is a snapshot count, it often underestimates the annual need for family beds. In addition, because each program comes with specific qualification and entry requirements, there is no guar-antee that the right kind of bed will be available for a family in need in the right area. Examining the complexity of housing needs in Massachusetts reflects the difficulty of planning and implementing programs that target specific segments of the homeless population and that focus on long-term solutions.

Welfare and Homelessness

Skepticism about public welfare and the idea that work is pref-erable to going "on the dole" are persistent themes in U.S. society. In their research on the functions of public welfare, Piven and Cloward (1993) suggest that relief is designed to regulate the political and economic behavior of the poor, main-tain civil order, and enforce work requirements. Relief in the form of enrollment in welfare programs is offered as a grudg-ing alternative to work opportunities during desperate times. During prosperous ones, relief dwindles, yet those on welfare, "the aged, disabled, insane—remain on the relief roles—and are so degraded there—that they instill fear and compliance in the laboring masses" (Piven and Cloward 1993, 3). Part of the shame of going on welfare is reflected in the applica-tion process, rules, and level of assistance, all of which mirror the inequality and racism still prevalent in U.S. society. For example, research studies have found that women of color are treated more harshly than white women in welfare application processes. This affects welfare policy, as well as who becomes poor and homeless, how their benefits are administered, and how much they receive.

Historically and currently, policy makers argue that the danger of welfare is that it encourages dependency, laziness, and delinquency and that it breeds a "culture of poverty" that threatens mainstream values centered around economic self-sufficiency. For this reason, forms of welfare that are the least controversial are entitlement-based programs tied to either employment history or being unable to work because of age or disability status. Benefits explicitly tied to poverty are "means tested" programs that depend on ascertaining whether or not an individual or family has the means to support itself or if welfare assistance is necessary. Over time, this means-testing approach has meant imposing restrictions that require work and training, dictate who can live with the recipient and for how long, and impose terms limiting the amount and duration of assistance. These requirements are set by the federal government but are adjusted by particular states, so receiving welfare can be difficult, informed by racial and regional biases, and confusing for recipients (Katz 2012).

The first reason that welfare is controversial is its expense. The drive to reduce cost is so pervasive, in fact, that it spans party lines, as some of the most restrictive welfare policies have been enacted by Democrats, who are usually seen as more liberal with respect to welfare and poverty policies. Critics contend, though, that making welfare a means-tested program in which poor people must demonstrate eligibility to receive financial assistance through tax dollars too often pits poor people against one another and against the middle classes and the working poor. This is because an increasing number of families experience financial struggle, yet only some qualify for assistance (Pal and Waldfogel 2016).

The second reason that welfare is controversial in U.S. society is that many Americans believe that offering assistance will erode the desire of recipients to find work and eventually achieve financial independence. They fear that if welfare benefits are too generous, people will live off them forever—or cheat the system by getting more assistance than they are entitled to receive. This shows the overall skepticism that some people feel about the morality of welfare recipients and informs many of the practices that restrict eligibility by limiting the amount or duration of assistance or imposing eligibility requirements that make qualifying for welfare stressful and uncertain. It also targets women of color for harsher treatment than white women, as research shows that sanctions are more often levied on African American and Latino women (Lee and Yoon 2012). Because welfare programs for poor and homeless people depend on establishing need and because they are designed to be temporary, keep benefits low, and return people to work as quickly as possible, there is also a stigma associated with welfare that is not found with Social Security, Medicare, or other entitlement programs enjoyed by middle-class and affluent Americans.

The third issue related to welfare is that the American welfare system is privatized in terms of delivery, meaning that even when the federal government provides funding for welfare programs, money is doled out as grants to states, which manage the funding locally, through block grants, and often contract out to multiple providers. This method of welfare spending is uneven and complicated, resulting in local restrictions that tighten already-rigid federal guidelines and call welfare's efficacy into question. Instead of an entitlement program, under TANF, states determine the terms and duration of a family's eligibility (Kyonne 2008) and end up spending more on the provision and coordination of services to manage poverty than solutions to end it. States are also beholden to the federal government to adhere to work participation rates or lose funding. This dynamic further contributes to the punitive nature of welfare administration in many areas.

The controversial change from AFDC to TANF occurred in 1996. The next section examines its legacy today, twenty-five years after the change. Examining the long-term effects of this policy change and additional policies to serve homeless families after the Great Recession shows that families that experience homelessness in the long term, face challenging barriers to exiting homelessness and poverty. Making the decision to change the structure and delivery of public welfare through the requirements imposed by TANF intensified an already-polarizing debate, with one side arguing that time limits and work incentives are essential to reduce welfare rolls and get people back to work, and the other side arguing for long-term assistance, training and education, and affordable public and mainstream housing. This section examines the legacy of the change from AFDC to TANF to see whether it leads women and children out of homelessness or leaves them trapped within its confines.

Welfare and Work

When Social Security was signed into law in 1935, its intent was to assist the aged, disabled, and widows in America's population. AFDC was Title IV of the Social Security Act. It was meant to keep women and children together instead of forcing mothers to meet demanding work requirements or consigning children to institutions. Male parents and widowers were included later in AFDC history. Over time, however, AFDC shifted from an entitlement program to a means-tested program. This means that assistance levels and eligibility requirements are set by the federal government and adjusted by individual states. They are increasingly tied to work requirements, with minimal support for child-care, training, and education programs needed to reach the ultimate goal of self-sufficiency.

From the 1960s to the 1970s, the mismanagement of welfare benefits and prejudicial treatment of AFDC applicants was exposed, leading to an overhaul of its eligibility requirements and intake procedures to make it more accessible. As a result, more women were granted welfare, poverty continued, and costs ballooned. At the same time, demonstrating the strength of arguments about the more deserving "working poor," the Earned Income Tax Credit (EITC) was implemented in 1975 as an antipoverty measure to support impoverished but employed Americans. While the EITC did decrease poverty and welfare dependence, it did not reach those facing deep, cyclical poverty, or benefit larger families (Mendenhall 2006). By the time Ronald Reagan took office in 1981, welfare had a poor national reputation as an inefficient, costly program that was robbing middle-class consumers of tax dollars. Reagan's changes to AFDC included allowing individual states to set work requirements. Although this and other changes would pale in comparison with the radical reforms implemented during Bill Clinton's presidency, it was during the Reagan years that the push to force welfare recipients to work began to gain real traction, informing and generating policies designed to reduce spending on social welfare programs and reinforce "traditional values."

The amount of welfare assistance women received under AFDC was not enough to keep families from experiencing insecure housing or homelessness. As a result, many women did "off the books" work to survive, only to be accused of dishonesty and "gaming the system" (Anderson 1999). This trend and judgments about it fueled the eventual changes to TANF.

In reality, academic studies (Cheng 2002) as well as journalistic accounts (Kotlowitz 1991) have provided important context for understanding women's "off the books" work, showing that women on welfare supplement assistance they receive from government agencies and programs with various forms of employment, contributions from friends or family, and legal and illegal employment. They do so not out of dishonesty but out of necessity (Cheng and Lo 2018). Cheng (2002) discusses four different adaptive strategies that people in poverty use to survive, ranging from complete dependency on welfare to complete autonomy. In between is the more common strategy of supplementation or the use of both employment and welfare to make ends meet.

In the same way that providing affordable housing can end homelessness, welfare benefits are instrumental in keeping people from becoming homeless and giving them the means to exit. The U.S. welfare system includes social insurance programs, Social Security retirement and disability insurance, unemployment insurance, and Medicare. It also includes means-tested transfer programs, which allocate benefits based on income and eligibility requirements and are specifically designed to serve low-income people. These include food assistance programs like the Supplemental Nutrition Assistance Program (SNAP), Supplemental Security Income (SSI), various tax credits including the EITC, housing assistance, and Medicaid. Social insurance or entitlement programs are less controversial than means-tested poverty programs in which people are not entitled to a specific amount or duration of benefits from the federal government. Means-tested programs are intended to keep people above the federal poverty line, but they don't typically offer more than bare-bones subsistence for homeless families. They also typically require that enrollees constantly prove their eligibility to receive benefits.

There are three main problems with forced work requirements for women on welfare, who are far more likely than men to be primary or sole caregivers for minor children. The first is that child-care options that would enable mothers to work are often unavailable, insufficient, or unaffordable. For women with several children or children who have disabilities or other special needs, they must qualify for additional benefits or choose between employment and child care. The second difficulty is that many women, particularly those experiencing chronic homelessness and housing instability, face their own challenges related to mental and physical health and histories of violence, abuse, and addiction (East and Bussey 2007). For women with these hurdles to face, securing and maintaining full-time employment is more difficult (Roschelle 2019). The third reason that forcing aid recipients to work is not feasible is that the training and education required for gainful employment are nearly impossible to achieve with limited assistance and tight timelines (Katz 2012). As a result, full-time education becomes secondary to short-term training or educational programs (Dave et al. 2012), and it is up to states to determine whether or not postsecondary education counts as a work-related activity.

AFDC to TANF

In 1996, the Personal Responsibility and Work Opportunity Reconciliation Act (PRWORA) officially replaced the AFDC program with the TANF program. The change in legislation placed a two-year contiguous limit and a five-year lifetime limit on cash assistance for poor and homeless families (Ozawa and Yoon 2005). TANF also imposed mandatory participation in work, education, and training programs overseen by individual states. In contrast, the AFDC program included cash benefits that were subject to federal guidelines, and families meeting the basic income eligibility could continue to receive benefits without imposed time limits or expulsion for remaining without employment.

Policies that reduce welfare benefits often do so by connecting the structure and provision of assistance with moral judgment of guilt or innocence, informed by social stigma. For example, welfare policies have for years restricted women's behavior according to moral grounds, like the "man in the house" rules that reduced benefits if men were present, whether they were contributing to household finances or not. The types of services offered were also tailored to assumptions about people on welfare as needing to be surveyed, policed, controlled, and forced to work. With the change to TANF, ending cash payments meant less choice for families and ensured that spending could be directed to avenues deemed more appropriate for people on welfare, like training over education.

To the present, policies legislating the everyday lives of welfare recipients extend not only to who they live with, what jobs and schools they belong in, but also what and how much they consume. Food stamps, now SNAP, is an in-kind benefit and is one the most generous and least contested form of assistance. It also restricts spending to ensure that recipients are not buying nonconsumable goods like tobacco and alcohol. Although there has been some attempt to destigmatize SNAP through the use of Electronic Benefits Transfer (EBT) cards that work much like ATM cards, low-income urban residents on welfare often lack access to grocery stores and other businesses selling healthy and nutritious foods; urban areas with shortages of healthy food choices are sometimes called "food deserts." Studies on children and college students who face food insecurity also show the wide-ranging, positive effects of a regular, balanced diet, including lower stress levels, lower health and nutritional deficiencies, and increased learning gains (Goldrick-Rab 2016; Pal and Waldfogel 2016). Maintaining a healthy diet is also an important way to stave off the cruel effects of poverty, which result in disproportionate health risks that reduce overall life chances (Fitzpatrick and LaGory 2000; Scott 2011).

Since 2009, fifteen states have required welfare recipients to submit to drug testing in order to receive benefits. In a study of this policy, Bjorklund et al. (2018) found that two things influence whether or not a state implements testing: declines in white labor force participation and having a Republican governor. This suggests that states enact these policies to manage a perceived racial and economic threat. Cheng and Lo (2018) corroborate this and note that the effects of imposing unfair sanctions or terminating welfare recipients are disastrous for women and children in particular. A reduction or loss of welfare assistance negatively affects the entire family, as it can precipitate a loss of Medicaid, leaving everyone at risk (Cheng and Lo 2018; Lee and Yoon 2012; Narain and Ettner 2017). Known collectively as "welfare to work," these eligibility requirements and restrictions have been criticized as actually being detrimental for workers and families (Cheng 2002), placing them at greater risk of cyclical poverty.

The two-year limit on assistance in the TANF program also means that a four-year degree, an increasingly important credential for sustainable employment, is off the table for many welfare recipients. This is evidenced by the decline in enrollment in full-time vocational education after welfare reform (Dave et al. 2012). This decline was emphasized by TANF critics who note that higher education can create opportunities for upward mobility, enabling families to withstand economic downturns like recession (Katz 2012). The education and training that welfare under TANF provides is often inadequate. In this sense, welfare assistance does not allow women experiencing long-term homelessness the training and education needed to secure full-time work, which is often unavailable. Entry-level jobs in the United States typically do not pay enough to afford basic housing. In addition to these issues, women on welfare may also face individual challenges associated with chronic poverty that stringent time limits do not take into account. As one observer noted, "Financial empowerment education with trauma informed peer support is more effective than standard TANF programming at improving behavioral health, reducing hardship, and increasing income" (Booshehri et al. 2018, 1594).

In a study of TANF leavers in Utah, a state with a strict thirty-six-month limit on benefits, one study found that women who received assistance for the full thirty-six-month period were less likely to have a high school diploma or GED, had poorer work histories, were more likely to have experienced severe domestic violence within the last year, and had more frequent mental and physical health problems (Taylor et al. 2006, 2). All of these challenges point to the need for longer-term support to surmount the deficits of long-term, generational poverty. Even for people who are not literally homeless and merely live in dilapidated housing in underfunded school districts, the physical and psychological effects of poverty are staggering (Austen 2019). Children in these neighborhoods experience personal and social challenges and trauma, greater health risks, criminalization, and fewer opportunities for social mobility. Even their daily safety is compromised (Conley 2000). Removal from welfare and cutting benefits are extremely stressful for families and feed into the instability that goes with long-term poverty and homelessness.

In summary, the change from AFDC to TANF has reduced the number of people receiving cash assistance, from sixty-eight out of one hundred families in poverty in 1996 to twenty-two out of one hundred families in poverty in 2018 (Center on Budget and Policy Priorities 2020). This decline has disproportionately affected families in deep poverty, black and Latino families, and those living in states with more stringent policies. In addition to cash assistance, the terms of the work requirement are also set by individual states. As detailed in a series of reports by the Center on Budget and Policy Priorities, imposing more stringent work requirements is a way of cutting expenses. It is also a way of reaching federally set work participation rates, which states must reach or face fiscal penalty. Similar to the way that standard reductions in numbers of homeless people are required to maintain federal funding, welfare rolls and expenses must trend downward, and work restrictions upward. These imperatives, say critics, cast considerable doubt about the accuracy of poverty statistics and trends.

American welfare policy has also required increasingly stringent proof and eligibility procedures that can be difficult for recipients to understand and follow, particularly for people without a fixed address. Even before the change to TANF many people eligible for welfare, an estimated 50 percent of those who qualified, did not receive it (Spetter 1996). The Center for Budget and Policy Priorities estimated in 2020 that an additional 2.4 million families would be receiving assistance if TANF had the same reach as AFDC (2020, 1). This reflects one of the pervasive trends in research on the implementation of TANF; it addresses fewer families temporarily, in a way that does not lift them out of poverty but rather causes stress and trauma. Ongoing systemic racism and individual biased treatment often determine the terms of assistance and impose sanctions (Bjorklund et al. 2018; Cheng and Lo 2018; East and Bussey 2007; Katz 2012). This has disastrous effects on mothers in their search for employment, education, and self-sufficiency (Lee and Yoon 2012) and creates barriers to exit, the ultimate goal of TANF.

The COVID-19 Crisis

The examination of criminalization, housing, and welfare so far shows that these closely intertwined structural features of

U.S. society limit opportunities, even for the populations they are designed to serve. The current section brings together the idea of crisis points discussed in the first chapter with the controversies included here, as ways of rethinking our approach to homelessness in U.S. society. The COVID-19 crisis shows how formative our ideas about poverty and homelessness are in shaping public policy. It also shows how the federal government is sometimes at odds with local and state officials over the best solutions: how much to spend, how and what to implement, and how to target assistance.

The COVID-19 pandemic is a public health crisis that set off a global recession. Solutions to controlling the pandemic emphasized social distancing. For homeless people living in shelters or on the street, though, this guideline presents a problem. Funding through the Coronavirus Aid, Relief, and Economic Security (CARES) Act, an economic stimulus package passed into law in March 2020, can be targeted to providing homeless people with private settings or semiprivate congregate settings so that they can socially distance. In the case of COVID-19, helping homeless people also helps the community, as it helps prevent widespread contagion. In this sense, providing assistance is an emergency measure, enacted during a crisis, but will it offer long-term solutions? In March 2021, the American Rescue Plan extended CARES Act provisions addressing homelessness, housing insecurity, and rental and utility assistance.

Like the crisis points discussed in the first chapter, how the government aligns itself with the common man during COVID-19 is a signature feature of the nation's political, economic, and social character. The American Dream, based on the notion of equal opportunity, is called into question when a global pandemic unfolds in ways that underscore how unequal and divided U.S. society is.

To examine how the current COVID-19 crisis affects homeless people, this section returns to the Skid Row neighborhood in Los Angeles, California. California is home to approximately

50 percent of the nationwide unsheltered population (HUD 2018). The Skid Row area of Los Angeles, meanwhile, has one of the country's largest concentrations of homeless people, and it is known for the proliferation of makeshift camps along its sidewalks. Unsheltered homeless communities, and tent cities in particular, have been documented in forty-six states, but they have reached crisis proportions on Los Angeles' Skid Row.

California's struggles with homelessness attracted the nation's attention when President Trump visited the state in 2020, derided the homelessness crisis as a "disgusting" problem, and blamed Democratic governor Gavin Newsom for failing to solve it. Many observers felt that Trump's attack on California was designed to take revenge on Democratic speaker of the house Nancy Pelosi, representative of California's Twelfth District, for launching an impeachment investigation against the president. Whether or not this is true, associating homeless people with filth and waste is a common and degrading stereotype that assumes poverty and deficient character go together. It also disregards the fact that it is because of a lack of accessible daytime housing or sanitation services like showers and bathrooms that homeless people are outside and unclean in the first place. It also neglects systemic barriers to the accumulation of wealth and access to equal opportunity that have been constants in U.S. society. Some critics have contended that Trump's condemnation of the state's management of homeless people, and his degradation of homeless people themselves, may have contributed to a subsequent rise in homeless hate crimes.

This highly publicized visit also drew attention to the sleeping and camping debate as an issue of public health, public safety, and legality. When homeless people sleep outside in a city's parks, parking lots, and beaches, or when they live in abandoned buildings or vehicles, other people may feel threatened. In reality, however, homeless people hurt themselves and one another far more than they do housed citizens. The health risks alone that people living on the streets or in shelters face are staggering, in both cold and warm weather areas

(O'Connell 2005), not to mention the risk of violence or trauma. The recently developed vulnerability index, a tool to prioritize people for housing based on mortality risk, shows how life-threatening homelessness can be. However, debates over whether homelessness is a manifestation of sickness and sinfulness, or evidence of the evils of an unequal, inefficient social system, continue to get more attention than efforts to address underlying causes (Gowan 2010).

The emergence of the COVID-19 virus in the United States illustrated how interrelated factors such as racism, inequality, and poverty all heightened potential exposure to the virus while reducing access to health care. The COVID-19 crisis also illuminated how people of color, people experiencing homelessness, the aged living in facilities, and prisoners all experienced greater vulnerabilities to the pandemic, including higher rates of loss of life. For people living in emergency shelters and on the street, the threat is a result of congregate living, which makes avoiding contagion almost impossible. This crisis also causes the nation to rethink its approach to housing homeless people, as large congregate shelters are temporarily off the table. When providing housing for people experiencing homelessness becomes a public good (by reducing community vulnerability to COVID-19, for example) rather than something that benefits a stigmatized population, how long will such housing last? Some communities use tents or motels as temporary housing, and some offer vouchers and new construction. Some target specific populations for subsidized housing, and others focus on offering long-term solutions.

But the COVID-19 crisis is about more than housing or congregate living. Transmission of the virus depends on contact. People experiencing poverty and homelessness are more likely to work in low-paying, frontline jobs at grocery stores and in hospitals, pharmacies, and restaurants, where they come into daily contact with hundreds of people. Not only do they lack access to better education, training, and employment but they are also more likely to lack personal protective equipment like masks and gloves. If they are substance abuse addicts or sex workers, their exposure to various kinds of contagion and risk is even more likely. Inadequate access to health care facilities and medication also makes homeless people less likely to recover if they are infected.

In this sense, the physical, financial, and mental health toll that the virus takes on people experiencing homelessness and poverty, as with other forms of crisis or downturn, is exponentially greater. This crisis also exposes structural inequalities, and for this reason, scholars at the Institute for Policy Studies linked the nation's response to the Great Recession with its response to COVID-19, asserting that the two events delivered a one-two punch to families of color. The institute pointed out that between 1983 and 2016, the racial wealth divide in America worsened. The average black family lost about half of its wealth, even after adjusting for inflation. The average white family saw a 33 percent increase (Collins et al. 2019).

Cities like Los Angeles have consistently struggled to provide adequate shelter for the homeless and have used criminalization as a way of controlling their homeless populations. Because of the large homeless and unsheltered populations in some cities, and the lack of social distancing that is typical of homeless communities, the virus threatened to spread rapidly in these areas. For this reason, several measures were considered to manage the threat. In this sense, COVID-19 forced the hand of communities that historically have not provided adequate housing and shelter to provide more and better housing or risk fresh outbreaks. Recall the *Martin v. Boise* decision preventing cities without adequate shelter from criminalizing sleep. Because of COVID-19, cities without enough housing and shelter to offer social distancing were forced to offer solutions that were previously off the table. Both Massachusetts and California turned to using motel beds and tent cities to allow homeless people to socially distance during the pandemic. Advocates for the homeless claim that these "shotgun solutions" show us what is possible when homelessness becomes a public issue demanding an immediate response and when it is seen as an issue that affects everyone, not just "them."

In Los Angeles in 2020, the homeless population numbered over 66,000 people, the vast majority of whom were unsheltered. Los Angeles' Project Roomkey was developed as a response to COVID-19 that attempted to prioritize homeless people for housing based on vulnerability. The criteria specified priority for people over 65 or who had one or more health conditions. The Los Angeles Homeless Services Authority (LAHSA) estimated that 4,056 people had been housed through Project Roomkey as of September 2020. Hotel and motel units were the most common units. Spending money to house homeless people in hotels and motels directly contributed to the hospitality industry, which was hard hit by the crisis. Homeless people were also housed in trailers, with the goal of moving 15,000 into permanent housing, and tent cities were temporarily permitted throughout the city. Apart from COVID-19, LAHSA shows great success rates in keeping homeless people housed through its programs, with an estimated 88 percent remaining in long-term housing rather than returning to homelessness.

LAHSA estimates the shortage of affordable housing units at over 500,000, meaning that a significant and sustained influx of resources is needed. Unfortunately, the duration and impact of the COVID-19 pandemic had yet to be fully felt in the general population and among people experiencing homelessness. Planning is currently underway at LAHSA to transition Project Roomkey participants into long-term housing. It also plans to offer outreach and services to people sleeping under freeways. How many people are placed into permanent housing is a question that cannot yet be answered. But one thing is clear: crisis events like the COVID-19 pandemic do two things. They expose our national and systemic failure in achieving safety and equity, and they offer new opportunities for change and innovative solutions.

Several related issues emerge from the case of California, both before and after COVID-19. Solutions developed to manage this crisis will have lasting implications for homelessness in the state and the nation. They emphasize the need to focus on underlying causes, instead of punishing effects. The first issue is politics. When state and governmental approaches to homelessness clash, the danger is that changing policies are both confusing and expensive to implement and do not lead to long-term change. If, for example, more conservative judges are appointed to the Ninth Circuit Court, criminalization may be revisited as a strategy for containing and removing homeless people. Advocates for the homeless also charge that prioritization of criminalization over housing, whether at the federal or state level, is indicative of a system in which data-driven policy goals that address inequality as well as structural racism, poverty, and homelessness remain a low priority.

Conclusion

Significant time, money, and myriad policies and programs have been used to focus on identifying and assisting people experiencing homelessness. Yet because homelessness still exists, it is easy to critique these efforts as inefficient or wasteful. Developing effective solutions is another matter entirely. As the controversies in this chapter show, solutions to homelessness are split between punishment and provision of assistance.

Approaches to housing and supporting homeless people can take the form of increasing shelter beds through public, private, and faith-based agencies; allocating and increasing public housing stock; and raising public awareness of the plight of the homeless. They can also take the form of legislation that imposes penalties for sleeping, sitting, and otherwise occupying public spaces. These responses are often considered together so that increased provisions to help the homeless often are accompanied by legislation that seeks to drive homeless populations to other cities and states. For example, in an effort to remove homeless people from public places, some cities offer "bus therapy," which gives homeless people bus tickets to facilitate their relocation, sometimes barring their return (Outside in America 2017). This is a controversial solution because simply moving the "problem" people from one place to another, within the same city or from one to another, does not address the root causes of poverty that most often result in homelessness.

Criminalizing people experiencing homelessness is a way of punishing its effects rather than addressing its causes. Instead of solving the problem of homelessness, critics assert that criminalization often prolongs it while feeding a growing prison industrial complex and allowing inaccessible employment, education, and housing markets to proliferate. They further contend that systems of criminalization are costly to implement over time and cause undue stress on people already overwhelmed by the effects of homelessness on the health, safety, and welfare on themselves and vulnerable family members, children in particular.

References

Anderson, Elijah. 1999. *Code of the Street.* New York: W.W. Norton & Company, Inc.

Aulette, Judy. 1987. "Police Harassment of the Homeless: The Political Purpose of the Criminalization of Homelessness." *Humanity & Society* 11(2): 244–256.

Austen, Ben. 2019. *High Risers: Cabrini Green and the Fate of American Public Housing.* New York: HarperCollins Publishers.

Belcher, John R. and Bruce R. DeForge. 2012. "Social Stigma and Homelessness: The Limits of Social Change." *Journal of Human Behavior in the Social Environment* 22: 929–946.

Bjorklund, Eric, Andrew P. Davis, and Jessica Pfaffendorf. 2018. "Urine or You're Out: Racialized Economic Threat and the Determinants of Welfare Drug Testing Policy in the United States, 2009–2015." *The Sociological Quarterly* (59)3: 407–423.

Booshehri, Layla G., Jerome Dugan, Falguni Patel, Sandra Bloom, and Mariana Chilton. 2018. "Trauma-Informed Temporary Assistance for Needy Families (TANF): A Randomized Controlled Trial with a Two-Generation Impact." *Journal of Child and Family Studies* 27: 1594–1604.

Burt, Martha. 2016. "Three Decades of Homelessness." In *Ending Homelessness: Why We Haven't, How We Can*, eds. D. Burnes and D. DiLeo, 47–66. Boulder, CO: Lynne Rienner Publishers.

Center on Budget and Policy Priorities. 2020. "Policy Basics: Temporary Assistance for Needy Families." https://www.cbpp.org/research/family-income-support/temporary-assistance-for-needy-families

Cheng, Tyrone. 2002. "Welfare Recipients: How Do They Become Independent?" *Social Work Research* (26)3: 159–170.

Cheng, Tyrone and Celia C. Lo. 2018. "Explaining Restrictive TANF Policies: Group Threat Hypothesis and State Economy Conditions." *Journal of Social Service Research* (44)4: 529–536.

Collins, Chuck, Darrick Hamilton, Dedrick Asante-Muhammad, and Josh Hoxie. 2019. *Embargoed: Ten Solutions to Bridge the Racial Wealth Divide*. Washington, DC: The Institute for Policy Studies.

Conley, Dalton. 2000. *Honky*. Berkeley, CA: University of California Press.

Council of Economic Advisers. 2019. "The State of Homelessness in America." Executive Office of the President of the United States.

Cresswell, Tim. 2001. *The Tramp in America*. London: Reaktion Books.

Cresswell, Tim. 2006. *On the Move: Mobility in the Modern Western World*. New York: Routledge.

Crowley. Sheila. 2003. "The Affordable Housing Crisis: Residential Mobility of Poor Families and School Mobility of Poor Children." *Journal of Negro Education* 72(1): 22–38.

Culhane, Dennis. 2002. "Public Service Reductions Associated with Placement of Homeless Persons with Severe Mental Illness in Supportive Housing." *Housing Policy Debate* 13(1): 107–163.

Culhane, Dennis, Jung Min Park, and Stephen Metraux. 2011. "The Patterns and Costs of Services Use among Homeless Families." *Journal of Community Psychology* 39(7): 815–825.

Dave, Dhaval M., Nancy E. Reichman, Hope Corman, and Dhiman Das. 2012. "Effects of Welfare Reform on Vocational Education and Training." *Economic Education Review* 30(6): 1399–1415.

Dear, Michael and Jennifer Wolch. 1987. *Landscapes of Despair*. Princeton, NJ: Princeton University Press.

Dordick, Gwendolyn. 1997. *Something Left to Lose: Personal Relations and Survival among New York's Homeless*. Philadelphia: Temple University Press.

East, Jean F. and Marian Bussey. 2007. "I Was Scared Every Day: Surviving in the TANF Environment." *Journal of Policy Practice* 6(3): 45–64.

Fitzpatrick, Kevin and Mark LaGory. 2000. *Unhealthy Places: The Ecology of Risk in the Urban Landscape*. New York: Routledge.

Goffman, Alice. 2014. *On the Run: Fugitive Life in an American City*. New York: Picador.

Goldrick-Rab, Sara. 2016. *Paying the Price: College Costs, Financial Aid, and the Betrayal of the American Dream*. Chicago: University of Chicago Press.

Gowan, Teresa. 2010. *Hobos, Hustlers, and Backsliders: Homeless in San Francisco*. Minneapolis: University of Minnesota Press.

Heben, Andrew. 2014. *Tent City Urbanism*. Eugene, OR: The Village Collaborative.

Irvine, Leslie. 2013. *My Dog Always Eats First: Homeless People and Their Animals*. Boulder, CO: Lynne Rienner Publishers.

Jones v. City of Los Angeles, 444 F. 3d 1118 (9th Cir. 2006).

Katz, Sheila. 2012. "TANF's 15th Anniversary and the Great Recession: Are Low-Income Mothers Celebrating Upward Economic Mobility?" *Sociology Compass* (6/8): 657–670.

Kotlowitz, Alex. 1991. *There Are No Children Here*. New York: First Anchor Books.

Kyonne, Jinman. 2008. "The Philosophical Origins of the U.S. Welfare Policy: Controversial Ideologies behind the TANF Program." *The International Journal of Diversity in Organisations, Communities and Nations* (8)5: 93–98.

Lee, Kyoung Hag and Dong Pil Yoon. 2012. "A Comparison of Sanctions in African American and White TANF Leavers." *Journal of Evidence-Based Social Work* 9: 396–413.

Martin v. City of Boise, 902 F. 3d 1031, 1049 (9th Cir. 2018).

Melamed, David, Christopher E. Munn, Leanne Barry, Bradley Montgomery, and Oneya F. Okubowi. 2019. "Status Characteristics, Implicit Bias, and the Production of Racial Inequality." *American Sociological Review* (84)6: 1013–1036.

Mendenhall, Amy. 2006. "A Guide to the Earned Income Tax Credit: What Everyone Should Know about the EITC." *Journal of Poverty* 10(3): 51–68.

Mitchell, Don. 2020. *Mean Streets: Homelessness, Public Space, and the Limits of Capital*. Athens, GA: University of Georgia Press.

Narain, Kimberly and Susan Ettner. 2017. "The Impact of Exceeding TANF Time Limits on the Access to Healthcare of Low-Income Mothers." *Social Work in Public Health* (32)7: 452–460.

National Law Center on Homelessness and Poverty. 2017. *Tent City, USA: The Growth of America's Homeless Encampments and How Communities Are Responding*. Washington, DC: National Law Center on Homelessness and Poverty.

National Law Center on Homelessness and Poverty. 2019. *Housing, Not Handcuffs: The Criminalization of Homelessness in US Cities*. Washington, DC: National Law Center on Homelessness and Poverty.

O'Connell, James J. 2005. *Premature Mortality in Homeless Populations: A Review of the Literature*. Nashville, TN: National Health Care for the Homeless Council, Inc.

Outside in America. 2017. "Bussed Out: How America Moves Its Homeless." https://www.theguardian.com/us-news/ng-interactive/2017/dec/20/bussed-out-america-moves-homeless-people-country-study

Ozawa, Martha N. and Hong-Sik Yoon. 2005. " 'Leavers' from TANF and AFDC: How Do They Fare Economically." *Social Work* 50(3): 239–249.

Padgett, Donald K., Bruce F. Henwood, and Sam J. Tsemberis. 2016. *Housing First: Ending Homelessness, Transforming Systems, and Changing Lives*. New York: Oxford University Press.

Pal, Ipshita and Jane Waldfogel. 2016. "The Family Gap in Pay: New Evidence for 1967 to 2013." *The Russell Sage Foundation Journal of the Social Sciences* 2(1): 104–127.

Piven, Francis F. and Richard Cloward. 1993. *Regulating the Poor: The Functions of Public Welfare*. New York: Vintage Books.

Pottinger v. City of Miami, 720 F. Supp. 955 (S.D. Fla. 1989).

Roschelle, Anne. 2019. *Struggling in the Land of Plenty*. London: Lexington Books.

Scott, Janny. 2011. "Life at the Top Isn't Just Better, It's Longer." In *The Inequality Reader: Contemporary and Foundational Readings in Race, Class, and Gender,* Second

Edition, eds. David B. Grusky and Szonja Szelènyi, 614–621. Boulder, CO: Westview Press.

Snow, Don and Leon Anderson. 1993. *Down on Their Luck: A Study of Homeless Street People*. Berkeley: University of California Press.

South Shore Network to End Homelessness: Regional Report Card for April 2009–September 2010.

Spetter, Victoria C. 1996. "As Government Assistance Decreases, Homelessness Increases: A Closer Look at Welfare, Housing, and Homelessness." *Hybrid* 3(1): 111–150.

Steele, Claude. 2011. "Stereotype Threat and African American Student Achievement." In *The Inequality Reader: Contemporary and Foundational Readings in Race, Class, and Gender,* Second Edition, eds. David B. Grusky and Szonja Szelènyi, 276–281. Boulder, CO: Westview Press.

Taylor, Mary Jane, Amanda Smith Barusch, and Mary Beth Vogel Ferguson. 2006. "Heterogeneity at the Bottom: TANF Closure and Long-Term Welfare Recipients." *Journal of Human Behavior in the Social Environment* 13(2): 1–14.

U.S. Department of Housing and Urban Development. 2009. *Annual Homeless Assessment Report to Congress*. Washington, DC: Office of Community Planning and Development.

U.S. Department of Housing and Urban Development. 2017. *Annual Homeless Assessment Report to Congress*. Washington, DC: Office of Community Planning and Development.

U.S. Department of Housing and Urban Development. 2018. *Annual Homeless Assessment Report to Congress*. Washington, DC: Office of Community Planning and Development.

U.S. Department of Housing and Urban Development. 2019. *Annual Homeless Assessment Report to Congress*. Washington, DC: Office of Community Planning and Development.

U.S. Interagency Council on Homelessness. 2010.
*Opening Doors: Federal Strategic Plan to Prevent and End
Homelessness*. Washington, DC: U.S. Interagency Council
on Homelessness.

Wagner, David. 2005. *The Poorhouse: America's Forgotten
Institution*. New York: Rowman & Littlefield Publishers, Inc.

Wakin, M. 2008. "Using Vehicles to Challenge Antisleeping
Ordinances." *City and Community* 7(4): 309–329.

Walters, Edward J. 1995. "No Way Out: Eighth Amendment
Protection for Do-Or-Die Acts of the Homeless." *The
University of Chicago Law Review* 62: 1619–1649.

Wright, T. 1997. *Out of Place: Homeless Mobilizations,
Subcities, and Contested Landscapes*. Albany: State
University of New York Press.

This chapter includes leading perspectives on four of the most important struggles facing individuals and families experiencing homelessness today: structural racism as a barrier to accessing education and welfare, homelessness among K–12 and college and university students, the criminalization of homelessness and the right to housing and urban spaces, and innovative state and national solutions to homelessness.

Complementing the focus on crisis points and controversies in the first two chapters, this one begins by detailing the experiences of women seeking welfare and education in an unequal, racially biased society. Anne Roschelle examines how welfare policy in the United States excludes women of color more often than white women, exposing them and their families to homelessness and generational poverty. Her essay offers a critical focus on how the welfare system, often seen as a way out of poverty, can itself become a barrier to exit that reaffirms and perpetuates marginality and homelessness. Her essay is followed by the firsthand experiences of Sefora Alcindor, a student seeking higher education as an immigrant from Haiti, who benefited from a university program for homeless youth. Her experiences show how deeply the scars of violence and insecurity run, causing her to doubt even her own abilities.

A homeless man sits among his possessions in Times Square, New York. Homeless people in public places are often subject to criminalization, which prolongs rather than ends their time on the street. (Dirk Ott/Dreamstime.com)

Yet she manages to persevere and go on to pursue a master's degree and become a homeowner. Alcindor is living proof of the grace of the human spirit and the transformative power of higher education.

Continuing the theme of education, Ronald Hallett and Katy Abel offer related essays on the needs of homeless students in K–12 and higher education settings, where they increasingly lack access to basic necessities and other targeted supports. Hallett details the multiple needs and challenges facing homeless students in K–12 settings, suggesting a wholistic, trauma-informed approach to supporting students. This approach has proven to be a successful, tailored way of removing barriers to education that can offer pathways out of homelessness and poverty. Working from a state-level policy perspective, Katy Abel provides an overview of an innovative pilot program implemented in Massachusetts to house students experiencing homelessness in college and university settings. Abel's essay details the prevalence of hunger and homelessness among students enrolled in institutions of higher education and shows how partnerships between schools and community agencies can offer comprehensive, wraparound support services including counseling and mental health assistance. Her exploration of this pilot program shows that it leads to increased stability and engagement with the higher education community, to the benefit of student participants.

In the third thematic section of this chapter, Maria Foscarinis and Colby King examine the legal and social response to homeless people in city spaces. King explores the idea of place character as a way of marking urban spaces as inclusive or exclusive zones. His essay suggests that rethinking public place branding offers a pathway for heightening accessibility and inclusion for marginalized populations in public places instead of excluding them to maximize the location's potential profitability. Maria Foscarinis, founder of the National Law Center on Homelessness and Poverty (renamed the National Homelessness Law Center), follows this essay with an examination of the important role of the law in helping homeless people find and secure essential services, including shelter and housing. Her central involvement in the fight for homeless rights at the federal level has won unprecedented support and protections for individuals and families experiencing homelessness. This essay discusses these gains as well as the ongoing drive to make housing a human right.

The final section of this chapter includes two essays from people on the front lines of service provision for the homeless, one as the leader of an emergency shelter and the other as a psychiatrist leading an outreach/treatment team. April Connolly begins this section with a firsthand view of how Massachusetts emergency shelters in the towns of Quincy and Brockton responded to the COVID-19 crisis. Despite significant challenges, the quick response of a statewide coordinating team effectively saved lives and avoided a surge in the virus among the homeless populations in these two locales. Her essay is an important way of highlighting the instrumental work of service providers in supporting and ultimately saving the lives of people experiencing homelessness. Finally, Sam Tsemberis, founder of the Housing First Initiative and Pathways to Housing, New York, offers an overview of the differences between a housing first and a treatment first model in combating homelessness. By describing the primary components of the Housing First model, this essay emphasizes the need for consumer participation and control as designing principles for homeless housing. This transformative approach has shown success nationwide and internationally and remains a cornerstone of the nation's overall response to homelessness.

Shut the Front Door: Welfare Reform and Homeless Mothers
Anne R. Roschelle

This essay focuses on the structural racism inherent in the 1996 Personal Responsibility and Work Opportunity Reconciliation Act (PRWORA) and its impact on homeless women. By examining the underlying ideology of this legislation and the sanctions it imposed, including punishment or termination for not complying with welfare rules, it shows that women of color are subject to more frequent and ongoing sanctions in comparison with white women, making them more likely to become homeless.

Racialized Welfare Reform

Throughout the 1980s and 1990s, a popular narrative swept the nation that demonized impoverished black and Latina mothers as lazy and welfare dependent. Conservative politicians and policy analysts introduced this conversation to promote their racialized antiwelfare agenda. Even Bill Clinton, a political moderate, jumped on the bandwagon during his presidential campaign when he pledged "the end of welfare as we know it." President Clinton made good on his campaign promise in 1996, when he signed the PRWORA, ushering in an era of punitive welfare reform. The underlying ideology of this radical reform was to eliminate welfare dependency, promote heterosexual marriage, discourage abortion, reduce nonmarital births, and compel poor women to go to work.

The new federal legislation put a maximum five-year lifetime cap on welfare receipt, although some states chose to implement a more punitive two-year cap. Despite more than twenty years of research confirming that the majority of welfare mothers are not long-term recipients but rather cycle on and off as their family and work lives necessitate (Bane and Ellwood 1994; Edin and Lein 1997; Gottschalk et al. 1994), the underlying assumption behind the change to PRWORA was that women of color are lazy and don't want to work. While there is a small subset of women who are long-term welfare recipients, it is not because they are indolent. Long-term recipients come from extremely poor families with young children and usually have little to no work experience, health problems, high rates of exposure to violence, chronically ill kids, housing insecurity, and little education, which are the real reasons they are chronically poor.

In addition to the work requirement, PRWORA legislation also promoted abstinence and heterosexual marriage, discouraged abortion and nonmarital births, and set aside $50 million per year to subsidize state abstinence education programs. In addition, $100 million was set aside to be shared annually by the five states that have the best record of reducing nonmarital births without increasing their abortion rates. Not surprisingly, however, the legislation did not include funding for birth control or family planning education (Hays 2003). Regrettably, however, it did include a family cap that excludes benefits to any children born to mothers who are already receiving benefits. These state-level rewards and punishments reflected the ideological viewpoint of policy makers that poor women of color were out of control breeders in need of restraint.

(Racialized-) Welfare Sanctions

PRWORA imposes harsh sanctions for women who do not comply with the new requirements. Given the racialized discourse that portrays black women as chronically dependent welfare queens, it is not surprising that they are significantly more likely than white women to be sanctioned for noncompliance by their caseworkers (Casey 2010). Research indicates that caseworkers, who are typically white, often fail to distinguish between minor procedural violations and willful substantive violations. In addition, studies have found that caseworkers tend to apply sanction rules narrowly, are skeptical of any legitimate exception claims (Lens 2008), have internalized the racist discourse on welfare recipients, and oversanction the most disenfranchised women (Cherlin et al. 2002; Kalil et al. 2002). Not surprisingly, homeless welfare recipients are particularly disadvantaged and have found it exceedingly difficult to comply with the requirements of the PRWORA (Roschelle 2019).

Once sanctioned, women on welfare have a greater risk of food insecurity, child hunger, hospitalization, utility shutoff, eviction, and ultimately homelessness. Although sanctions are intended to provide women with disincentives for refusing to work, it turns out that a majority of sanctions are for late or missed appointments, not filing paperwork, and other minor infractions (Cherlin et al. 2002). For homeless women who are also victims of intimate partner violence, the relentless imposition of sanctions has been disastrous. Many battered homeless women are sanctioned and lose their benefits as a result of their partners' harassment, stalking behavior, emotional abuse, unreliable parenting, and physical violence (Brandwein and Filiano 2000; Raphael 2000; Scott et al. 2002; Staggs and Riger 2005; Taylor and Barusch 2004). Although sanctions are promoted as a way of enforcing work requirements, they are in fact meant to punish poor women of color for their perceived laziness. Whether intended or not, the consequences of this legislation have been disastrous for countless Latina and black women who have been forced off the welfare rolls into the arms of abusive men and ultimately onto the streets (along with their children).

The Welfare State and the Reproduction of Race, Class, and Gender Inequality

Although poor white women also suffered under the changes contained in PRWORA, black women and Latinas suffered more extensively, as they are more likely to be chronically poor and to be victims of intimate partner violence (Copp et al. 2015; Richie 2012; Roschelle 2017; Sokoloff and Dupont 2005). The five-year lifetime limit on welfare receipt was also disastrous for women of color who, because of institutional racism, are more likely to use up their allotment more quickly. Similarly, women of color are also more likely to be sanctioned than white women (Casey 2010), embedding them in the lowest recesses of the social structure and ultimately perpetuating generational poverty. This generational cycle of poverty is particularly likely to trap women who come from the most economically disadvantaged backgrounds, including homeless women, who often lack the education, training, and cultural capital needed to survive in today's job and housing markets. Subsequently, these women are less able to comply with the rules of PRWORA, find work that pays a living wage, and leave abusive relationships—all of which make them more likely to become homeless. Race, class, and gender intersect under the tyranny of the welfare state, which further re-creates socially structured race, class, and gender inequality.

References

Bane, Mary Jo and David T. Ellwood. 1994. *Welfare Realities: From Rhetoric to Reform*. Cambridge, MA: Harvard University Press.

Brandwein, Ruth A., and Diana M. Filiano. 2000. "Toward Real Welfare Reform: The Voices of Battered Women." *Affilia* 15(2): 224–243.

Casey, Timothy. 2010. "The Sanction Epidemic in the Temporary Assistance for Needy Families Program." *The Women's Legal Defense and Education Fund*, www.legal momentum.org. New York: Legal Momentum.

Cherlin, Andrew J, Karen Bogen, James M. Quane, and Linda Burton. 2002. "Operating within the Rules: Welfare Recipients' Experiences with Sanctions and Case Closings." *Social Services Review* 76(3): 387–405.

Copp, Jennifer E., Danielle C. Kuhl, Peggy C. Giordano, Monica A. Longmore, and Wendy D. Manning. 2015. "Intimate Partner Violence in Neighborhood Context: The Roles of Structural Disadvantage, Subjective Disorder, and Emotional Distress." *Social Science Research* 53: 59–72.

Edin, Kathryn and Laura Lein. 1997. *Making Ends Meet: How Single Mothers Survive Welfare and Low-Wage Work*. New York: Russell Sage Foundation.

Gottschalk, Peter, Sara McLanahan, and Gary D. Sandefur. 1994. "The Dynamics and Intergenerational Transmission of Poverty and Welfare Participation." In *Confronting Poverty: Prescriptions for Change*, eds. Sheldon H. Danziger, Gary D. Sandefur, and Daniel H. Weinberg, 85–108. New York: Russell Sage Foundation.

Hays, Sharon. 2003. *Flat Broke with Children: Women in the Age of Welfare Reform*. Oxford: Oxford University Press.

Kalil, Ariel, Kristen S. Seefeldt, and Hui-Chen Wang. 2002. "Sanctions and Marital Hardship under TANF." *Social Service Review* 76(4): 642–662. https://doi.org/10.1086/342998

Lens, Vicki. 2008. "Welfare and Work Sanctions: Examining Discretion on the Front Lines." *Social Service Review* 82(2): 197–222.

Raphael, Jody. 2000. *Saving Bernice: Battered Women, Welfare, and Poverty*. Boston: Northeastern University Press.

Richie, Beth E. 2012. "The Matrix: A Black Feminist Response to Male Violence and the State." In *Arrested Justice: Black Women, Violence, and America's Prison Nation*, ed. Beth E. Richie, 125–156. New York: NYU Press.

Roschelle, Anne R. 2017. "Our Lives Matter: The Racialized Violence of Poverty among Homeless Mothers of Color." *Sociological Forum* 32(S1): 998–1017. DOI: 10.1111./socf.12365

Roschelle, Anne R. 2019. *Struggling in the Land of Plenty: Race, Class, and Gender in the Lives of Homeless Families*. Boulder, CO: Lexington Books.

Scott, Ellen K., Andrew S. London, and Nancy A. Myers. 2002. "Dangerous Dependencies: The Intersection of Welfare Reform and Domestic Violence." *Gender & Society* 16(6): 878–897.

Sokoloff, Natalie J. and Ida Dupont. 2005. "Domestic Violence at the Intersections of Race, Class, and Gender." *Violence against Women* 11(1): 38–64.

Staggs, Susan L. and Stephanie Riger. 2005. "The Effects of Intimate Partner Violence on Low-Income Women's Health and Employment." *American Journal of Community Psychology* 36(1/2): 133–145.

Taylor, Mary J. and Amanda S. Barusch. 2004. "Personal Family and Multiple Barriers of Long-Term Welfare Receipt." *Social Work* 49(2): 175–183.

Anne R. Roschelle is professor of sociology and chair of the Department of Women's, Gender, and Sexuality Studies at the State University of New York at New Paltz. Dr. Roschelle is the author of No More Kin: Exploring Race, Class, and Gender in Family Networks, *which was a recipient of* Choice Magazine's *1997 Outstanding Academic Book Award. Anne is an antiracist, feminist ethnographer whose research publications focus on racial ethnic families; poverty and homelessness; race, class, and gender inequality; welfare reform and domestic violence; and gender, work, and tourism in Cuba. Dr. Roschelle's book* Struggling in the Land of Plenty: Race, Class, and Gender in the Lives of Homeless Families *was published in 2019. Anne has also recently published her current research on unaccompanied minors in the Hudson Valley and is conducting research on Central American immigrants in the Hudson Valley and deportees in Guatemala. In addition, Anne is writing a book (with Sharina Maillo-Pozo) on the legacy of Dominican scholar Camila Henriquez Ureña.*

Struggles and Strengths
Sefora Alcindor

Coming to America, I never imagined myself becoming homeless. When you hear that you will be coming to America, you think of living what they call "the American Dream." For me, it was the idea of having my own room, going to a school that doesn't require a uniform, and eating unlimited pizza. It would also mean being with a family that I hardly knew, which was a dream come true! I was finally going to be around my mother's family with a bunch of cousins and aunts to love me.

My homeless story started when one of my aunts approached me and told me that her husband asked her to kick me out because his children were coming to live with him and the house was too small for everyone. I reached out to my friends to see if I could stay with them temporarily. Later that day, I was dropped off at my friend's house. She and her mom were living in a government-funded house where visitors were not allowed. That day, I had only two black plastic trash bags full of clothes. The next day I had to hide under her bed because her case manager came for an unexpected home visit.

Throughout my time in the United States, I really never had a place to call home, a place where I felt the unconditional love of people who care without expecting something back. When I enrolled at Bridgewater State University (BSU), I was relieved because I knew that I would have a place in which to be myself and to meet others while still being safe. Some days, when I was doing assignments for school, I could hardly focus because I kept worrying about when the person I was living with would ask me to leave. There was always that fear in the back of my mind, but I never stopped working hard in school. When I interviewed to become part of the Bridgewater Scholars Program at BSU, a program that would cover my room and board, tuition, and fees, I felt relieved because I was finally going to have a place I could call my own for longer than ninety days. But even my first day on campus was bittersweet.

I had not yet started classes when I received a call from the lady I was staying with. Before I left to move onto the campus, she promised to keep my room for as long as I wanted. She said that whenever I needed a break from school, I could always come back to her home and her family. Around 10 p.m. on that first night, she called to ask me to come get the rest of my stuff, stating that it was starting to be a bother to have in her home. With tears rolling down my cheeks, I heard myself saying, "I do not have transportation to pick them up at the moment, can you leave them outside for me?" She said, "If you don't pick them up tonight, I am throwing everything away." That was the last time I ever heard from her. I had no choice but to let her throw everything away because I was unable to go pick it up.

My years in college were extremely difficult, nothing like television shows that make it look easy. I attempted suicide twice, as depression really hit me, especially on holidays. Each time we had break periods, I had nowhere to go. I did not have a family that was willing to welcome me on Christmas Day to even have a nice warm meal. I kept thinking about the day that I could finally say "this is my home," the day I would have the power to do everything that I never could in "my home." When I arrived at BSU, I met a lot of amazing people who really helped me get through my four years. There, I felt a sense of community. Almost every professor had an open-door policy. They always wanted to help, whether to refer me to see a therapist right on campus, to get help outside of campus, and even to recommend me to programs that could benefit me in the future. With an open mind, I accepted all their help with a mind-set that forever helped me in life. Because of being around people who really cared for not only my well-being but also my education, I vowed to always do great and be great. This really gave me hope that one day I can give back to the world the knowledge that I received from each and every one who believed in me during my years as an undergraduate student.

Obtaining my psychology degree has everything to do with my time at BSU and the experiences I had. My goal is to continue with my studies until I receive my doctoral degree and become a well-known and respected therapist-educator. I would love to use my degree to teach others that it is possible, even in the darkest moments, to find what gives you purpose in life. For me, education was my purpose, because I knew it would give me the freedom that I needed in life to succeed. Today I get to be part of people's lives and make a difference for them. I have used everything that I learned in my psychology courses to help people who cannot help themselves.

Looking back, I am very grateful that I went through the experiences that I went through because they all made me stronger, and now I can share my story with others who are going through similar situations. One thing that helped me was to make connections with faculty members. I got invited to some of their houses for Christmas, winter breaks, birthdays, and Easter dinners. After I completed my undergraduate degree, I promised myself that I would never be homeless again. I worked hard during college, and there were many bumps along the way: rejection from family members and close friends, dealing with depression, suicidal thoughts, and rape. I was afraid to reach out to get the help that I needed from mental health professionals, but I accepted the fact that I needed more than just therapy. I educated myself about the culture clash I experienced, as Haitian people do not always believe in taking care of their mental health. I knew I had to take care of myself if I was going to succeed and continue to work hard to achieve my dreams.

Two months before I graduated with my undergraduate degree, I signed my first lease to rent an apartment—a dream come true! Having my own apartment made me feel excited. I felt home. I felt like I deserved this. But I was not stopping there. There was no way I was going to allow myself to stop there. I quickly registered to start working toward a graduate degree in clinical mental health counseling, and I could not be any prouder. This all helped me realize that with struggles come strengths, and with strength, all is possible. I know this because I am a product of struggles and strengths.

Sefora Alcindor is currently completing her master's degree in clinical mental health counseling at Southern New Hampshire University (SNHU). She was born in Port-au-Prince, Haiti, and lived there until she was 14 years old, when she came to the United States. She attended Brockton High School for four years and met wonderful teachers and counselors who inspired her current career choices. After graduation, she was accepted to BSU and gained entry to a prestigious scholarship program offering mentorship and support. She is a lifelong member of the Bridgewater Scholars Program and still returns to mentor incoming scholars. Although graduating from BSU was a struggle, Sefora persevered and remained strong, drawing on the memory of her mother's strength and the support of her love. Sefora's dedication to her studies is meant to show those who have supported her that their faith in her is not misplaced. While studying for her master's degree, Sefora is applying the skills she learned while pursuing her bachelor's degree, working as a program manager overseeing a staff of ten people. Her goal is to pursue a PhD in psychology, with a focus on counseling, to be able to teach others and share her knowledge and experience.

Increasing Educational Access and Success for Students Experiencing Homelessness
Ronald Hallett

Many common notions and images of homelessness exclude students. The most visible homeless people tend to be adults living on the street who may have mental health and substance abuse issues. Although these individuals warrant attention and support, narrowing the definition of homelessness to only its most visible forms leads to the creation of policies, practices, and services that neglect the needs of students and families experiencing homelessness. Because of the challenges faced by individuals experiencing homelessness, some argue that education should be considered secondary to other forms of social support. This essay suggests that access to education is an issue of equity and justice. In order to create long-term solutions that break the generational cycle of homelessness, interventions need to include efforts to improve educational outcomes.

Students and families are an important and central part of conversations about homelessness. In the United States, 40 percent of the homeless population comprises families with children (U.S. Department of Housing and Urban Development

2014). During the 2016–2017 academic year, approximately 1.4 million students in kindergarten through high school experienced homelessness (U.S. Department of Education 2018). While postsecondary institutions are not required to track housing insecurity, emerging estimates range from 5 percent to 15 percent of college students experiencing homelessness, with many more living in unstable housing situations (e.g., Goldrick-Rab et al. 2017; Silva et al. 2017; Wood et al. 2017).

Homeless initiatives that do not prioritize educational access result in short-term interventions that rarely lead to sustained housing stability for students and families. For example, focusing on access to food or emergency shelters allows for meeting basic needs but does not create a pathway to long-term stability. Young people experiencing homelessness consistently comment on how much they value education, but they often cannot get past the barriers to schooling that exist (Tierney et al. 2008). Student homelessness is associated with lower academic outcomes in math and reading, lower graduation rates for high school students, and lower academic outcomes in comparison to low-income students (Low et al. 2015). The impact of homelessness on academic performance is so severe that effects can persist for up to three years after the student regains secure housing (Institute for Children, Poverty, and Homelessness 2016). Educators and administrators can play important roles in creating structures, pedagogical approaches, and resources that encourage academic retention and success for students experiencing homelessness (Hallett and Skrla 2017).

While addressing the barriers to high school graduation are essential, that is not where the conversation about educational access should end. In order to encourage the long-term economic and residential stability of individuals experiencing homelessness, most will need some form of postsecondary degree or credentials, which includes both community colleges and four-year institutions (Hallett et al. 2019). In this essay, I discuss some of the barriers and opportunities related to increasing educational access and success for individuals experiencing homelessness.

Federal Law

The McKinney-Vento Homeless Assistance Act (42 U.S. Code §§11431–11435) provides federal protections related to educational access for students experiencing homelessness in preschool through high school. The McKinney-Vento Act was reauthorized in 2015 as part of the Every Student Succeeds Act (ESSA) to offer greater homeless access to education by changing any policies or practices deemed limiting. In addition to protections, McKinney-Vento defines homelessness in a more expansive way than the U.S. Department of Housing and Urban Development (HUD). The definition of a student experiencing homelessness is anyone without fixed, regular, and adequate nighttime residence. This includes individuals living in shelters, hotels, cars, abandoned buildings, tents or campers, and public spaces. The law also covers individuals living "doubled-up," a term for when multiple families share a residence as a result of economic crisis (Hallett 2012).

Through ESSA, current federal law focuses on educational opportunities for students in preschool through high school, including mandates to offer high school students experiencing homelessness priority access to college preparation programming and information about the process of applying for financial aid. However, a comprehensive federal policy for college students experiencing homelessness does not currently exist. As a result, some states and postsecondary institutions have begun creating protections related to housing, tuition, hygiene, and enrollment (Hallett et al. 2019). In California, for example, college students experiencing homelessness can access their campus's shower facilities and receive priority enrollment. Many advocates and educators have been pushing for a federal law that outlines protections for college students. Currently, efforts to support access and success in higher education tend to be piecemeal and do not fully address the challenges of attending college while experiencing homelessness.

Moving from Trauma to Support

Homelessness is associated with shame in American society (Tierney and Hallett 2012). People are made to feel embarrassed when they are unable to secure consistent housing. This feeling of humiliation or self-consciousness often takes a toll on their mental health and social relationships. In addition, the context of homelessness may be connected to violence, abuse, and malnutrition. Simply the experience of being without stable housing is a traumatic experience for most individuals. Young people feel particular pressure to fit in with their peers. Being homeless impacts their social connections, which also influences how they engage with the educational process. Students in primary, secondary, and postsecondary institutions benefit from a holistic approach to homelessness that addresses underlying trauma as well as provides academic supports.

Educational institutions can employ a trauma-informed approach in preschool to high school contexts (Hallett and Skrla 2017) as well as in postsecondary education settings (Hallett et al. 2019). A trauma-informed approach recognizes that individuals have a life outside of the educational institution. Individuals who experience trauma, such as those associated with homelessness, may not be able to fully participate in the educational process without some additional supports. Generally speaking, a trauma-informed approach involves thinking about students holistically, and all students—regardless of background—benefit when institutions use this to inform how they do their work.

The California State University, Long Beach (CSULB) Basic Needs Program focuses on providing wraparound support for students who experience homelessness. In addition to providing access to food and emergency housing, the program also coordinates with counseling resources and the health center on campus. Using a case management approach, CSULB attempts to identify the multifaceted needs that exist when a student is homeless. A coordinated approach like this can and should be developed at all levels of education, as ending homelessness requires collaboration. Instead of considering the discreet needs of individuals experiencing homelessness and developing individual policies to address each need, we should move toward a holistic intervention. This means bringing together practitioners and policy makers across the spectrum of social service agencies. Educational institutions should be an integral part of these interventions and policies.

References

Goldrick-Rab, Sara, Jeb Richardson, and Anthony Hernandez. 2017. *Hungry and Homeless in College: Results from a National Study of Basic Needs Insecurity in Higher Education*. Madison: University of Wisconsin, Wisconsin HOPE Lab.

Hallett, Ronald E. 2012. *Educational Experiences of Hidden Homeless Teenagers: Living Doubled-Up*. New York: Routledge.

Hallett, Ronald E., Rashida M. Crutchfield, and Jennifer J. Maguire. 2019. *Addressing Homelessness and Housing Insecurity in Higher Education: Strategies for Educational Leaders*. New York: Teachers College Press.

Hallett, Ronald E. and Linda Skrla. 2017. *Serving Students Who Are Homeless: A Resource Guide for Schools, Districts and Educational Leaders*. New York: Teachers College Press.

Institute for Children, Poverty, and Homelessness. 2016. *Aftershocks: The Lasting Impact of Homelessness on Student Achievement*. New York, NY: Institute for Children, Poverty, and Homelessness.

Low, Justin A., Ronald E. Hallett, and Elaine Mo. 2015. "Doubled-Up Homeless: Comparing Educational

Outcomes to Low-Income Students." *Education & Urban Society* 49(9): 795–813.

Silva, Meghan R., Whitney L. Kleinert, A. Victoria Sheppard, Kathryn A. Cantrell, Freeman-Coppadge, Elena Tsoy, and Melissa Pearrow. 2017. "The Relationship between Food Security, Housing Stability, and School Performance among College Students in an Urban University." *Journal of College Student Retention* 19(3): 284–299.

Tierney, William G., Jarrett T. Gupton, and Ronald E. Hallett. 2008. *Transition to Adulthood for Homeless Adolescents*. Los Angeles: Center for Higher Education Policy Analysis.

Tierney, William G. and Ronald E. Hallett. 2012. "Social Capital and Homeless Youth: Influence of Residential Instability on College Access." *Metropolitan Universities Journal* 22(3): 46–62.

U.S. Department of Education. 2018. *ED Data Express* (Data tool). https://eddataexpress.ed.gov.

U.S. Department of Housing and Urban Development (HUD). 2014. The 2014 Point-in-Time Estimates of Homelessness. The 2014 Annual Assessment Report to Congress, Vol. 1. Washington, DC: Author.

Wood, J. Luke, Frank Harris III, and Nexi R. Delgado. 2017. *Struggling to Survive—Striving to Succeed: Food and Housing Insecurities in the Community College*. San Diego: Community College Equity Assessment Lab.

Ronald Hallett is a professor of organizational leadership in the LaFetra College of Education at the University of La Verne and a research associate in the Pullias Center for Higher Education at the University of Southern California. A former school teacher, he now researches the educational experiences that marginalized youth face in their pursuit of completing high school and transitioning to college. Specifically, he has spent over a decade studying the educational experiences of youth experiencing homelessness.

*In addition to publishing several research articles and book chap-
ters on the topic, he recently authored or coauthored three books
related to youth homelessness:* Educational Experiences of Hidden Homeless Teenagers *(2012);* Serving Students Who Are
Homeless: A Resource Guide for Schools, Districts, and Educational Leaders *(with Linda Skrla, 2016); and* Homelessness
and Housing Insecurity in Higher Education *(with Rashida
Crutchfield, 2018).*

Housing for Homeless Students: A Statewide Pilot
Katy Abel

While many colleges and universities are grappling with the
growing incidence of student homelessness, the Massachusetts
Campus Housing Security Pilot, which this essay describes,
was the first in the nation to address the issue as a matter of
intentional, state-level public policy involving an entire system
of public higher education. The pilot was launched in 2019
following the release of a 2018 survey of Massachusetts public
colleges and universities conducted by the HOPE Lab at the
University of Wisconsin (now the Hope Center for College,
Community, and Justice at Temple University).

Collected as part of a larger national survey of student basic
needs security, data showed that during the previous year,
49 percent of Massachusetts community college students and
32 percent of the state's four-year university students had experienced housing insecurity, defined by researchers as "unaffordable housing, poor housing quality, crowding, and frequent
moves" (Goldrick-Rab et al. 2019). In terms of outright
homelessness, 13 percent of community college students and
10 percent of four-year university students said they had experienced homelessness. The survey also found that 23 percent
of community college students said they had experienced both
food and housing insecurity. Causes of homelessness among
students include family violence as a leading factor—and one
that is especially prevalent among LGBTQ youth rejected by

their families. Research studies also emphasize rising levels of income inequality due to the lasting impact of the Great Recession, soaring college costs, and unprecedented levels of student debt as influential factors in the growth in student homelessness (Goldrick-Rab 2016).

In Massachusetts, campus staff felt they were making strides in combatting student hunger through increasing the use of food pantries and the launch of the meal swipes program to fund meals for students in need. But on the issue of housing homeless students, they felt stymied. Local shelters were viewed as an inappropriate option for students, and few youth shelter beds were available. But the campuses themselves had a significant resource, if funds could be tapped to utilize it: vacant beds in residence halls. Since 2011, enrollments at higher education institutions had declined by 11 percent (National Student Clearinghouse Research Center 2019), freeing up needed dorm space. If money could be found to pay for those beds, there would be space for students to live on campus.

Beginning in January 2019, the Massachusetts Unaccompanied Homeless Youth Commission agreed to fund the cost of housing homeless students in twenty dorm beds in four regions of the state. The plan, designed by staff from the Youth Commission, the Department of Higher Education, and campus staff, called for pairing a residential state university with a nearby community college that would refer eligible students. A separate funding stream from the Youth Commission flowed to local community organizations that would provide case management services to the pilot participants. Campuses would cover meal costs.

Campus teams took applications from homeless students and grappled with issues such as how to transport community college students to and from the residential campuses where they would live, how to provide food during spring and summer breaks when dining halls closed, and whether to require grade point average (GPA) thresholds and full-time enrollment as conditions for remaining in the program. Such questions forced campus and community partners to ask: Is this a degree completion program or a housing program? For most campus staff, the answer was the former. As the pilot program was designed and then refined, its mission became clearer: to keep vulnerable students on track to commencement day, with the hope that they will achieve economic self-sufficiency and future housing stability once they've earned postsecondary credentials.

Massachusetts governor Charles Baker's public launch of the pilot received widespread media attention. Reporters were captivated by the dramatic stories of students who were couch-surfing or living in cars or tents or public spaces. They were vulnerable in many respects, but these students also demonstrated tremendous tenacity to remain enrolled in school. One such student was Dilon, a participant in the pilot program from Quinsigamond Community College in Worcester. By the time he entered college, Dilon had decided that it was essential to get away from his abusive father. He left home and began couch-surfing with friends, texting a different friend each night from his job at a restaurant, asking if he could crash at their place once his shift as a waiter ended. Not having a reliable place to sleep created deep embarrassment and anxiety. Within a few weeks, his grades began to plummet.

"One of my professors asked me what was up because it had been two weeks and she hadn't gotten any work from me," Dilon recalls. "I was lucky I had someone who noticed and cared. All the anger went away and I was left with this overwhelming sadness as I realized I'd been dealing with this by myself this whole time." The same professor put Dilon in touch with Quinsigamond's dean of students, who was looking for homeless students to join the new pilot program to address student housing insecurity. Dilon was accepted into the program and moved into an apartment suite at nearby Worcester State University. He commuted back to his classes at Quinsigamond, and within a short time of securing housing, his grades rebounded.

"I slept like a baby," he calls of that first night in the dorm. "I wasn't going to bed feeling guilty. And I haven't gotten a C since I've been in the pilot."

Individual successes like Dilon's were enhanced by campus-community partnerships that gave Massachusetts' response to student homelessness its unique character. The support that students received from local community service organizations augmented the support received on campus. From material goods such as laptops, bedding, and gift cards to counseling and financial literacy, community agencies made a difference in the lives of student participants. Dilon loved the support and attention he received from his case managers at LUK, Inc., a social service agency in Worcester, Massachusetts. "It's like someone's always there and always listening and I loved all of my case managers," he recalled.

The supplemental funds to community organizations also served as a reminder to campuses that they would not be expected to shoulder the burden of caring for a high-need student population on their own. This was and will remain very important, as funding for public higher education in Massachusetts and other states is always weighed against competing priorities such as health care coverage, pension liabilities, and mass transit improvements. One early goal of the pilot was to safeguard it against economic downturns, providing enough external financial support so that no college's chief financial officer (CFO) had to recommend the program's cancellation due to budget constraints. To that end, all students in the pilot were granted the right to remain on campus throughout the COVID-19 epidemic.

Of the pilot's first cohort, seventeen of the nineteen students who began in the program were retained and planned to re-enroll—a positive sign for the pilot, as homelessness is a barrier to college completion. Based on this and other early success indicators, the Massachusetts Department of Housing and Community Development agreed in the fall of 2019 to repurpose a state-leased group home, previously used by clients of the Department of Mental Health, as a residence for up to eleven homeless students from four Boston campuses. The K House Scholars program in Malden, Massachusetts, offers a different model for students. Under this program, students who are accepted as tenants must pay a small portion of their income in rent. While the goal is to expand housing options for students in Boston's ultra-expensive housing market, K House will also give the Department of Higher Education a window into the benefits and liabilities of off-campus housing solutions. The on-campus pilot expanded by two additional regions in January 2020 to accommodate thirty students from a total of twelve institutions. Later in 2020, the Department of Higher Education began using federal housing vouchers to place students in additional on- and off-campus housing, based on a model developed at San Diego State University.

The Massachusetts Campus Housing Security Pilot, unsurprisingly, is having both intended and unintended consequences. Homeless students are by no means the only high-need student population on campus; what we're learning about the keys to success for these students, such as the introduction of case management by community providers, may yield important takeaways for campus staff working with other cohorts. Our next step is to have the pilot programs in their various forms fully evaluated by researchers and then to utilize the results to develop a state strategic plan for basic needs security, one that addresses not only student homelessness and hunger but child-care and transportation needs as well. As the Commonwealth's Commissioner of Higher Education, Carlos E. Santiago, routinely explains to legislators and other stakeholders, serving vulnerable students is not only a matter of social justice but an economic imperative as well, especially in a state with an aging population and a pressing need for college graduates to fill jobs in high-skilled industries that drive growth. Cast in such a light, the outcome of the pilot program has implications for all Massachusetts residents, whether they are properly housed or not.

References

Goldrick-Rab, Sara. 2016. *Paying the Price: College Costs, Financial Aid, and the Betrayal of the American Dream.* Chicago: University of Chicago Press.

Goldrick-Rab, Sara, Christine Baker-Smith, Vanessa Coca, Elizabeth Looker, and Tiffany Williams. 2019. *College and University Basic Needs Insecurity: A National #Real College Survey Report.* Philadelphia, PA: The Hope Center.

National Student Clearinghouse Research Center. 2019. *Current Term Enrollment Estimates.* https://nscresearch center.org/current-term-enrollment-estimates-2019/

Katy Abel is association commissioner for External Affairs and Special Projects at the Massachusetts Department of Higher Education. She oversees strategic communications, media and government relations, and pilot programs to support homeless students across the Commonwealth. A lifelong resident of Boston, Abel was a journalist working in radio, television, and print for twenty years before joining state government.

Place Character and Making Space for People Experiencing Homelessness
Colby King

Cities invest money and effort to make and remake their images, to create a place brand that attracts investment, economic development, and tourism (Ward 1998). These place branding efforts are overt exercises in managing how cities are perceived (Govers and Go 2009; Kavaratzis 2004). The related development of themed environments, such as Las Vegas Casinos, Dollywood, and entertainment districts in cities across the United States, illustrates how specific consumer audiences are targeted in these efforts to shape the meanings associated with a place. Like cities, these environments similarly co-opt and privatize the character of a place, attracting specific audiences in the process (Gottdiener 2001; Gottdiener et al. 2019). As cities are commercialized and public space is privatized, homeless people are pushed out, often through laws targeted at limiting their use of public space (Amster 2008). This essay argues that our understanding of the character of a city should be shaped as much by who the city marginalizes as by who the city invites in.

City branding is related to the broader concept of place character. Place character can be used to understand how the "seemingly ineffable set of qualities of a place," like whether it is considered hip, expensive, or welcoming illustrates what life is like on the ground in those places (Paulsen 2004). A city's place character is continually renegotiated through institutional marketing and public discussion as well as everyday interaction among residents (King and Crommelin 2013; Medway and Warnaby 2008). Together, cities and their residents make decisions about the ways in which they welcome or exclude people, which effects whether they stay or leave, allowing residents to re-create or reinvent the qualities of their places. Homeless people are as much a part of their city as other residents, however, and their struggles to find a place to live, and the ways in which policies and police further marginalize them, should also be understood as important reflections of the character of a place.

In cities across the United States, commercialization and the privatization of public space have hastened the criminalization of homelessness. Amster (2008) closely studies the development and implementation of ordinances, which criminalize particular activities, from panhandling and sleeping to even sitting on sidewalk curbs. He also describes a range of exclusionary antihomeless laws and practices that cities adopt, including the installation of spikes on surfaces that might otherwise be used for sitting or sleeping. As Mitchell wrote ten years earlier, "If homeless people can only live in public, and if the things one must do to live are not allowed in public space, then homelessness is not just criminalized; life for homeless people is made impossible" (1998, 10). From this, Amster argues that public space is "the sole site of guaranteed access in the city" and that it "stands materially and metaphorically as the essence of pluralism, political participation, and personal freedom" (2008, 45). In this way, we can see that the space, power, and voice that a city affords its residents are important aspects of the character of that city.

Of course, those with lower socioeconomic status have fewer resources and less political clout with which to shape these decisions. As a result, homeless residents are often pushed to the margins of their communities, while those with resources are more easily able to exercise their preferences or just leave. Herron (2007) showed how the decline of Detroit, Michigan, was created as much by those who left the city as by its remaining residents. Desmond (2017) showed how eviction processes exclude impoverished residents from housing and erode access to community life in Milwaukee, Wisconsin. Attempting to exclude or make space for poor and homeless people highlights the ways in which exclusionary forces are based on inequalities across social categories. Those who are marginalized in society are often not afforded space in the places we live and are literally pushed to the margins of cities, leading to criminalization and cyclical poverty.

What these examples highlight is how those groups that have been marginalized and excluded in myriad ways across our society are also those that are most in need of access to space. These tensions are all made more explicit when tourism and economic development groups publicly raise concerns about how the presence of homeless people in public space can impact a city's brand image. After organizing a convention that brought 6,300 pharmacists and their families to Seattle in 2018, the American Pharmacists Association (APhA) wrote a letter to Visit Seattle raising concerns about the city's homeless population (Horcher 2018). The following year, in an effort that reflects the character of APhA members as well as the city of Seattle, APhA returned to Seattle and partnered with

Mary's Place, a local organization that helps homeless women, children, and families. APhA members volunteered time and raised money to support the homeless in Seattle (Palmer 2019).

Over the past few years, many cities passed sanctuary city ordinances to protect undocumented immigrants from prosecution or deportation (Foerster 2018), but in what ways do these cities make space for citizens without housing? This question highlights the interrelatedness of the struggle of marginalized people to obtain access to public space and housing amid the commercialization of cities through place branding and privatization of space. Discussing the construction of spiked fences in otherwise public spaces, Amster (2008) notes how "a spike out is not a hand up" (22). As cities continue to rebrand themselves, we ought to consider how the city supports or excludes homeless people and other residents on the margins as critical aspects of the character of that place. While a city's branding campaign would likely not include images of the city with these spiked surfaces in sight, the spiking itself reflects the character of that city.

References

Amster, Randall. 2008. *Lost in Space: The Criminalization, Globalization, and Urban Ecology of Homelessness*. El Paso, TC: LFB Scholarly Publishing.

Beebeejaun, Yasminah. 2016. "Gender, Urban Space, and the Right to Everyday Life." *Journal of Urban Affairs* 39(3): 323–334.

Connor, Eric. "Greenville County Anti-Gay Resolution a Relic of History after Council Vote." *Greenville News*. https://www.greenvilleonline.com/story/news/2020/03/11/greenville-county-anti-gay-resolution-no-longer-applies-after-council-vote/5019899002/

Desmond, Matthew. 2017. *Evicted: Poverty and Profit in the American City*. New York, NY: Broadway Books.

Foerster, Amy. 2018. "Solidarity or Sanctuary? A Global Strategy for Migrant Rights." *Humanity & Society* 43(1): 19–42.

Gilbert, Melissa R. 1998. " 'Race,' Space, and Power: The Survival Strategies of Working Poor Women." *Annals of the Association of American Geographers* 88(4): 595–621.

Gottdiener, Mark. 2001. *The Theming of America: Dreams, Media Fantasies, and Themed Environments*, 2nd ed. Boulder, CO: Westview Press.

Gottdiener, Mark, Randolph Hohle, and Colby King. 2019. *The New Urban Sociology*, 6th ed. New York, NY: Routledge.

Govers, Robert and Frank Go. 2009. *Place Branding: Glocal, Virtual and Physical Identities, Constructed, Imagined and Experienced*. New York, NY: Palgrave MacMillan.

Herron, Jerry. 2007. "Detroit: Disaster Deferred, Disaster in Progress." *South Atlantic Quarterly* 106(4): 663–682.

Holder, Sarah. 2018. "Why Are So Many People in San Jose Fighting Housing for Teachers?" *CityLab*, October 17. https://www.citylab.com/equity/2018/10/san-jose-trying -build-low-cost-housing-teachers/572665/

Horcher, Gary. 2018. "Letter to Seattle Convention Leaders: Your Program Is Out of Control." *KIRO*. https://www .kiro7.com/news/local/letter-to-seattle-convention-leaders -your-homeless-problem-is-out-of-control/770150626/

Kavaratzis, M. 2004. "From City Marketing to City Branding: Towards a Theoretical Framework for Developing City Brands." *Place Branding and Public Diplomacy* 1(1): 58–73.

King, Colby and Laura Crommelin. 2013. "Surfing the Yinzernet: Exploring the Complexities of Place Branding in Post-Industrial Pittsburgh. *Place Branding and Public Diplomacy* 9(4): 264–278.

King, Colby and Laura Crommelin. 2019. "A Different Perspective on Post-Industrial Labor Market Restructuring in Detroit and Pittsburgh." *Journal of Urban Affairs*. Published online August 16. https://www.tandfonline.com /doi/full/10.1080/07352166.2019.1645569

Lambert, Diana and Daniel J. Willis. 2019. "California's Teacher Housing Crunch: More School Districts Building Their Own." *San Francisco Chronicle*, April 22. https:// www.sfchronicle.com/bayarea/article/California-s-teacher -housing-crunch-More-13783401.php

Loewen, James W. 2005. *Sundown Towns: A Hidden Dimension of American Racism*. New York, NY: New Press.

Massey, Douglas and Nancy Denton. 1993. *American Apartheid: Segregation and the Making of the Underclass*. Cambridge, MA: Harvard University Press.

Medway, Dominic and Gary Warnaby. 2008. "Alternative Perspectives on Marketing and the Place Brand." *European Journal of Marketing* 42(5/6): 641–653.

Merlan, Anna. 2020. "After the End of the World: The Eerie Silence of the Las Vegas Strip." *Guardian*, April 14. Las Vegas. https://www.theguardian.com/world/2020/apr/14 /las-vegas-strip-closed-coronavirus

Mitchell, Don. 1998. "Anti-Homeless Laws and Public Space: Begging and the First Amendment." *Urban Geography* 19(1): 6–11.

Palmer, Barbara. 2019. *How One Event Professional is Helping the Homeless*. Chicago, IL: pcma.org/helping-homeless -windy-christner

Paulsen, Krista. 2004. "Making Character Concrete: Empirical Strategies for Studying Place Distinction." *City & Community* 3(3): 243–262.

Rice, LaVon. 2006. "Shedding Light on Sundown Towns." Footnotes. American Sociological Association, March. https://www.asanet.org/sites/default/files/savvy/footnotes /mar06/fn5.html

Rothstein, Richard. 2017. *The Color of Law: A Forgotten History of How Our Government Segregated America*. New York, NY: Liveright.

Spain, Daphne. "Gender and Urban Space." *Annual Review of Sociology* 40: 581–598.

Ward, S. 1998. *Selling Places: The Marketing and Promotion of Towns and Cities, 1850–2000*. London: Routledge.

Colby King teaches and studies social inequality and social class, work, and urban sociology, including place character, city branding, and homelessness, as well as strategies for supporting working-class and first-generation college students. Dr. King has published research on postrecession shifts in occupational structures in the Pittsburgh and Detroit metropolitan regions in the Journal of Urban Affairs, *the geography and demographics of the working class in the* Journal of Working-Class Studies, *DIY place branding in deindustrialized cities in* Place Branding and Public Diplomacy, *and efforts to support development of students' social and cultural capital in* Teacher-Scholar: The Journal of the State Comprehensive University. *He is currently serving as secretary of the Working-Class Studies Association, is a member of the American Sociological Association's Task Force on First-Generation and Working-Class People in Sociology, and is a co-PI for the SEISMIC grant program at Bridgewater State University, funded by the National Science Foundation's S-STEM program (NSF-DUE 1643475). He is also a regular contributor for the Everyday Sociology Blog.*

Law and Homelessness
Maria Foscarinis

What does law have to do with homelessness? Don't homeless people just need housing and not lawyers?

Law and lawyers have played a critical role in addressing the modern crisis of homelessness in America. A lawsuit filed in

1979 resulted in a consent decree guaranteeing a right to shelter in New York City, spurring the creation of a shelter system that today accommodates over 60,000 people. The case, *Callahan v. Carey*, also helped launch homeless advocacy efforts in New York City and other cities around the country.

By the mid-1980s, it was clear that homelessness was a national crisis. At the time, I was a young lawyer at a big law firm in New York City, where I had volunteered for a pro bono case representing homeless families on Long Island. We argued successfully that the families were entitled to shelter under a federal law as it was then implemented in the state of New York. Having seen the positive impact that law could make on this crisis, I left my firm and moved to Washington, DC, to help organize a campaign for a federal response to homelessness.

As a lawyer, I played a lead role in drafting proposed new legislation and lobbying Congress; I also recruited a powerful law firm to help pro bono. In 1987, following a big campaign, and partnering with grassroots activists, the first major federal legislation addressing homelessness was enacted. The Stewart B. McKinney Homeless Assistance Act (now known as the McKinney-Vento Homeless Assistance Act) authorized $1 billion in aid over two years and created new legal rights: a right to education for homeless children and a right for service providers to acquire vacant federal property at no cost to use to aid homeless people.

While lobbying Congress, I also filed litigation to enforce existing federal laws to benefit homeless people. Before the McKinney-Vento Act, there were very few such laws. But I spent many hours in the law library, and in one notable case, I successfully sued the U.S. Department of Defense to force it to carry out an existing law to use vacant property to help homeless people.

In 1989, I founded the National Law Center on Homelessness and Poverty, focused on two key goals: implementing the McKinney-Vento Act and moving national policy beyond it. The McKinney-Vento Act was meant to be a first step in a comprehensive federal response, focused mainly on emergency relief; the bulk of funding went to shelter. Together with many of the groups I had worked with previously, the new Law Center outlined goals focused on housing, income, services, and civil rights for people experiencing or at risk of homelessness.

To move these goals forward, we devised a strategy to push for amendments to existing "mainstream" programs to aid homeless people and prevent homelessness. One important example of this is the inclusion of housing rights in the Violence Against Women Act (VAWA) of 1994. This provision was designed to prevent domestic violence survivors from having to choose between abuse and homelessness and to address a leading cause of homelessness for women.

The first goal of the National Law Center on Homelessness and Poverty, implementing the McKinney-Vento Act, sometimes meant litigation. One early key issue was the education rights of homeless children; our first case, *Lampkin v. D.C.*, established that the right is enforceable in court, setting national precedent. At the same time, we and others worked with members of Congress to strengthen the law. Over time, school access for homeless children has improved, and we've also worked to amend other laws to open access to other education resources, such as special education programs.

Another early piece of litigation was to enforce the right to vacant federal property. To date, some 500 vacant properties have been turned over by federal agencies to service providers to reuse as housing, shelter, foods banks, day care centers, and many other facilities that aid about 2 million people a year. But it took ongoing litigation by the Law Center to get the agencies to comply with the law—and litigation continues to this day.

In the 1990s, a trend to enact and enforce punitive laws against homelessness intensified, and advocates began focusing on preparing challenges to them. At the Law Center, we began tracking laws "criminalizing" homelessness—such as laws making it a crime to sleep, sit, or lie down in public—which, in the absence of housing or shelter, homeless people have no choice but to do. We published reports, focused media attention, and began litigating to challenge such laws on constitutional grounds, joining local-level advocates. We used law as a policy tool to require federal attention on criminalization trends and to use federal funding to discourage local criminalization.

In *Martin v. Boise*, a case we first filed in 2009, the U.S. Court of Appeals for the Ninth Circuit—which covers not just Idaho, where the case arose, but also nine states, including California—ruled that criminally punishing people for sleeping, sitting, or lying in public when they have nowhere else to go is unconstitutional. Despite a big push from the city of Boise, the U.S. Supreme Court declined review and the ruling stands. The *Martin v. Boise* decision is binding in the Ninth Circuit and sets an influential precedent nationally.

Of course, our goal is not for people to live on the street. Our goal has always been to end homelessness, and this means increasing the supply of permanent, affordable housing. But the U.S. legal system is often described as a system of negative rights—freedom from government intervention—as opposed to positive rights to aid and support. This means our tools as lawyers are often more suited to fighting against harmful actions—like criminalization—than for positive ones, like ensuring housing.

But unlike U.S. law, international human rights law does explicitly recognize economic and social rights like housing, as well as the right to education, health, and a living wage—and in the mid-1990s, we began advocating for a right to housing in the United States.

Recently, after years of advocacy, the "right to housing" began to enter mainstream policy discourse. In 2019, four major presidential candidates called for it, as did state and local leaders. In 2020, a bill was introduced in the California state legislature to amend that state's constitution to include a right to housing—the first in the nation. And the Housing Is a Human Right Act was introduced in the U.S. Congress to address homelessness.

Then came the pandemic, which is especially devastating to homeless people who already suffer disproportionately from health problems and are thus very vulnerable. How do you stay at home if you have no home? How do you wash your hands if you have no sink?

Again, lawyers are playing a leadership role in driving the response to this crisis. At the Law Center, COVID-19 only made our existing goals even more urgent, and we adjusted them to address the pandemic directly, with recommendations for government and private response. The Centers for Disease Control and Prevention (CDC) adopted several of our recommendations, including urging communities not to "sweep" encampments but rather to offer housing to their residents.

Most important, we have redoubled our call to acknowledge the human right to housing here in the United States. Lawyers have played a critical role in ending homelessness, but we need to push our legal system to recognize that housing and other economic needs are basic rights. The pandemic has made clearer than ever before that housing is essential to health and to life itself—not only for those who lack it but also for all of us.

Let's use this moment of crisis to advocate for the human right to housing—to the benefit of everyone.

References

Callahan v. Carey, No. 79–42582 (Sup. Ct. N.Y. County, Cot. 18, 1979).

Lampkin v. District of Columbia, 886 F. Supp. 56 (D.D.C. 1995).

McKinney-Vento Act. 2006. *NCH Fact Sheet No. 18.* Washington, DC: National Coalition for the Homeless.

"People Experiencing Homelessness." Centers for Disease Control. https://www.cdc.gov/coronavirus/2019-ncov/need-extra-precautions/homelessness.html

Robert Martin v. City of Boise, No. 15–35845 (9th Cir. 2019).

UN General Assembly. 1948. *Universal Declaration of Human Rights* (217 [III] A).

VAWA—(Title IV, sec. 40001–40703 of the Violent Crime Control and Law Enforcement Act, H.R. 3355). Reauthorization in 2015.

Maria Foscarinis is an American lawyer who has advocated for legal and policy responses to end homelessness in the United States since 1985. She is a primary architect of the McKinney-Vento Act, the first major federal legislation addressing homelessness; she has also led successful litigation to secure the legal rights of homeless persons. Ms. Foscarinis has published dozens of articles, book chapters, and opinion pieces; testified before Congress on numerous occasions; and speaks regularly about legal and policy issues affecting homeless persons. She is the founder of the National Homelessness Law Center (formerly known as the National Law Center on Homelessness and Poverty), a not-for-profit organization and the only national organization dedicated solely to using the power of the law to end homelessness in America. Ms. Foscarinis served as the organization's executive director from its founding in 1989 until March 2021. She holds an adjunct appointment at Columbia Law School, where she teaches a seminar on law and policy of homelessness. She is currently working on a book about national advocacy and policy responses to modern homelessness.

Saving Lives: A Coordinated Response to COVID-19
April Connolly

I am writing this submission in April 2020, one month after President Trump declared the COVID-19 pandemic a national emergency. Even prior to this, from its arrival in the United States in January, COVID-19 has infected over 31 million people nationally and 663,000 in Massachusetts, killing over 559,000 nationally and 17,413 in Massachusetts as of mid-April 2021 (Centers for Disease Control and Prevention 2021). In Massachusetts, responding to the pandemic means protecting people from infection while they are experiencing homelessness, which presents tremendous challenges. Only through unprecedented collaboration across multiple systems, including state agencies, municipalities, health care providers, and nonprofit organizations, has our region controlled and minimized the spread of COVID-19, protecting people experiencing homelessness who are often stigmatized, ignored, and invisible. This pandemic has shone a light on the housing crisis in this country and specifically in Massachusetts, emphasizing the need to address the overcrowded, underresourced homeless emergency response system, now and permanently.

With the outbreak of the COVID-19 virus, particular attention has been paid to the uniquely vulnerable homeless population, given their overlapping forms of physical and mental health challenges, posing an increased risk of serious health conditions. Complicating matters is the overcrowded emergency shelter system in Massachusetts, which accommodates individuals in congregate settings. In these settings a highly contagious virus can rapidly spread through the population with just one infected person.

Father Bill's & MainSpring (FBMS) operates two individual emergency shelters 24 hours per day, 365 days per year in two communities in southern Massachusetts, serving 250 people a night in highly concentrated spaces. In general, individual emergency shelter programs across Massachusetts are under-resourced and overutilized, experiencing overflow year-round with guests relegated to sleeping on mats on the floor when all the beds are full. The average space afforded between individuals in sleeping quarters is limited to 3–4 feet in order to accommodate as many people as possible and not turn anyone away. Emergency shelters are a social safety net, and decisions about occupancy are based on local fire codes and saving lives.

The proximity between bunk beds is a critical concern, as it makes the social distancing needed to mitigate the spread of COVID-19 virtually impossible.

Best practices indicate that depopulating these overcrowded facilities is the best option to prevent widespread viral infection among this highly vulnerable population. When alerts of this outbreak reached FBMS, we knew we had to act fast to prevent widespread infection. Beginning in mid-March 2020, FBMS partnered with the local municipalities, health care providers, as well as state public health and emergency management agencies to strategize and execute depopulation sites to allow for the requisite social distancing. Each of these stakeholders came to the table with different perspectives; for example, health care providers focused on reducing hospitalizations. But we had one common goal: keep our most vulnerable neighbors and the communities they reside in as healthy as possible. Together we were able to create two fully operational depopulation sites, where homeless people could socially distance outside of congregate shelters, inside of two weeks; one in Quincy and the other in Brockton, Massachusetts, a tremendous undertaking. Not only did these partnerships allow us to prevent the spread of COVID-19 through enabling social distancing but we were also able to test all remaining shelter guests, thanks to our health care partners.

Organizing across our region, working collaboratively, and taking proactive steps to manage this public health crisis were life saving for people experiencing homelessness. Although infection rates among homeless people across the Commonwealth of Massachusetts average around 30 percent, thanks to the proactive efforts in our region, we have been able to keep that rate at 16 percent. Part of this is also due to the mobilizing capacity of people working to end homelessness in our region, including FBMS. Of the two locations in Quincy and Brockton, the rate of infection in Quincy is below 5 percent, thanks to the rapid response by city officials and commitment by a partner nonprofit.

In addition to saving lives, one of the many successes of this effort is the inspiring commitment of the staff working to support our most vulnerable neighbors. The teams at FBMS, as well as in homeless service organizations across the Commonwealth, have put themselves at daily risk in order to make sure that guests can still access a safe place to rest their heads at night. This commitment to an already-challenging mission has been awe-inspiring. I have never worked alongside so many partners with different ways of operating, different objectives in their day-to-day business, and different expertise yet unified under one purpose, one goal, one mission. I am awestruck and grateful for the power of our collective and personal dedication. Whether it is the emergency management coordinator calling on a Saturday to warn of impending inclement weather, the local health center doctor dedicating their weekend to test our guests, the local hotel manager opening their doors to our guests, or the local YMCA offering their field house as a secondary site for depopulation, these and so many other examples demonstrate the power and impact of partnerships for a common good.

There have been many challenges in coordinating these efforts. Delays in decision-making have been shown to have detrimental effects on infection rates. When navigating multiple stakeholders, cooperation and developing a shared agenda take time. We have had to double our workforce to support multiple sites in a high-risk environment that operate 24/7 at a time when many people are getting sick and are scared of exposure. We have also had to deal with the unpredictability of New England weather during a changing season while accommodating people in tents (in our depopulation sites). And we still face many uncertainties ahead. We are advised that social distancing will be a standard, best practice to prevent infection; we suspect that repopulating the emergency sites after the initial phase of this crisis passes will only lead to another surge in infection.

How do we sustain a depopulated emergency shelter system with limited space, resources, and an anticipated increased demand? How do we plan for longer-term strategies and programming to serve the highly vulnerable homeless population and provide emergency services when we are still learning about this virus and the information seems to evolve almost daily? Without long-term partnerships and resource commitments at the local, state, and federal levels, nonprofit homeless providers will be limited in our capacity to provide these essential services now and into the future. The COVID-19 crisis has emphasized what we have known for years, that the practice of warehousing people experiencing homelessness in large, overcrowded emergency shelters is simply not sustainable and not a solution. Providing safe, affordable, and permanent housing with no barriers remains the best solution to ending homelessness. Only time will tell how we as a society adapt and reprioritize how we take care of ourselves and one another.

Reference

Centers for Disease Control and Prevention. 2021. "Morbidity and Mortality Weekly Report (MMWR)." cdc.gov/mmwr /index.html.

April Connolly joined the FBMS team after completing her MSW at BSU in May 2008. She had previously graduated summa cum laude from BSU's Bachelor's in Social Work program in 2007. Determined to pursue social work practice from a macro perspective, she became interested in homelessness as an intern at the United Way of Greater Plymouth County in 2006. April began her career with FBMS by coordinating the daytime guest services at the Mainspring House in Brockton. In a few, short years, she took on the role of housing programs director where she was responsible for the oversight of operations and clinical services for over 300 units of supportive housing for individuals and families. Today, as the chief operating officer, she oversees the programming and day-to-day operations for the entire organization, including Housing, Individual and Family Sheltering, developing and improving programs and services in pursuit of FBMS' mission to end homelessness through a Housing First approach.

Housing First: Ending Homelessness and Supporting Social Integration
Sam Tsemberis

This essay describes the Pathways Housing First (PHF) program, developed in 1992 by Pathways to Housing, New York. It presents evidence on program effectiveness and provides recommendations for taking PHF to scale to end homelessness nationwide. Popularly known simply as "Housing First," PHF is a program that provides home and support services for individuals or families experiencing homelessness and coping with clinical challenges such as health, mental health, and/or addiction. This subgroup of the homeless population is only 10–15 percent of the total, but it is a group that utilizes approximately 50 percent of homeless service resources (Culhane et al. 2002). PHF has two main program components: (1) a rent subsidy to immediately secure housing and (2) a community-based case management team to support program participants after they are housed. The four core principles of the PHF model are consumer choice, separation of housing and supports, a recovery orientation, and community integration.

For most of us, a home is not only a physical structure but also where our lives and relationships happen. People living without a home are described as "the homeless." This label pits "us" against "them," putting "the homeless" in a pathological category that blames their current circumstances on individual problems such as mental illness or substance use instead of viewing neoliberal social and economic policies as forces that create and perpetuate homelessness (Willse 2015).

In the United States, the current era of homelessness began in the early 1980s as a direct result of the Reagan administration's drastic cuts to funding and support for the development of public housing. This enormous loss, from an estimated 350,000 units built each year to less than 50,000, was followed by a tremendous boom in the real estate market, which resulted in rapidly rising rents. Economic forces, therefore, combine with political ones to leave growing numbers of people on disability or other fixed income priced out of the rental market, as they remain to the present. In 2020, the average disability income is $783/month and the average monthly rent for studio/one bedroom is $1,022 (Technical Assistance Collaborative 2020).

Before Housing First

Before Housing First, permanent supportive housing was offered only *after* consumers successfully proceeded through a series of programs starting with outreach or drop-in centers followed by emergency shelters and transitional housing. While empirical studies show that Housing First is a more effective strategy for ending homelessness, the treatment first approach still dominates the field of homeless services.

This traditional approach to housing for people with psychiatric disabilities is based on several inaccurate assumptions: (1) clinicians are the experts and know which type of housing is best suited to meet consumers' needs, (2) consumers with psychiatric and/or addiction problems require around the clock supervision, (3) consumers with a diagnosis of severe mental illness are not capable of managing independent housing even

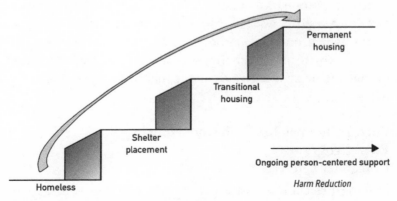

Figure 3.1 The Housing First Approach

with supports, and (4) consumers must first receive skills training for independent living in order to learn how to live in independent housing. Contrary to these assumptions, PHF is based on empirical evidence indicating that consumers with psychiatric disabilities and/or addiction issues can set and attain their own goals and, with support, can live independently and effectively manage their housing, mental health, addiction, employment, and much more.

Randomized control trials conducted in the United States (Stefancic and Tsemberis 2007; Tsemberis et al. 2004), Canada (Aubrey et al. 2015), and France (Tinland et al. 2013) and numerous pre-post studies report that PHF programs achieve an average of 85 percent housing retention compared with 40 percent for the "treatment as usual" groups, which require a period of sobriety and psychiatric treatment as preconditions for housing.

Born out of the limitations of the traditional "treatment first" approach, the PHF model has changed the landscape of what is considered possible for people with psychiatric disabilities and/or addiction who have remained chronically homeless (Tsemberis 2015). PHF provides immediate access to permanent affordable housing coupled with support and treatment services after the person is housed. PHF is based on the belief that housing is a basic human right rather than a reward for treatment compliance or good behavior. This program philosophy emerges from a social justice and consumer rights perspective in which program participants do not have to prove that they are worthy or deserve housing and instead are empowered to make their own decisions about their housing and recovery plans.

Core Principles for Pathways Housing First Program
Consumer Choice

Making life choices and experiencing their consequences are fundamental to the processes of learning for everyone. Yet most traditional supportive housing programs are averse to trial-and-error learning in which clients make decisions about how and where they want to live or who they want to live with. Traditional permanent supportive housing programs operate with a risk-aversive approach, as they are highly structured and supervised. They offer program participants few options and little choice regarding day-to-day activities. Programs are typically operated in large single site buildings with an emphasis on maintaining daily routines and not on community integration.

These programs are based on long-held assumptions that individuals with psychiatric disabilities require this type of "therapeutic milieu" to better manage their illnesses. These congregate programs, which emphasize treatment first, are especially challenging as they often do not use an individualized harm-reduction approach for treating drug and alcohol use. Instead, everyone must be abstinent or take medication for the sake of the tranquility of the community, and relapses can result in eviction.

PHF programs, on the other hand, are driven by consumer choice, as consumer preference and active participation are fundamental to its program philosophy. Instead of assuming that "we know what's best" for the client, we work together to choose the neighborhood, the apartment, furniture and household items, and whether or not they want to live with someone or their pet. PHF's two program requirements are (1) consumers must adhere to the terms and conditions of a standard lease and pay 30 percent of their income, usually Supplemental Security Income (SSI) toward their rent, and (2) consumers must agree to regular home visits by program staff.

Separation of Housing and Services

Most PHF consumers live in their own scattered site apartments integrated into the community. Support services are provided by staff who live off-site but make frequent home visits. The use of normal working-class rental housing is the model most preferred by consumers. Housing integrated within the community also reduces the likelihood that people with psychiatric disabilities will be stigmatized, a possible outcome if they reside in buildings that are dedicated to housing a disabled population. The PHF program does not rent more than 10–20 percent of the units in any one apartment building in an urban area, with some variance in suburban or rural areas.

Another advantage of separating housing from service is evident when consumers must change from one apartment to another, whether for positive or negative reasons. Positive moves include entering a relationship and wanting to move in together or being reunified with children who had previously been in placement. Negative reasons for moving or relocating include eviction after relapse, having too many guests disrupting the neighbors, or interpersonal behavioral problems with neighbors. In these latter instances, the PHF staff will try to address these issues, but if a move is required, the staff support the consumer in securing another apartment. Because the support services team is separate from the apartment building, staff can effectively continue to provide support even as consumers move to a different apartment.

In some instances, such as when the consumer is hospitalized, arrested, or jailed, the staff can visit the client, provide support while the client is institutionalized, and then continue their support when the client returns home. There is no break in support because of a change in residential status. Changes or breaks in residence do not mean a break from service support, and consumers are not discharged or terminated from the program. In fact, PHF programs generally operate with a "no discharge" policy. In addition, the PHF support services are available on call on a 24/7 basis and are offered for as long as a consumer needs them.

Recovery-Oriented Services

PHF embodies a recovery orientation that has become a cornerstone of mental health service reform (New Freedom Commission on Mental Health 2003). PHF services are characterized by a philosophy that conveys respect for the homeless and the hope that people will be able to overcome their difficulties. Longitudinal research studies of rates of recovery from mental illness consistently report that between 47 percent and 67 percent of individuals diagnosed with schizophrenia experience significant improvements over time, and many are recovered fully (Harding et al. 1987). Part of this is due to establishing control and choice. Studies of PHF programs have shown that when consumers exercise choice in decision-making, they develop a sense of mastery over their lives, which results in a reduction of psychiatric symptoms (Greenwood et al. 2005). Choice and mastery are considered cornerstones of recovery.

For PHF, having a recovery focus means that staff are aware that life is more complex and interesting than managing an illness and stand ready to support consumers in pursuing their social, educational, artistic, cultural, leisure, and other goals and interests (Rowe and Davidson 2015). The journey of recovery begins with an urgent plan to immediately help a person experiencing homelessness into housing, but this program soon develops into a journey to build a life in the community, not as a client of a program but as a neighbor, a relative, an employee, a volunteer, or any other "regular" person. One dimension of recovery is to expand one's social role participation in their community.

Community Integration

One of the most important aspects of the PHF model is that it promotes community integration, which fosters establishing normative relationships beyond those with program staff, including landlords, neighbors, store owners, and other natural supports. This model is also consistent with antidiscriminatory legislation such as the Americans with Disability Act (ADA) and the *Olmstead* Supreme Court decision, which mandates that people with disabilities live in the least restrictive settings. Both the ADA and the *Olmstead* decision promote social inclusion and community integration (Sloan and Gulrajani 2019).

Future Directions

Today, PHF programs are operating throughout the United States, Canada, Europe, Australia, and New Zealand (Padgett et al. 2016). Some countries, notably, Finland and Norway, have adopted a PHF approach and have for the most part ended street homelessness. The key to their success was that they made an evidence-based decision and adopted a highly effective program model that espouses the values of consumer choice and housing as a basic right. Finally, their success was due to investments in funding for housing subsidies and support services.

In the United States, we have an excellent example of what is possible with political support in the case of veterans experiencing homelessness. In 2009, the Obama administration estimated that 70,000 veterans were experiencing homelessness nationwide. Congressional approval was obtained to provide rental subsidies and funding for case management teams for the Veterans Administration. To date, more than 56,000 veterans have been housed, and 78 communities and 3 states have ended veterans' homelessness (U.S. Interagency Council on Homelessness 2020). In general, the United States has not taken the same approach with the general homeless population as it did with veterans.

Today, the focus is not on the structural factors that continue to make people homeless every day. There is no consensus about how to reduce income disparity, housing is still regarded as a commodity instead of as a basic human right, and wages and benefits are not keeping up with rental markets. Most important, since the 1980s, the federal government has refused to develop large-scale public housing. To make matters worse, in spite of enormous empirical evidence, the Trump administration urged a return to the 1980s view of people experiencing homelessness as having made poor choices and not working hard enough. If we are going to end homelessness in the United States, it will take great political will. We the people who have homes will have to stop averting our eyes when we see a person experiencing homelessness, address the shortcomings of our ineffectual policies, and start demanding that we put an end to homelessness because we have the tools and the resources to do so.

References

Aubrey, Tim, Sam Tsemberis, Carol E. Adair, Scott Veldhuizen, David Streiner, Eric Latimer, Jitender Sareen, Michelle Patterson, Kathleen McGarvey, Brianna Kopp, Catharine Hume, and Paula Goering. 2015. "One Year Outcomes of a Randomized Controlled Trial of Housing First in Five Canadian Cities." *Psychiatric Services* 66(5): 463–469.

Culhane, Dennis, Stephen Metraux, and Trevor Hadley. 2002. "Public Service Reductions Associated with Placement of Homeless Persons with Severe Mental Illness in Supportive Housing." *Housing Policy Debate* 13(1): 107–163.

Greenwood, Ronni Michelle, Nicole J. Schaefer-McDaniel, Gary Winkel, and Sam Tsemberis. 2005. "Decreasing Psychiatric Symptoms by Increasing Choice in Services for Adults with Histories of Homelessness." *American Journal of Community Psychology* 36(4): 223–238.

Harding C. M., J. Zubin J., and J. S. Strauss. 1987. "Chronicity in Schizophrenia: Fact, Partial Fact, or Artifact?" *Hospital Community Psychiatry* 38: 477–486.

New Freedom Commission on Mental Health. 2003. *Achieving the Promise: Transforming Mental Health Care in America. Final Report.* DHHS Pub. No. SMA-03–3832. Rockville, MD: U.S. Department of Health and Human Services.

Padgett, Deborah K., Bruce Henwood, and Sam Tsemberis. 2016. *Housing First: Ending Homelessness, Transforming Lives, and Systems Change.* New York: Oxford University Press.

Pathways to Housing. https://www.pathwayshousingfirst.org/

Rowe, Michael and Larry Davidson. 2015. "Recovering Citizenship." *Israeli Journal of Psychiatry and Related Science* 53: 14–21.

Sloan, Laura and Chinmoy Gulrajani. 2019. "Where We Are on the Twentieth Anniversary of *Olmstead v. L.C.*" *Journal of the American Academy of Psychiatry and the Law* 47(4): 408–413.

Stefancic, Ana and Sam Tsemberis. 2007. "Housing First for Long-Term Shelter Dwellers with Psychiatric Disabilities in a Suburban County: A Four-year Outcome Study of Housing Access and Retention." *Journal of Primary Prevention* 28: 265–279.

Technical Assistance Collaborative (TAC). 2020. *Priced Out, 2020.* https://tac.org

Tinland, Aurelie, Cecile Fortanier, Vincent Girard, Christian Laval, Benjamin Videau, Pauline Rhenter, Tim Greacen, Bruno Falissard, Themis Apostolidis, Christophe Lancon, Laurent Boyer, and Pascual Anquier. 2013. "Evaluation of the Housing First Program in Patients with Severe Mental Disorders in France: Study Protocol for a Randomized Control Trial." *Trials* 14 (309). https://doi.org/10.1186/1745-6215-14-309

Tsemberis, Sam. 2015. *Housing First: The Pathways Model to End Homelessness for People with Mental Illness and Addiction.* Center City, MN: Hazelden Press.

Tsemberis, Sam, Leyla Gulcur, and Maria Nakae. 2004. "Housing First, Consumer Choice, and Harm Reduction for Homeless Individuals with a Dual Diagnosis." *American Journal of Public Health* 94: 651–656.

Willse, Craig. 2015. *The Value of Homelessness: Managing Surplus Life in the United States.* Minneapolis, MN: University of Minnesota Press.

Sam Tsemberis is a clinical-community psychologist who originated the "Housing First" program that effectively ends homelessness for

individuals with psychiatric and addiction problems. Housing is provided as a basic human right, not as a reward that must be earned through treatment compliance or other demonstrations of worthiness. Dr. Tsemberis serves as CEO of Pathways Housing First Institute, executive director of the VA-UCLA Center of Excellence for Training and Research, and clinical associate professor, UCLA Department of Psychiatry and Biobehavioral Sciences. Dr. Tsemberis consults across the United States, Canada, the EU, Australia, New Zealand, and South America. He has published articles, book chapters, and two books on homelessness and mental illness, and his work has been recognized by the National Alliance to End Homelessness, American Psychiatric Association, American Psychological Association, and the Lieutenant Governor of Canada.

This chapter begins with an overview of the primary governmental organizations dedicated to ending homelessness. Each profile highlights the contributions of members and founders, as well as the general mission and impact of each agency. Because homelessness is such a pervasive problem in the United States, this chapter follows profiles of government agencies with national organizations. These are nonprofit organizations that have contributed to ending homelessness for the population overall, or for specific subpopulations, at the national level. Each profile explains the history of the organization and details its activities, leaders, critics, and controversies.

Many of the organizations profiled in this chapter began in the 1980s and are a direct outgrowth of that particular crisis point in the history of homelessness. Collectively, the organizations included here spearheaded the McKinney-Vento Homeless Assistance Act, the annual point-in-time (PIT) count, and the continuum of care (CoC) planning process. They also began the drive to develop ten-year plans to end homelessness. They have informed the nation's data collection procedures and assisted in defining focus areas and targeting populations and approaches to ending homelessness. They also offer important tools for communities to work against the criminalization of

---

Substance abuse is both a cause and a result of homelessness. National organizations that address substance abuse recognize that homeless people often experience multiple, co-occurring risk factors. (Syda Productions/ Dreamstime.com)

homelessness, access affordable housing, and provide protection and support. The organizations included here do not cover specific state and local efforts to end homelessness. Instead, they offer a national profile of the structure of homeless assistance. In this sense, these profiles provide a macro-level orientation to homelessness.

This chapter is organized around three basic ideas: (1) the federal government plays an instrumental role in defining homelessness and mobilizing resources to end it; (2) basic needs resources like housing, health care, education, and quality of life must be considered in tandem with all other solutions; and (3) national and grassroots organizations influence public opinion and federal policy to address specific issues and populations and to explore innovative approaches to ending homelessness. The McKinney-Vento Homeless Assistance Act, the only federal legislation directly addressing homelessness, established the U.S. Interagency Council on Homelessness (USICH) as the coordinating agency for all federal efforts to end homelessness.

The first profile in this chapter offers a summary of the history, goals, and accomplishments of the USICH. It follows with profiles of the key member agencies that offer housing (the U.S. Department of Housing and Urban Development [HUD]), education (the Department of Education [ED]), and services geared toward special populations, including veterans (Veterans Administration [VA] and Department of Labor [DOL]) and people involved with the criminal justice system (U.S. Department of Justice [DOJ]). It also examines federal agencies in charge of the nation's food supply and distribution (U.S. Department of Agriculture [USDA]) and responsible for managing assistance efforts in times of national disaster (U.S. Federal Emergency Management Agency [FEMA]).

National nonprofit organizations directly inform the federal government in its efforts to end homelessness and address special issues and populations, basic needs, and basic rights.

Some organizations, like the National Alliance to End Homelessness (NAEH) and the National Coalition for the Homeless (NCH), focus on ending homelessness and on specific initiatives related to data collection, training, and community awareness. This is also true for the Urban Institute, a nonpartisan think tank on federal policy issues affecting urban, low-income communities.

Other organizations focus on specific issues, like the National Law Center on Homelessness and Poverty (NLCHP), later renamed the National Homelessness Law Center, which examines criminalization and how the law impacts homeless people, or the National Low-Income Housing Coalition (NLIHC), which focuses on affordable housing. Still other agencies focus on specific populations, including children and youth (National Association for the Education of Homeless Children and Youth [NAEHCY]. Additional contact information for each organization, and a review of publications and resources, can be found in Chapter 5.

The final section of this chapter offers a brief profile of people who pioneered early approaches to the study of homelessness or developed policy to end it. This section focuses on the roots of homeless research and specifically on quantitative and qualitative data collection. Aside from Nels Anderson, all these profiles are of women. Highlighting women's important contributions to understanding homelessness, poverty, and housing insecurity helps us question our taken-for-granted beliefs about why women get interested in issues of poverty and homelessness in the first place and what their overall contribution can be. Stereotypically, the reason women are interested in homelessness and poverty is because of personal sympathy, feelings, or experience. Rarely is it associated with a skill set, a research tradition, an empirical question, or a political standpoint. Yet, these are exactly the issues that have driven the women in these profiles to pursue homelessness as an area of research and study and to create the provisions and structures still used to guide national policy and ideally end homelessness in the United States.

Government Organizations
U.S. Interagency Council on Homelessness (USICH)

The USICH was officially authorized in 1987, as part of Title II of the McKinney-Vento Homeless Assistance Act. The USICH works with nineteen member organizations to coordinate the nation's response to homelessness. Member organizations work with states and local jurisdictions on service delivery, data collection, and reporting. The USICH coordinates twenty-three programs across nine of its member agencies (Cunningham et al. 2017). The USICH also submits an annual performance report and budget justification to Congress to show progress toward meeting the nation's goals in reducing homelessness. These goals are determined in concert with the current administration and spelled out in the Federal Strategic Plan to End Homelessness.

Throughout its history, the USICH has played an instrumental role as leader and coordinator, catalyst, and facilitator. Sometimes it takes the lead in shaping federal policy, and other times, particularly in times of crisis, it works with limited support. Because the USICH depends so heavily on Congress and the government for funding and direction, its role has changed over time, along with federal priorities. Federal funding to address homelessness goes primarily to HUD, U.S. Department of Health and Human Services (HHS), and the VA. Additional funding goes to the USICH and DOL and DOJ and to FEMA and the USDA for emergency and food assistance.

The 1980s drew attention to the complex issues veterans faced, and national attention to this issue grew over time. In the late 1980s and early 1990s, the primary activities of the USICH focused on collecting and reporting reliable data, coordinating food assistance, and ending homelessness among the severely mentally ill and military veterans. Congress also reauthorized McKinney-Vento Act in 1990 and 1994 to offer better coordination and access to educational services at the state and local levels. These focus areas progressed during the Clinton administration and became even more finely tuned, as services were eventually coordinated through the CoC planning process. This eased the path to full educational access through additional provisions and funding. More accurate, reliable data was also collected and disseminated, and the nation began to address critical health issues among the homeless population.

By 2002, the focus on permanent housing and support services helped build support for the goal of ending chronic homelessness in ten years. In addition, the Homeless Veterans Comprehensive Assistance Act, which was signed in 2001, authorized funding and coordination to end homelessness among veterans. The goals of ending chronic and veteran homelessness, and the development of ten-year plans to do so, would become an important part of the USICH mission for years to come.

Philip Mangano became the executive director of the USICH in 2002. Popularly known as the "homeless czar," Mangano helped advance the ten-year planning process, the Housing First initiative, and a focus on ending chronic homelessness. The USICH established ten regional coordinators to oversee this work, including Matthew Doherty, who would go on to lead the USICH in 2015. The agency's focus on ending homelessness, a monumental task, has been advanced through over 300 ten-year plans throughout the country. Agency achievements also include the end of veteran homelessness in at least seventy-eight communities, three states, and counting. Although the NAEH was the originator of the ten-year plan idea, the official endorsement of the USICH has made it part of the national conversation and helped translate goals into policy.

The role of the USICH changed under the 2009 Homeless Emergency Assistance and Rapid Transition to Housing (HEARTH) Act to allow for the development of the *Federal Strategic Plan to Prevent and End Homelessness*, called *Opening Doors*. *Opening Doors* lays out the nation's plan to end homelessness among distinct subpopulations, including veterans, youth, families, and chronically homeless people. Part of the reason for including families in this reauthorization is that the subprime mortgage crisis brought the plight of families hurt by the Great Recession into the spotlight. Many families, over-whelmingly families of color and in deep poverty, who had worked hard to accumulate wealth lost everything because of predatory lending. In addition to addressing families, ending homelessness for "all other individuals" is also a part of the plan, but the plan's goals and timeline here are less specific. Focusing on categories of people highlights the fact that policy choices often reaffirm a separation between those seen as deserving or undeserving of assistance.

Part of what helps establish someone as deserving or worthy is being part of a group that the nation cares about protecting. In cases like this, it is easier and less controversial to provide support. Veterans, youth, and families with children are all seen as deserving of assistance and have been specifically targeted for additional resources. Chronically homeless people, on the other hand, are usually considered less deserving at best and personally culpable for their circumstances at worst. As a result, and because of the complex needs and risks they face, justifying support for chronic homelessness is more difficult. The primary argument that has worked to justify focusing on chronically homeless people is that it saves taxpayer money by providing housing over emergency services. This view, which is backed up by the work of Dennis Culhane et al. (2002), is supported by the USICH and the Housing First initiative.

Housing First was pioneered in the 1990s in New York City by Pathways to Housing. It is a data-driven strategy that eliminates the typical stepwise progression of outreach and emergency shelter to transitional housing and finally to permanent housing. The Housing First approach, by contrast, offers housing as a first step for the most-difficult-to-serve populations. It is a trauma-informed, harm-reduction approach to factors that may accompany homelessness like addiction or mental illness, which are typically seen as barriers to remaining housed permanently. The Housing First approach has experienced long-term success in keeping people housed and engaged in support services. It has been codified into the national funding and reporting process. This means that CoC regions implementing the Housing First approach can retain existing funding and garner additional resources. However, advocates question whether or not pressure to conform to these requirements means rushed planning and implementation, compromising program outcomes and the overall integrity of the approach.

The logic of separating homeless people into categories prioritized for assistance is that specific groups have unique needs that set them apart from other homeless people. We also prioritize these groups as more important to our nation and thus more deserving of resources than people in other categories. There is no specific mention, for example, of structural racism or domestic violence, although we know that women and people of color are at greater risk of homelessness and are already overrepresented in its ranks. Although international agreements, like the United Nations' Millennium Development Goals, explicitly focus on gender equality, *Opening Doors* supports women who are in families, with children, or who are chronically homeless or in another prioritized category.

The split between deserving and undeserving symbolized by the focus on special populations is both a strength and a weakness of *Opening Doors*. Focusing on specific populations ignores the cyclical nature of homelessness and the systemic inequality that created it. Yet, given the enormity and complexity of the problem and long-standing controversy over U.S. welfare spending, perhaps the most effective way of managing homelessness is piece by piece. Experts acknowledge the revolving door that extreme poverty and homelessness have become. But the path toward ending homelessness for the entire population remains an elusive goal, without specific benchmarks. By 2018, *Opening Doors* was significantly revised and titled *Home, Together*. It included the general goal of ending chronic homelessness among people with disabilities and among unaccompanied youth. Released as an update, *Home, Together* eliminated all timelines associated with its goals.

Beginning in 2019, the Trump administration leveled unfounded critiques of Housing First, decrying it as expensive and inefficient. Even as the administration touted progress toward ending veteran homelessness—gains that had been accomplished to a significant extent through Housing First—it suggested that a rise in permanent supportive housing had not succeeded in ending homelessness and was therefore suspect. It also espoused a criminalization-driven approach to homelessness, suggesting that permissiveness and the shelter system itself were responsible for the population's high numbers and visibility. California received specific attention for what President Trump called a "disgusting" and "disgraceful" problem. Criticizing this insulting, punitive approach to homelessness led to the resignation of Matthew Doherty, executive director of the USICH, who was asked to leave by the Trump administration. He went on to serve as a consultant on homeless issues in California and Texas.

Ron Marbut replaced Doherty as executive director of the USICH in 2019. Marbut's leadership of the USICH reflected the rejection of Housing First and a turn toward congregate, warehouse style shelters where beds must be earned through program compliance. Marbut also espoused additional criminalization measures designed to punish people sleeping on the street and organizations providing food for homeless people, to prevent them from getting too comfortable. Members of Congress, as well as the NLIHC, published letters of objection to Marbut's appointment. Advocates and long-term homeless policy makers also expressed disappointment with Doherty's removal and concern with the Trump administration's overall approach to homelessness. Marbut resigned from the USICH in February 2021, a month after Democrat Joe Biden, who defeated Trump in the November 2020 presidential election, was inaugurated as the country's forty-sixth president.

U.S. Department of Housing and Urban Development (HUD)

Prior to the creation of HUD in 1965, the federal government oversaw the nation's supply of affordable housing through various agencies and programs. Early focus areas included providing loans and mortgage insurance, developing low-rent housing to replace dilapidated slum dwellings, and providing senior housing. Over time, HUD's established goals expanded to promote urban housing development and to ensure affordability and equity and social and racial justice. Homelessness is one of eight initiatives related to the provision of housing that HUD oversees.

HUD was created in 1965, as part of the War on Poverty that was launched under the Johnson administration. Its establishment coincided with the ongoing civil rights movement and the Watts riots that occurred in the same year. Robert Weaver was the inaugural secretary of HUD and the first African American to sit on the president's cabinet. HUD headquarters are currently housed in a federal building bearing Weaver's name. When HUD was established, discrimination in housing was legal, and it remained so until 1968. By that time, the ills associated with slum housing had garnered national attention as symbols of urban blight and racial inequality. While white homeowners enjoyed suburban housing and affordable home mortgages throughout the postwar era, many African Americans were relegated to substandard urban rental housing and cut off from the ability to accumulate wealth. This is a primary reason that people of color, and African Americans in particular, are overrepresented in the homeless population, along with other "at risk" categories.

The Fair Housing Act of 1968 was designed to reduce residential segregation and put an end to discrimination in rental housing and home ownership. Yet, it was not until the 1970s that the Equal Credit Opportunity Act and the Community Reinvestment Act prevented discrimination in mortgage lending and the redlining of black neighborhoods (Rothstein 2017). In the wake of this new legislation, HUD had the difficult task of ensuring fairness and equity throughout its programs, many of which created inequality to begin with. Part of evaluating HUD's record in serving homeless people is reflected in its policies to reduce discrimination. Like the USICH, HUD's reach and focus depend on the current administration's fiscal and ideological support. HUD secretaries are nominated by the president and approved by the Senate and are typically members of the same political party as the president. Understanding how HUD's approach to housing and homelessness has evolved over time demonstrates the enormous impact that the federal government has in determining the size and composition of the homeless population and people in poverty.

When homelessness became recognized as a national social problem in the 1980s, the USICH was established and HUD became one of its charter members. HUD's oversight of homelessness includes establishing national definitions and benchmarks; collecting, analyzing, and disseminating data; overseeing the federal funding and application process; and providing coordination and other support for CoC regions throughout the country. HUD also administers the Community Development Block Grant (CDBG) program through the office of Housing and Community Development and the housing voucher and subsidy program known as Section 8. It is important to note that both CDBG funding and Section 8 are not limited to homeless people but are also for low- and moderate-income households. This profile reviews the history and specific impact these programs have had on homelessness in the United States.

In addition to distributing funding for homeless shelters and services to CoC regions nationwide, HUD coordinates the annual PIT count, which began in 2005. The PIT count is required as part of an application for federal funding. It is a one-time, "snapshot" count estimating the size and demographics of the homeless population in the region in question. HUD offers guidance for CoC regions and uses PIT count data to coordinate reporting for the Annual Homeless Assessment

Report (AHAR) to Congress. HUD guidance includes establishing official definitions, subpopulations of interest, and specifics on how to count and record information. The purpose of this is to ensure consistent reporting within and across years and regions. This is a monumental task, as there are over 400 CoC regions in the United States, with multiple stakeholders and unique circumstances that make national comparisons difficult.

In 2009, the HEARTH Act consolidated McKinney-Vento Programs and established new definitions of homelessness and chronic homelessness. It also identified those "at risk of homelessness," to guide future services and funding. It includes the goal of returning newly homeless families to permanent housing within thirty days and the less specific goal of providing affordable housing for all. Chronically homeless people, who consume more in emergency dollars than it would cost to house them, are also a focus of the HEARTH Act.

HUD defines chronic homelessness as having "a substance use disorder, severe mental illness, a developmental disability, PTSD, cognitive impairment from a brain injury, or chronic physical or developmental disability." This definition also specifies the length of time one must be homeless to be considered "chronic." It must be "for at least 1 year or on at least four separate occasions in the last 3 years," including less than ninety days in jail or in an institution (HUD 2015). Any shelters that do not collect this information and document it using the Homeless Management Information System (HMIS) can lose federal funding. Establishing an official definition of chronic homelessness is challenging, but the benefits of doing so are that national data comparisons ideally lead to improved policies and housing opportunities.

An ongoing challenge related to the definition of chronic homelessness is that estimating the length of homeless "episodes" is difficult. People who are chronically homeless often withdraw from the rhythms of settled life and may find it more difficult to keep track of their time (Wakin 2020).

Documenting this information is also time-consuming for providers, who worry that time spent on documentation takes away from service delivery. In addition, providers fear that focusing on chronic homelessness over other risk categories will lead to empty beds waiting for designated populations rather than beds that can be provided to anyone in need.

The Emergency Shelter Grant (ESG) Program is one of several homeless programs that HUD oversees. It was renamed the Emergency Solutions Grants Program in 2012. The ESG is funded through a process separate from the CoC. The other programs that HUD oversees include Housing Opportunities for low-income Persons with Aids (HOPWA) and the Rural Housing Stability Assistance Program (RHSP). RHSP consolidates homeless assistance programs under the HEARTH Act.

More recent programs include Pay for Success. This initiative is a collaboration with the DOJ to direct funding to programs supporting permanent housing as a way of breaking the link between homelessness and involvement in the criminal justice system. The Youth Homelessness Demonstration Program is another pilot program that began in 2018, with twenty-three communities participating to end youth homelessness. HUD oversees a related initiative for veterans, in collaboration with the VA, to offer housing vouchers and services for those experiencing homelessness. This program is known as the HUD-VA Supportive Housing (HUD-VASH).

HUD also oversees several "legacy programs," including the ESG Program, mentioned previously. Until 2012, it also included the Homeless Prevention and Rapid Re-Housing Program (HPRP), which was designed to respond to the subprime mortgage crisis and focus on quickly rehousing newly homeless families and individuals. Three existing programs, consolidated under the HEARTH Act, complete the list of legacy programs. They are the supportive housing program (SHP), the shelter plus care program (S + C), and the Section 8 moderate rehabilitation single rent occupancy program.

Using the most recent AHAR to evaluate HUD's progress toward reducing or ending homelessness reveals mixed results. It also reflects a growing polarization between categories of homeless people seen as deserving and those regarded as undeserving of assistance. The undeserving are presumed to have caused their own homelessness and, in the latest AHAR, are blamed for its national resurgence. Deserving populations typically get a larger share of direct housing and service dollars and better programs, and their numbers subsequently decrease. As the 2019 AHAR shows, the number of veterans experiencing homelessness declined by over 36,000 since 2018. This is due to increased funding and policies targeting veterans, a shift in emphasis that ramped up under the Obama administration. Other groups that experienced moderate declines include homeless families with children, who saw a decrease of 8,700 people from 2018 to 2019 and an overall decline of more than 68,000 since 2007, and unaccompanied youth, whose numbers decreased by over 3,500 since the baseline count in 2017.

In contrast with these decreases, the number of people experiencing long-term chronic homeless has risen in the past four years. From 2018 to 2019 alone, over 16,000 additional people were classified in this category. California is specifically mentioned in the report as having the highest increase in homelessness overall, as well as among the chronically homeless. This report raises the question of how best to permanently house people in this category. HUD lauds its own record of producing permanent supportive housing and implementing Housing First, yet these successes have clearly not been enough to address the problem. This is particularly true for warm weather states with high-priced housing, like California (Shinn and Khadduri 2020). The AHAR puts annual increases of chronic homelessness into perspective by noting that it is down 20 percent from 2007 to 2019. Yet, because early PIT counts took time to coordinate across CoC regions, some of this decrease is due to changing methodology and not population changes. As the nation experienced the COVID-19 pandemic, the limitations of HUD's tools to manage affordable housing became evident, renewing claims that the country has a glaring need for universal basic housing.

U.S. Department of Justice (DOJ)

The DOJ works to reduce the criminalization of homeless people. DOJ programs focus on offering targeted assistance including mental health counseling and addiction services as an alternative to arrest and incarceration. These diversion measures not only reduce jail and prison stays but also save money spent on enforcement over treatment. The Pay for Success Permanent Housing Demonstration Program focuses on people defined as chronically homeless, with multiple jail or prison stays and physical or behavioral health problems.

Pay for Success was launched in 2016. It is an outcomes-based program informed by the philosophy of Housing First. It involves a complex partnership among HUD, the DOJ, local governments, private investors, and independent evaluators. Private donors and philanthropic organizations pay for housing and are reimbursed by the government for meeting various benchmarks that determine success. Local demonstration projects are designed to prevent recidivism and chronic homelessness and reduce costs by offering housing and wraparound services. The DOJ used funding allocated through the Second Chance Act of 2008 focusing on diversion and re-entry to support this program.

The first set of competitive grants totaling $8.7 million were distributed to seven sites, two in Alaska, and one per state in California, Oregon, Texas, Maryland, and Rhode Island. Each individual demonstration site could receive up to $1.3 million. To be eligible for funding, projects offered no less than one hundred permanent supportive housing units. These projects minimized the cost of emergency services by providing permanent housing. Grant money paid for feasibility studies, as well as the implementation of new projects and permanent housing. Some of the ongoing challenges of Pay for Success are that success is often difficult to measure consistently across diverse programs. In addition, although Pay for Success shows positive outcomes, it serves only a small fraction of the population in need. The Pay for Success program was evaluated by the Urban Institute in 2018, the program's second year. This evaluation examined the costs and benefits of the program in terms of its meaning for participants as well as its literal costs and successes. The evaluation showed that this program produced benefits such as increased collaboration and data sharing but that significant challenges remain, chief among them the considerable investments of time and money that Pay for Success programs require.

One of the most positive aspects of Pay for Success is the multisector collaboration it fostered between local stakeholders. Once participants eliminated structural barriers to sharing information, this improved collaboration. Participants noted, however, that this took significant staff time, often far exceeding what was originally budgeted for. One of the initial challenges of this program was identifying the target population. Demonstration sites used a variety of data collection tools to prioritize participants based on risk. An additional challenge demonstration sites faced was establishing the feasibility and cost-effectiveness of their programs. Although most programs showed initial cost savings, these gains were often offset by long-term costs. In addition, the overall savings to organizations was not significant enough for most projects. Because program funding depends on success, evaluation remains a key challenge.

In addition to Pay for Success, the DOJ oversees the Office of Violence against Women (OVW). This office was established in 1994, with the passage of the Violence Against Women Act (VAWA). Its programs are for victims of sexual assault, domestic violence, dating violence, or stalking. This disproportionately affects women, people of color, youth, and people experiencing poverty and can result in heightened risk of homelessness. Domestic and sexual violence are underreported and represent an ongoing threat to women and children. In 2018, OVW awarded $269 million in awards to fund programs designed to assist victims and hold perpetrators accountable. Programs provided staffing and supportive services including housing and shelter beds, hotline calls, victim advocacy, crisis intervention, civil legal advocacy, and criminal justice advocacy (DOJ, OVW 2018).

U.S. Department of Health and Human Services (HHS)

The HHS is a USICH member. Like many agencies that are USICH members, HHS addresses the needs of the nation, as well as specific populations, including individuals and families experiencing homelessness. In terms of its organizational structure, HHS oversees eleven operating divisions that include the Substance Abuse and Mental Health Services Agency (SAMHSA) and the National Institutes of Health (NIH), which oversees the National Institute on Alcohol Abuse and Alcoholism (NIAAA) and the National Institute on Drug Abuse (NIDA).

The HHS also funds and directs programs that directly focus on people experiencing homelessness. These include the Health Care for the Homeless (HCH) Program, Projects for Assistance in Transition from Homelessness (PATH), and grants for the benefit of homeless individuals and runaway and youth. These programs are designed to offer homeless people access to mainstream services and health care benefits. They are also designed to serve populations with addiction and/or mental illness, homeless children and youth, and other special populations. Finally, HHS focuses on better coordination of service delivery, including innovative approaches to outreach and engagement.

Funding for HHS initiatives related to homelessness comes from the federal government and often includes interagency partnerships and matching funds from states and localities. Federal funding for HUD for homeless programs hovers around the $3 billion mark, and HHS funding is about one-third of that. HHS oversees programs for homeless people through its member agencies, which also serve the general population. The Health Resources and Services Administration (HRSA) oversees the HCH Program. SAMHSA oversees homeless prevention and housing programs as well as the PATH program. Finally, the Administration for Children and Families (ACF) is in charge of Head Start and Runaway and Homeless Youth Programs and Service Connections for Youth. This profile briefly reviews each of the six programs HHS oversees, with additional detail in the profiles of these member organizations.

The HCH Program funds outpatient health centers that offer health care, substance abuse treatment and prevention, and referral services. This program was initially authorized in 1987, with the passage of the Stewart B. McKinney Homeless Assistance Act, later renamed Mckinney-Vento Homeless Assistance Act. In 1996, health centers for the homeless were combined with three existing facility types: community health centers, health centers for residents of public housing, and migrant health centers. In 2015, health centers served 24.3 million patients in total. Just over 22 million patients went to community health centers, 890,283 to health centers for the homeless, 833,271 to migrant health centers, and 487,034 to health centers for residents of public housing (Heisler 2017, 15). In the same year, more than 60 percent of patients had incomes at or below the federal poverty line or were racial or ethnic minorities. Finally, about half of all patients were receiving Medicaid, and about one-quarter were uninsured.

Funding for health centers reflects a focus on the general population, as approximately 80 percent of funding goes to community health centers, over the other types. A minimum of 8.7 percent goes to health centers focusing on homeless people. These centers must rely on a combination of other funding sources to support their operating costs, as only about one-fifth of a health center's operating budget comes from HCH funding. The rest comes from Medicaid (42.2 percent), followed by HHS grants (22 percent); state, local, and private funding (13.9 percent); and reimbursements from private

insurance (9 percent) (Heisler 2017). In 2017, the HCH program supported the work of approximately 300 health centers and addressed the needs of 1 million homeless people. The
National Association of Community Health Centers reports
that an additional 1.4 million homeless people were served by
health centers not receiving federal funds.

Throughout the HCH Program's history, its main contributions are in the areas of outreach and engagement, community
collaboration, case management, medical respite care, and consumer advisory boards (Zlotnick et al. 2013). These approaches
were developed through research and supported with federal,
state, and local funding. They inform current research studies and service delivery. The Patient Protection and Affordable Care Act of 2010 further improved health care access for
homeless people, one of several previously uninsured populations targeted for assistance in the law. Yet, ongoing challenges
remain. The prevalence of co-occurring disorders, long-term
and chronic homelessness, ongoing health conditions, and lack
of access to basic needs remain some of the most prominent
problems confronting homeless people and health care providers. In addition, the health care community remains divided
on how best to deliver health care services to special populations, by bolstering mainstream services or offering separate
ones. In addition to the HCH Program, HHS oversees several
programs through SAMHSA, which is discussed elsewhere in
this chapter.

The ACF oversees the Head Start and Early Head Start
programs. These programs focus on early learning experiences that promote school readiness, support basic access to
health care and food assistance, and improve overall family
well-being. This program developed in the 1960s and 1970s
and expanded in the 1980s. Head Start, as it is known today,
officially began in 2007, through the Improving Head Start
for School Readiness Act. Its most substantial revision was in
2016, when ACF updated performance standards to meet the
needs of local populations. Children from birth to age 5 who

are experiencing homelessness or are designated low-income are eligible for Head Start programs, and Early Head Start programs serve women and families with children under 3. There are over 1 million children in the United States who qualify for these programs. Head Start is tailored to the specific needs of the community and usually operates in local schools or child-care centers. According to the ACF, there are 1,700 community agencies in the United States that deliver these services.

Substance Abuse and Mental Health Services Administration (SAMHSA)

SAMHSA is one of eleven operating divisions under the HHS, a USICH member agency. Although many of the eleven HHS divisions work in collaboration to address issues related to homelessness, none are specifically dedicated to the homeless population. This includes SAMHSA. In its most recent strategic plan, covering the years 2019–2023, its objectives include addressing the opioid crisis, substance abuse, serious mental illness, and data collection and training. The plan recognizes the fact that substance abuse, mental illness, and homelessness often go together. It also appreciates the challenges involved in providing prevention, treatment, recovery, education, and employment. An overall focus of the plan is to increase access to permanent housing for the service population.

The main homeless program that SAMHSA oversees is PATH. PATH is a block grant program that distributes money to states, which contract out to providers to deliver services. PATH was first authorized through the Stewart B. McKinney Homeless Assistance Amendments Act of 1990. It was later reauthorized in 2016 under Section 9004 of the 21st Century Cures Act (P.L. 114–225). PATH funding covers homeless assistance activities ranging from street outreach to educational services. It addresses mental illness and substance abuse, outreach and service participation, and data and documentation. PATH is a matching grant program, meaning that all grant recipients must contribute at least $1 for every three received from the federal government. Many contribute more. Overall, federal costs for PATH programs are estimated annually at over $64 million, with matching funds coming from local, state, or other funding sources.

Communities receiving PATH funding must adhere to strict guidelines including HMIS participation and annual reporting. This allows SAMSHA to evaluate the success of PATH and better track the demographics of the population served. The 2019 annual report shows that, of the 66,458 people enrolled in PATH programs, just over 39 percent were unsheltered and considered chronically homeless. Over 40 percent were identified as having co-occurring disorders. These survey results show the dramatic overlap among addiction, mental illness, homelessness, and living unsheltered. PATH outreach and services reached just over 106,000 new people in 2019, with just over 66,000 people contacted through street outreach. The focus on outreach and engagement reflects a recognition that PATH is intended for one of the most hidden and difficult-to-serve populations. The most common services provided through PATH are screening and case management, clinical assessment, and community mental health.

The Center for Mental Health Services (CMHS) oversees the PATH program. It is one of five homeless programs offering grants and services through SAMHSA. Others include Cooperative Agreements to Benefit Homeless Individuals (CABHI), Grants for the Benefit of Homeless Individuals (GBHI), Treatment for Individuals Experiencing Homelessness (TIEH), and SSI/SSDI Outreach, Access, and Recovery (SOAR). Together, these initiatives focus on the service and housing needs of people experiencing homelessness with serious mental illness, emotional disturbance, substance use, or co-occurring disorders. The various funding these programs offer gives communities the tools to organize and deliver services and to assist patients in accessing mainstream assistance, like SSI and SSDI, through SOAR. They provide individuals and service providers with targeted housing and greater access to various kinds of assistance.

SAMHSA programs address the mental health and sub-stance use issues of the nation. In so doing, SAMHSA serves an important preventative role in keeping new populations from becoming homeless, as mental illness and substance use are pri-mary risk factors. SAMHSA also works to build capacity in communities nationwide and to reinforce equity and integra-tion as key goals. Part of this involves data collection and analy-sis. The Center for Behavioral Statistics and Quality (CBHSQ) collects national data, as a subsidiary of the Census Bureau. Behavioral health data sets include the National Survey on Drug Use and Health, the National Survey of Substance Abuse Treatment Services, the National Mental Health Services Sur-vey, Mental Health Client-Level Data and the Mental Health Treatment Episode Set, and the Uniform Reporting System for individual state data.

In service of better data collection, SAMHSA works closely with other organizations including the National Institute of Mental Health (NIMH) and the National Center for Health Statistics. These collaborations allow for a more coordinated approach to basic issues as well as crises like opioid addiction and the COVID-19 virus. In 2018, SAMHSA received a bud-get increase to implement new programs related to the opi-oid crisis. This required a revision of its overall business plan, application and review process, and provision of training and technical assistance. This important initiative overlaps with homelessness, as early city-specific studies show that as much as 81 percent of overdose deaths among homeless people are caused by opioids (Baggett et al. 2013).

National Institute of Mental Health (NIMH)

Today, NIMH is one of twenty-seven centers and institutes within the NIH, a biomedical research agency housed within the HHS. NIMH uses research and evaluation to develop new programs and services to address the nation's mental health issues (Levine and Rog 1990). The primary difference between NIMH and SAMHSA is that NIMH focuses on mental health disorders and SAMHSA on the broader issue of behavioral health. Mental and behavioral health issues are primary risk factors leading to homelessness, and homelessness is a predictor of future mental health issues. The cost associated with managing and treating mental health issues is also a risk factor that can contribute to homelessness.

NIMH was officially established in 1949, three years after the passage of the National Mental Health Act. Throughout the 1950s and 1960s, as the nation's understanding of mental illness advanced, NIMH gathered important information on its primary causes. NIMH also conducted research on specific issues including suicide, schizophrenia, child and family mental health, aging, minority group and urban problems, and delinquency and crime. Many of these areas overlap with homelessness and are considered contributing factors. By 1963, the general trend in the United States was away from hospital care for mental illness and toward treatment centers in local communities. Among the problems associated with mental hospitals included the dangers of involuntary confinement and a withdrawal from community life. The cost of treating mental illness was also seen as a critical issue and a drain on the nation.

With the passage of the Community Mental Health Centers Act in 1963, the federal government officially supported situating mental health care and services in local communities. This approach was designed to allow patients to remain in their own homes, with family and friends, instead of being removed to an institution. Establishing mental health centers came with challenges including how to assess the local prevalence of mental illness and where to locate treatment facilities. In addition, as the nation became more aware of how substance abuse, poverty, and homelessness overlap with mental illness, the need for better information intensified.

To address a growing national concern with addiction, two new institutes were established, the NIAAA in 1970 and the NIDA in 1972. Both institutes are housed within NIMH. By the 1980s, NIMH extended its research to examine mental and addictive disorders with a focus on prevalence and service use. By this time, it was clear that the closure of mental hospitals through what is known as "deinstitutionalization" was a contributing factor to the increase in America's homeless population.

In 1981, the Omnibus Budget Reconciliation Act established block grants to states to address mental health issues within their borders. While the government continued to provide technical assistance, training, and support, states were charged with planning and administering all treatment and rehabilitation programs. Legislation specifically mandated a focus on prevention and early intervention. Increased attention to mental health and addiction issues coincided with the emerging national homelessness crisis in the 1980s. Both NIMH and its counterparts in NIAAA and NIDA contributed to research addressing the overlapping issues related to mental illness and addiction within the homeless population. Some researchers argue, however, that this focus overemphasized the prevalence of mental illness among homeless people (Jones 2015).

Despite this critique, NIMH research in the 1980s led to a greater understanding of the mental health issues facing people experiencing homelessness. Studies conducted between 1982 and 1986 showed that approximately one-third experienced severe mental illness, and about half also had substance abuse issues (Levine and Rog 1990). Research also showed that people who were both mentally ill and homeless often went untreated and unsheltered and that many became involved with the criminal justice system. Overall, NIMH research emphasized the complexity of needs and risks facing this population and the need for better coordination of services.

With the passage of the Stewart B. McKinney Homeless Assistance Act in 1987, two additional provisions addressed homelessness and mental illness. The first offered funding for demonstration projects to better understand service needs in the areas of: street outreach, long-term case management, mental health treatment, staffing and operating supportive living programs, and management and administrative activities.

The second act authorized NIMH to administer block grants to states for similar services to address homeless people with chronic mental illness. This work was administered with the Alcohol, Drug Abuse, and Mental Health Administration (ADAMHA), which was eventually replaced by SAMHSA, NIAAA, and NIDA.

In 1989, a new Office of Programs for the Homeless Mentally Ill was established within NIMH. This office advanced research on homeless families and children and distributed over $3 million in grant money for individual projects. By 1992, Congress passed the ADAMHA Reorganization Act, abolishing ADAMHA and creating SAMHSA. NIMH rejoined NIAAA and NIDA, under the umbrella of the NIH. By 1990, funding for programs related to homelessness through NIMH, NIAAA, and NIDA reached $74 million (Jones 2015). Throughout the 1990s, as NIMH reorganized and focused its research agenda, the homeless service system was also emerging. Early efforts focused on establishing definitions of homelessness, understanding causes and solutions, and developing reliable data collection mechanisms.

After its reorganization in the 1990s, NIMH's research and grant programs expanded to include new areas of research. It also re-evaluated its public education program to allow better integration of public opinion to shape future directions. By 1997, NIMH restructured its extramural research program to encompass three new research divisions: Basic and Clinical Neuroscience Research; Services and Intervention Research; and Mental Disorders, Behavioral Research, and AIDS. NIMH also supported intramural research through the work of hundreds of scientists at the NIH Clinical Center. Research in the above areas continued into the 2000s along with an emphasis on diversity, education, and public outreach. NIMH also stepped forward to help treat mental health issues that arose among people affected by Hurricane Katrina and prevention issues to address mass violence.

NIMH continues to partner with SAMHSA (NIDA and NIAAA) to research issues related to both behavioral and mental health. Their research supports initiatives that include addressing and treating serious mental illness, managing the opioid crisis, and responding to the COVID-19 pandemic. Legislation to address the opioid crisis in 2016 initiated new funding streams and organizational partnerships involving both NIMH and SAMHSA. These efforts directly address the homeless population, as studies show that as many as 30 percent have both mental illness and substance abuse issues (Burt et al. 1999). The opioid crisis is also particularly deadly for the homeless population, as discussed in the SAMHSA profile. Because of the increased exposure to violence and trauma that often accompany homelessness, developing effective solutions is particularly challenging. With NIH funding, NIMH partnered with SAMHSA to study opioid deaths. The overall goal of this project was a 40 percent reduction in the number of deaths across the national population.

In conclusion, NIMH research is expansive, focusing on the causes, diagnosis, treatment, management, and prevention of mental illness. NIMH research has advanced the nation's understanding of the scientific causes of mental illness through clinical research. The impact of this research on the homeless population has led to a greater understanding of the prevalence of major depression, trauma, schizophrenia, suicide, and the general category of mental illness. It has also led to increased support for harm-reduction approaches and initiatives designed to reach the overall homeless population as well as specific subgroups.

National Institute on Alcohol Abuse and Alcoholism (NIAAA)

NIAAA began in 1970, along with SAMHSA, NIMH, and NIDA. It is one of twenty-seven centers and institutes within the NIH. Like other government institutes described in this chapter, NIAAA's overall goals and mission address the entire U.S. population, not only or specifically homeless people. Nevertheless, its research has proven relevant to efforts to reduce homelessness. The agency conducts research in the areas of genetics, neuroscience, epidemiology, prevention, and treatment throughout the life course. Its overall goal is to discover the biological and sociocultural causes of alcohol addiction, as well as the risks faced by specific populations, and to assess various approaches to treatment. To fulfill this goal, the NIAAA provides funding and training opportunities to support and disseminate research and reduce the stigma of substance abuse.

NIAAA research has both internal and external components, under the larger umbrella of HHS and the NIH. Internal research is conducted through the Division of Intramural Clinical and Biological Research. The NIAAA also distributes federal grant money to state and local agencies, which comprises the vast majority of its annual budget. Four extramural research divisions oversee the areas of epidemiology and prevention, metabolism and health effects, neuroscience and behavior, and treatment and recovery (Heilig et al. 2010). NIAAA research targets special populations including under-aged youth, college students, women, older adults, minorities, those with health disparities, people with other psychiatric disorders, and those with HIV/AIDS. Homeless people are under the broader category of minorities and those with health disparities. This category also includes Hispanics, blacks, Native Americans, and rural and economically disadvantaged populations. Homeless people experience economic disadvantages and are also frequently members of one or more of these other categories. Research on alcohol addiction suggests that at least 35–40 percent of those experiencing homelessness have alcohol-related problems, in comparison with about 26 percent of adults in the general population.

The challenges involved in outreach and engagement to homeless people with substance abuse are numerous. Outreach activities bring providers into direct contact with the service population with the overall goal of engaging them in treatment. The high attrition rate and hidden, stigmatized nature of homelessness and addiction are two of the most common barriers to outreach. Engaging homeless people comes with its own challenges, including disaffiliation or a lack of social ties, isolation, distrust of authorities, and dual-diagnosis or co-occurring disorders (Zerger 2002). Homelessness has also been found to be both a reason for and a consequence of addiction, making effective substance abuse treatment both crucial and complicated. The NIAAA's approach to researching addiction is that clinical, scientific research can lead to better treatment, even for the most-difficult-to-serve populations.

The NIAAA approaches substance use among homeless people as a medical issue. It emphasizes systemic inequality rather than focusing on individual causes or blame. This is an important contribution to research on addiction because homelessness is so often seen as a personal failure. This trend is reflected in the research. Studies show that research focusing on the health problems of homeless people decreased from 77 percent of all homelessness-related research from 1984 to 1988 to 41 percent between 1994 and 1998. In the same time period, research on personal risk factors increased from 15 percent to 44 percent (Zerger 2002, 11). Part of the reason for this shift is that the nation's understanding of homelessness increasingly focuses on subpopulations and individual causes, making the need for NIAAA research paramount.

The primary NIAAA initiative that was directly related to homelessness began in 1987 with the passage of the Stewart B. McKinney Homeless Assistance Act (known since 2000 as the McKinney-Vento Homeless Assistance Act). Section 613 of this act authorized new funding for the NIAAA in conjunction with NIDA, to establish Community Demonstration Grant Projects for Alcohol and Drug Abuse Treatment of Homeless Individuals (Lubran 1989). Administration of these grants follows the same structure as other federal funding, meaning that states and localities coordinate and evaluate their own programs and the NIAAA offers training and guidance. Community Demonstration Projects offered a total of $9.2 million in 1987 and an additional $4.5 million in 1989 to explore innovative approaches to address addiction among homeless people.

The Community Demonstration Projects produced nine two-year demonstration projects in eight cities (Orwin et al. 1994). Seven of these projects received additional support in 1989. Aside from the one in Anchorage, Alaska, all funded projects were located in cities with fewer than 250,000 people. Community Demonstration Projects focused on innovative approaches to treatment including intensive case management, street and shelter outreach, and additional services and assistance including literacy training, vocational education, employment counseling and job placement, financial counseling, child care, and housing assistance (Lubran 1989). They also focused on specific populations, including women and children, people dually diagnosed with substance abuse and mental illness, and racial minorities including Native Americans and Alaskan Natives.

Given the experimental nature of these programs and approaches, funding also came with a mandate to spend 25 percent of the award on evaluation. To ensure standardization across programs, all awardees used the Addiction Severity Index. This is an interview tool that measures risk factors including medical status; drug and alcohol use; family, social, legal, and psychiatric status; and employment and support. Because of the multifaceted, emergency nature of the problem of homelessness, the NIAAA did not prescribe a single, uniform treatment protocol (Huebner et al. 1993). Community Demonstration Projects showed that the goal of decreasing alcohol and drug abuse among homeless people needed to be combined with addressing basic needs. This includes treatment for physical and mental health issues and access to shelter, housing, and employment.

Lessons learned from the Community Demonstration Projects included the need to allow adequate start-up time for new programs, a longer project duration to allow for outcomes assessment, and the need to track individual program users after exit. Another challenge was that agencies often found themselves competing for scarce resources. While government organizations struggled to produce a coordinated approach, states and localities were exploring how best to collaborate across agencies offering complimentary homeless services. Despite these challenges, the Community Demonstration Projects were groundbreaking in their attempt to address the multiple, co-occurring risk factors facing homeless people and to explore innovative forms of treatment.

Following this set of projects, in 1990, the NIAAA provided a total of $48 million in new funding for fourteen projects over a three-year period. This round of projects was known as the Cooperative Agreement Program. It emphasized effective treatment methods and better coordination with NIAAA for program management and evaluation. The NIAAA also created standardized reporting tools for funding recipients and used additional survey tools to measure alcohol dependence and collect personal histories. Projects focused on initial outreach and long-term activities including housing and employment (Huebner et al. 1993). Approximately 6,000 people experiencing homelessness were targeted under the Cooperative Agreement Program. The majority of those receiving services were minority men, women with children, chronically homeless people with co-occurring issues, and veterans.

Results from the Cooperative Agreement Program examined differences in efficacy between medical and social detoxification programs and different approaches to service and engagement. Medical detoxification or "detox" programs are costlier and are typically administered through hospitals, where patients stay for the duration of treatment. Social detox programs may include twelve-step programs or those that emphasize harm-reduction strategies and peer support. Cooperative Agreement Programs did not suggest one uniform approach to treatment as more successful than the others. However, case management was used more often than other approaches. Because the training and oversight of case managers were inconsistent across programs, this approach was seen as better targeted to serve specific local subpopulation needs.

One of the ongoing challenges that the NIAAA faces is that focusing on homeless people takes coordination among federal, state, and local agencies. It also takes substantial, ongoing funding, oversight, and evaluation. Collaboration with other agencies in the areas of mental health, other forms of addiction, community prevention, health care, addiction among veterans, and the criminal justice system is a primary way that NIAAA research can be tailored to meet specific needs. Because the NIAAA's primary focus is on addiction in the general population, its research debunks the stereotype that homeless people are more frequent substance abusers. In fact, alcohol addiction in particular has been shown to be more common in some segments of the U.S. population, including college students. NIAAA research on alcohol and drug abuse among welfare recipients also shows that their use levels are consistent with and not in excess of the general population.

Despite their use level, all homeless people who abuse alcohol face additional challenges related to meeting basic needs. They may also face risk factors including mental illness and various experiences with trauma and abuse, in addition to other identity-based risk factors. The consequences of substance abuse are also more serious for homeless people and can range from criminal justice problems to loss of employment, shelter, housing, medical care, and financial assistance. These losses can affect entire families and perpetuate the cycle of poverty. Although determining which approaches will work for a majority of the homeless population remains challenging, NIAAA research consistently shows that long-term, chronically homeless people with co-occurring disorders remain the most difficult to serve.

National Institute on Drug Abuse (NIDA)

Like NIAAA, NIDA was established in 1970. Its overall focus is on the science of drug use in the general population. Throughout its history, NIDA has advanced the nation's understanding of drug use in the areas of prevention and treatment. It also focused on the effects of addiction on behavior and mental and physical health. NIDA mobilizes its resources to research drug use trends in the general population and explore the most viable solutions to drug abuse and addiction. Through its internal and external grants and research, NIDA focuses on issues like the HIV/AIDS crisis and opioid addiction, specific drugs, and special populations like veterans, youth, and prisoners. Drug use and addiction are recognized as both causes and consequences of homelessness.

NIDA has always been a close companion of NIAAA, as both are part of the HHS. They are also close partners because of the overlapping nature of addiction to alcohol and other drugs in the general population and among homeless people. Developing research to address homeless people specifically usually occurs in tandem with crisis points or to focus on specific subpopulations of interest. In the 1980s, as the nation's understanding and awareness of homelessness were increasing, NIAAA and NIDA collaborated on the Community Demonstration Grant Projects and the Cooperative Agreement Program to examine the nature of addiction among homeless people and innovative approaches to outreach and engagement. The need for this was uncontested in the 1980s, as research suggested that homeless people often did not access government benefits to which they were entitled and that they suffered additional health and safety risks related to homelessness and addiction.

The three primary challenges in service design that the Community Demonstration Projects revealed include the difficulty of providing accessible services for active users, as many shelters require sobriety before entry. Projects also highlighted the need for comprehensive and continuous care, typically through case management. Finally, they highlighted the need for permanent housing as a necessity, along with ongoing treatment (Baumohl and Huebner 1991). While some of the projects under this grant program offered unique approaches to these challenges, their service populations were always small. For this reason, the approach that began to win the day was to increase access to mainstream services for homeless and low-income people and to use basic needs services as means of engagement. The profile on NIAAA, included in this chapter, has additional information on early grant programs.

Although homelessness has been of national concern since the 1980s, the cost and complexity of developing and evaluating specific services to address the problem are daunting. Instead, homelessness is considered in tandem with other drug-related issues, like opioid addiction, or health crises, like the rise of HIV/AIDS or the COVID-19 pandemic. It is considered in relation to special populations like youth and veterans. Homeless people are also included in the general category "low-income," although they may lack access to the same resources as people with greater levels of housing stability. Approaches to treatment generally focus on causes and on prevention and detection.

After the 1990s, specific populations, like chronically homeless people, also became national priorities. This focus begins with the Bush administration, which in 2003 took notice of the finding that chronically homeless people consume more in emergency service dollars than they would if permanently housed (Culhane et al. 2002). Other studies emphasize the relationship between substance use, homelessness, and morbidity, noting that homeless people have comparatively higher rates and greater severity of drug use than mainstream patients (Doran et al. 2018). Studies also show that the myriad issues homeless people face make it necessary to bolster mainstream services instead of spending more on targeted ones. The need for reliable, comparable national data also became a federal priority, with the annual PIT count beginning in 2005.

When the USICH was established in 2005, it took over the job of coordinating the federal response to homelessness. Housing First was one of the emerging approaches to treatment that addressed the most-difficult-to-serve segment of the homeless population, those with severe mental illness. Housing

First reverses the usual, linear path from outreach and shelter to housing and instead offers housing immediately in conjunction with ongoing services. It does not always or exclusively focus on addiction, emphasizing the need for ongoing research to determine how addiction is best addressed. This need is also corroborated by the risk factors that homeless people face related to health and addiction, in comparison with the general population. People experiencing homelessness have an increased likelihood of hospitalization, illness, and premature death. One study found that a homeless person's life expectancy is between forty-two and fifty-two years (Maness and Khan 2014), far lower than that of the U.S. general population.

One factor leading to the lower life expectancy of homeless people is that they face a disproportionate number of health risks in comparison with the general population. These include cognitive disorders and brain injury, violence and trauma, infectious diseases and sexually transmitted infections, skin and foot problems, and exposure-related conditions (Maness and Khan 2014). Addiction can be a cause and a result of homelessness, but it universally makes existing conditions worse, and the consequences can be fatal. NIDA develops solutions to addiction that involve drug innovations to combat the use of opioids or to address the high rate of nicotine use among homeless people. Addiction research also addresses drug use among specific subsets of the homeless population, including women, youth, and members of the LGBTQ community.

NIDA continues to work in partnership with NIAAA, under the direction of the NIH and HHS, to provide solutions to addiction issues. They recognize the prevalence of coexisting or "comorbid" conditions, like mental illness, that often accompany drug abuse among homeless people. The primary behavioral therapies that have been shown to be successful in treating comorbid conditions include addressing harmful behaviors and beliefs, reducing self-harm, promoting community and individualized outreach, long-term residential treatment, and rewards for abstinence. The future of these innovations depends on ongoing NIDA research, in conjunction with federal, state, and local partners.

U.S. Department of Veterans Affairs (VA)

The VA was established in 1989. Its secretary is appointed by the president and is a member of the president's cabinet. The VA has three main divisions that focus on health benefits, general benefits and entitlements, and access to and maintenance of national VA cemeteries. Veterans in the United States can receive benefits to compensate for the effects of military service on their mental and physical health and ability status. The VA also offers services to assist them in the transition back to civilian life and routines, including access to gainful employment, affordable mortgages, and education and training opportunities. Veterans also receive military pensions, a benefit that covers their dependents and spouses.

The VA is similar to other government organizations because its goal is to provide for veterans in general, not specifically for homeless veterans. It is also unique in this sense because of the direct link between military service and homeless status, as well as various other postmilitary conditions, like posttraumatic stress disorder (PTSD) and service-related disability. For this reason, the VA focuses some of its resources on ending homelessness for veterans. Some homeless populations receive assistance because of the expense of emergency services, like chronically homeless people, or because of the sympathy they inspire, like homeless children. Veterans are unique because they are considered deserving of assistance because of their military service to their country. Their benefits may be entitlement based, in the case of service-related disability, or income based, depending on other resources and benefits they receive.

The VA offers general benefits to veterans like the GI Bill, passed in 1944. The GI Bill offers qualified veterans access to affordable mortgages and education and training opportunities, all of which act as security against poverty and homelessness. The VA, however, has also focused specifically on ending homelessness among veterans, as they are overrepresented in the general homeless population. In 2009–2010, the federal government and the VA both developed plans to end homelessness among veterans. In 2010, with the release of *Opening Doors: Federal Strategic Plan to Prevent and End Homelessness*, a path was set to end veteran homelessness by 2015. While this goal has not yet been achieved, significant progress has been made. Using the estimates provided in the AHAR, veteran homelessness has declined by about 50 percent since 2009. In addition, eighty-one communities and three states have ended veteran homelessness, with overall declines recorded in virtually all states in the nation.

Prior to the release of *Opening Doors*, the VA plan to end homelessness focused on outreach and education, prevention, income/employment/benefits, treatment, housing/supportive services, and community partnerships. These elements remain a central part of the effort to end veteran homelessness. Since *Opening Doors*, federal expenditures have risen exponentially and show impressive results. Currently, the VA requests about $1.9 billion annually for programs related to homelessness. The request for FY2021 asks for an $82 million increase from 2020.

There are seven federally funded programs, administered by the VA, that focus on homelessness. The Health Care for Homeless Veterans (HCHV) Program provides outreach and engagement services to transition veterans from precarious to stable housing. In 2019, the program moved over 6,300 veterans into permanent housing, with ongoing medical and mental health services. Its outreach activities are also extensive, including "stand down" events to provide supplies and services, and raise awareness in local communities. Over 75,000 veterans were reached through the 320 "stand down" events held in 2019. Outreach services reached close to 140,000 veterans in the same year, and "case management," a collaborative process of counseling, planning, and goal setting, reached over 10,750. Additional funding for medical and housing services were made available through the Coronavirus Aid, Relief, and Economic Security (CARES) Act, to protect veterans from the health risks associated with the COVID-19 pandemic.

This program is closely related to the Supportive Services for Veteran Families (SSVF) program for low-income veterans. SSVF is a rapid rehousing and homeless prevention program designed to offer benefits that keep families from becoming homeless and establish overall stability. Services available through this program are delivered through local nonprofit organizations that receive grant funding from the VA. Services are available in every state in the nation, and the VA estimates that more than 70,500 veterans received SSVF services in FY2019. Approximately 13 percent were women. In addition, this program demonstrates positive, sustained outcomes, as 82 percent of those served obtained permanent housing upon exit. Along with other grant programs administered through the VA, this one also receives funding through the CARES Act of 2020, which included provisions intended to prevent a new wave of veteran homelessness due to unemployment and evictions, negative economic effects of the pandemic.

Like the Supportive Services program, the Homeless Providers Grant and Per Diem Program also distributes grants to community organizations. Funding is directed toward acquiring or rehabilitating existing buildings to house and provide services for homeless veterans. Transitional housing is particularly important to this program, as it provides over 12,700 beds nationwide. Grant recipients typically provide 35 percent of the funding for these facilities, and the VA covers the additional cost. Services can include meals, transportation, showers, health and mental health care, counseling and case management, and job placement and training (Congressional Research Service 2018). The VA estimates that in FY2019, over 29,600 veterans received services, including 1,800 (6 percent) women. An additional 13,400 were moved to permanent housing after exiting service. A subset of this program provides for the development of programs for veterans with special needs, including those who are women or parents or who are suffering from a terminal illness or chronic mental health issues.

The largest program that the VA administers for homeless veterans involves a partnership with HUD called the HUD-VASH Program. This program began in 2008 with an emphasis on supportive housing. It espouses the principles of Housing First, which include housing placement prior to service engagement. HUD-VASH offers Housing Choice Vouchers as rental assistance for homeless families, through HUD, and the VA provides clinical and case management services in community facilities. Vouchers are awarded to communities depending on the size of the veteran homeless population. They are offered to public housing agencies with good performance records in close proximity to VA facilities. HUD estimates that since the beginning of HUD-VASH in 2008, more than 97,500 vouchers have been provided to public housing authorities.

The Domiciliary Care for Homeless Veterans Program addresses both sheltered and unsheltered veterans with clinical needs, including mental health issues and substance use disorders. It offers training and employment as well as mainstream services. It also fosters community among veterans and independent community living through its various facilities. Another innovative feature of this program is that it offers referral services to mainstream and VA housing programs. By 2020, this program had forty-seven sites, with more than 2,400 beds.

Related to this program, the Compensated Work Therapy/Transitional Residence Program is a twelve-month transitional housing program. Veterans who participate have access to lucrative employment opportunities and are assisted in reintegrating into the routines and responsibilities of community life. This is particularly necessary for veterans who may have chronic disabling conditions and are at risk of homelessness. The VA reports that in FY2019, over 9,300 veterans were gainfully employed after leaving homeless residential housing.

In addition to these programs, which have specific, dedicated federal funding, the VA runs several additional programs for homeless veterans. These programs address the multifaceted nature of veteran homelessness and provide outreach and education and referrals to help clients secure basic needs and basic health services. They also support research and planning to serve veterans experiencing homelessness and focus on prevention. The VA assists veterans who are in the criminal corrections system by offering legal clinics and outreach and assistance services. This is a preventative measure, designed to keep vulnerable veterans from becoming homeless.

Although the USICH coordinates the federal response to homelessness, the VA remains a member and close collaborator. The VA works with the DOL to ensure veteran access to mainstream employment through the Homeless Veterans' Reintegration Program (HVRP). This program provides "wraparound" assistance that includes outreach as well as follow-up after employment is established. Although most veterans are men, at approximately 90 percent of the total, women were added to this program in 2010, and child care was added to the list of services provided. This program is closely related to the Referral and Counseling Services Program, which provides counseling and other services for veterans transitioning from prison, mental institutions, or long-term care. Both programs are intended to prevent veterans who have found housing from returning to homelessness.

Finally, the presence of the VA in local communities is instrumental in engaging veterans and raising public awareness of veteran homelessness. Some of the notable programs that establish a presence in local communities are the Community Employment Services and Community Resource and Referral Centers. These services engage veterans in central locations. They ensure timely referral to various mainstream and VA benefits and a range of services targeting employment for homeless and chronically homeless veterans. Veterans also receive specialized dental care as well as Homeless Patient Allied Care Teams (H-PACT). H-PACT care teams ensure wraparound physical and mental health services that take care of the immediate needs of veterans while also working on their long-term reintegration and housing stability.

Related to these initiatives, the VA has taken measures to advance knowledge and raise public awareness of veteran homelessness. The VA established a National Call Center for homeless veterans that operates on a continuous basis to ensure immediate access to support services. This hotline is designed to assist veterans who are at risk of becoming homeless or already experiencing homelessness. The National Research Center is another important resource for the VA, as it employs researchers who examine innovative approaches to service and engagement for veteran homeless populations and analyze the effects of current policy.

Together, these myriad efforts demonstrate coordinated federal, state, and local support for veterans. This translates to wraparound services that are tailored to their unique needs, experiences, and challenges. It means a presence in local communities and a way of accessing immediate and long-term assistance. And it means sustained resources to continue this effort. The outstanding success of this concerted and unified national effort to end homelessness among veterans proves that it is possible to reduce or end it. It also justifies ongoing spending on these programs.

Despite an overall reduction in the number of homeless veterans, developing a precise timeline for ending veteran homelessness altogether has proven elusive. In addition, although significant gains have been made to reach out to women and other special populations within the armed forces, it is still a white, male-dominated institution. This is important in the context of homelessness because women, racial and ethnic minorities, and openly gay or transgender people, all of whom are underrepresented in the U.S. military, are actually overrepresented in the nation's homeless population. Of the 1.3 million active duty personnel in the U.S. military, approximately 16 percent are women. Hispanic Americans are over 17 percent, and black or African Americans are just over 13 percent. When we examine the various forms of assistance available to people experiencing homelessness, military service offers resources that benefit middle-class white men over all other groups.

U.S. Department of Labor: Homeless Veterans' Reintegration Program (HVRP)

Additional federal support for homeless veterans is available through the DOL and the DOJ. The DOL administers the HVRP, a program that focuses exclusively on veteran employment. It is a companion to the SSVF program, which is oriented toward finding permanent housing. HVRP has more than 150 grants operating in forty states, the District of Columbia, and Puerto Rico. HVRP includes a significant outreach component to identify potential employers, engage new participants, and raise community awareness of homeless issues.

Veterans in HVRP receive job training and placement and long-term follow-up services. Total annual program funding is approximately $50 million, and individual grants can reach as high as $500,000. Approximately 18,000 veterans are served through this program, and it has a job placement rate that is consistently over 60 percent. In 2010, a separate HVRP was created for women veterans and veterans with children, funded at $1 million per year through 2020. Agencies serving these subgroups or serving incarcerated veterans also receive grants through the HVRP program.

U.S. Department of Education (ED)

Support for students experiencing homelessness is authorized under Subtitle VII-B of the Stewart B. McKinney Homeless Assistance Act of 1987. This act was amended in 1990 and reauthorized in 1994, by the Improving America's Schools Act. In 2000, it was renamed the McKinney-Vento Homeless Assistance Act, and it was reauthorized again in 2002 by the No Child Left Behind Act and by the Every Student Succeeds Act (ESSA) in 2015. Overall, this legislation reduces barriers to immediate school enrollment and provides flexible, wrap-around services for homeless students and families.

Through McKinney-Vento, local liaisons coordinate and deliver program provisions and publicize available forms of assistance. State coordinators are hired to centralize services and offer training and information to ensure compliance, implementation, and evaluation of McKinney-Vento provisions. The Education for Homeless Children and Youth (EHCY) is the main federal program that awards grants to individual states. The National Center for Homeless Education offers technical assistance and information about the EHCY program.

When a state receives an EHCY subgrant, it distributes competitive funding to local school districts based on overall need and the quality of the application. EHCY also offers a national data profile of the needs and characteristics of students receiving services. The EHCY program focuses on the idea that children experiencing homelessness should have free and equal access to public education. To meet this goal, EHCY reduces barriers to immediate enrollment, like a lack of identification, immunization or prior school records, and other documents. It also preserves school selection and allows children and families to choose to remain enrolled in their school of origin. Local homeless education liaisons coordinate all of EHCY's provisions. They coordinate transportation and facilitate the recovery of documents. They identify homeless students and work on a case-by-case basis to maximize student participation in all school activities. In this sense, local liaisons are a bridge among the family, the school, the district, and homeless service agencies in the state. They make families aware of McKinney-Vento provisions and mainstream resources and collaborate with schools on policies and procedures.

There are over 17,600 local liaisons across the United States, one for each public school district. The ED surveyed local liaisons in 2012 and found that the vast majority of their time was spent identifying homeless students and providing basic school supplies and referrals to other services and organizations. Local liaisons work closely with state coordinators, who collect and report aggregate statewide data. State coordinators keep an updated list of local liaisons and provide them with training and assistance on the legal provisions of McKinney-Vento. They also support them in understanding state-specific reporting procedures and in troubleshooting in individual cases. In a data summary released in February 2019, the EHCY program estimated the number of homeless students enrolled in public schools across the United States at just over 1,350,000. Annual program funding reached over $101 million in 2020, with states providing an average of $54 per student and large discrepancies between states.

The definition of homeless students used to determine federal assistance includes those who are temporarily "doubled up" with others, sleeping on couches or in cramped spare rooms in shared or precarious housing. It also includes those who are housed in shelters, hotels or motels, or in other locations not designed for human habitation. This definition is more expansive than the HUD definition used for the annual PIT count, so EHCY numbers of homeless students are often higher than in other official reports, like the AHAR. In addition to general information on homeless students, EHCY collects information on subgroups of interest. These include unaccompanied homeless youth, migratory students, English learners, and children with disabilities.

Unaccompanied youth are defined as any K–12 students who are not in the physical custody of a parent or guardian. Services for these students focus on access and include college preparation and readiness and payment of fees for various entrance exams. Migratory children are defined by frequent mobility and low-income status. Understanding the needs of particular student subgroups like these is one of the primary goals of the EHCY program. Studies show that students in these subgroups are typically overrepresented within the homeless population and may require additional services.

The numbers of homeless students and students in subgroups with higher vulnerability to homelessness continue to rise. From 2014 to 2017, the nation saw large increases in the number of unsheltered students (by 27 percent); unaccompanied youth age 18–24, not in the physical custody of a parent or guardian (25 percent); English learners (19 percent); and students with disabilities (14 percent) (EHCY Federal Data summary SYS 2014–2017). These trends are of grave concern, particularly since students in these subgroups face additional challenges in accessing consistent educational services. Homeless students in general face educational barriers related to a precarious living environment. Results from school years 2014 through 2017 show that approximately 75 percent of homeless students reported living in "doubled up/couch surfing" conditions, followed by 14 percent in shelters, 6 percent in hotels or motels, and 4 percent unsheltered. These circumstances make school attendance, enrollment, and participation an ongoing challenge. This is an important issue to address, as studies show that children in more precarious housing environments, or who experience frequent mobility or trauma, are more likely to experience educational delays.

The additional challenges posed by rising numbers of homeless students in the wake of the COVID-19 pandemic are staggering. They illustrate the dramatic impact of housing insecurity on educational access, an issue well established before the pandemic. Although federal support for EHCY has remained consistent, more funding is needed to address growing inequities. Because of the challenges posed in locating and conducting outreach and engagement with homeless children, less than 10 percent of eligible students under age 6 receive EHCY services. This pattern extends to school districts, where only 24 percent receive EHCY subgrants. All of this was true before COVID-19, but these problems increased in severity during the pandemic, which sent poverty and unemployment higher and forced a seismic shift in schools toward online learning, which is often beyond the reach of impoverished students in homeless or transient shelter situations. EHCY funding is also competitive, meaning that school districts best prepared to produce quality applications are first in line for funding. Education advocates call for an increase in funding to meet the current barriers and reach additional districts, students, and families that will inevitably need service.

Provisions are also available for students pursuing higher education. Students can verify their independent status on the Free Application for Federal Student Aid (FAFSA). Doing this means that their financial aid package is based on their own income, not the income and assets of their parents. This typically results in additional financial aid for the student. Additional state and federal assistance is available for youth in foster care. Over twenty-five states have tuition waiver programs that cover partial or total costs for students who have aged out of foster care.

U.S. Department of Agriculture (USDA)

The USDA is one of the top five largest agencies in the federal government. In 2019, the USDA spent about 19 percent of its total budget, or $27 billion, on the discretionary food programs included in this profile. The USDA was established in 1862, when the majority of the nation's population was living in rural areas and subsisting on agricultural income. Today, over 80 percent of the population lives in urban areas and farming and agriculture account for only a small percentage of total employment. Ensuring food quantity, quality, and access is an instrumental part of managing changes in population and supporting urban development. Early USDA initiatives championed the basic rights and agricultural prosperity of rural farmers. From providing irrigation to electricity, the focus was on sustaining the nation's domestic farming capacity and production and supply chains. The USDA also supported farmers during times of crisis like the Great Depression. Since its beginning, the USDA has always focused on reducing barriers that prevent Americans from accessing quality food.

The USDA administers The Emergency Food Assistance Program (TEFAP), which is the largest source of federal support for emergency feeding organizations (Congressional Research Service 2020). The USDA oversees other food assistance programs, including the Supplemental Nutrition Assistance Program (SNAP), the Nutrition Program for Women, Infants, and Children (WIC), and the Commodity Supplemental Food Program for low-income elderly people. Eligibility for these programs is determined by income and other requirements detailed in this profile and varies from state to state. In addition to USDA-administered programs, FEMA runs the Emergency Food and Shelter Program (EFSP), detailed separately in this chapter. Low-income populations are more likely to cycle in and out of homelessness and need emergency services. Discussing the various food programs is a way of evaluating how successful they are in reducing poverty and homelessness.

TEFAP began in 1983 with the passage of the Emergency Food Assistance Act. This act was signed into law to reduce government food surpluses and to offset the impact of recession (Congressional Research Office 2018). It is authorized annually through farm bills that extend funding; manage food surpluses, donations, quality, and distribution; and attempt to reduce food waste. TEFAP distributes food and funding to state agencies including food banks, homeless shelters, food pantries, and soup kitchens and a smaller amount in cash assistance. Local organizations often coordinate distribution and determine overall need. In some cases, food is directly distributed to households. TEFAP agencies can include summer camps and child nutrition programs, those that serve the elderly, or focus on disaster relief, so there is some overlap between homeless populations and those in immediate emergency or distress.

Although eligibility for TEFAP varies by state, a common general guideline is that recipients' income must be at or below 130 percent of the poverty guidelines. In 2019, this would mean that a family of three would need an income of $27,000 or less per year to qualify. Additional requirements are typically placed on those who receive meals directly, rather than in a service setting, to limit eligibility to the neediest.

Formerly known as "food stamps," SNAP has existed in some form since the Great Depression. Today's SNAP focuses on supplementing low incomes with federally provided nutrition benefits. It is the largest antihunger program and third-largest antipoverty program in the United States (Nestle 2019). Recipients receive an Electronic Benefits Transfer (EBT) card that can be used like a bank-issued debit card, exclusive of some items (alcohol and tobacco products as well as hot food, dietary supplements, and nonfood items are off-limits). The switch from actual food stamps to the EBT card in 2004 was meant to reduce the stigma of receiving federal assistance. Yet, SNAP remains controversial because of its rigid eligibility requirements, which are difficult to understand and have been accused of reflecting racial bias. Additional ongoing debates focus on what foods are permitted under SNAP. Some states seek additional bans on sweetened beverages, arguing that they are a direct cause of obesity (Bamhill 2011). Once families qualify for SNAP, children are typically eligible for free school meals. This is also the case if families are enrolled in TANF, Head Start, the Food Distribution Program on Indian Reservations, or the foster care program.

Another controversial regulation is the SNAP work requirement, implemented in 1996 as part of the Personal Responsibility and Work Opportunity Reconciliation Act (PRWORA). Work requirements were always a part of food and welfare assistance, but after the passage of PRWORA, they became even more restrictive. Currently, all adults receiving SNAP benefits who are between the ages of 16 and 59 and are able to work must register for work, participate in SNAP Employment and Training (E&T) or workfare as assigned by a state SNAP agency, take a suitable job if offered, and not voluntarily quit a job or reduce work hours below thirty a week without a good reason. How this is determined is left to case managers. Exceptions are made for people who are mentally or physically unable to work, who are in a drug or alcohol treatment program, or who are caring for someone who is disabled or a child under 6 years old. About two-thirds of all SNAP recipients cannot work because they are elderly, disabled, or children. For the other one-third, who do not adhere to SNAP work requirements, benefits can be temporarily or permanently cut. States can also adjust these restrictions and set benefit levels according to income or other assets.

For people experiencing homelessness, the documentation required to qualify for SNAP, including proof of residency, immigration status, medical history, and assorted other records, can be extremely daunting. Understanding the requirements and restrictions of SNAP benefits is also a challenge. Assistance in meeting work requirements is limited because many states do not adequately fund training or education programs or pay a living wage. Studies show that SNAP recipients often work low-wage, frontline work in the service and health industries. Although SNAP is intended to supplement low and intermittent wages, it often does not lead to a permanent lift out of poverty. Studies also show that more rigid work requirements reduce SNAP spending on enrollees. As Ku et al. (2019) found, the implementation of rigid work requirements caused approximately 600,000 participants to lose benefits from 2013 to 2017. This is a reduction of $2.5 billion in SNAP outlays. In fact, reduced participation in SNAP was evident throughout much of the 2010s, and spending has fallen annually since 2014.

Despite these limitations, SNAP is oriented toward extremely low-income people, as just over half of all SNAP benefits in 2019 went to households at or below half of the poverty line, translating to $10,390 for a family of three. Food insecurity has also become more widespread, and studies show that it extends to unexpected populations, like college students (Freudenberg et al. 2019). Many advocates argue that SNAP should be expanded and be more flexible to meet the needs of these groups as well. It is important to point out that SNAP contributes to the nation's GDP because families put money back into the economy when they purchase food. Over 90 percent of SNAP benefit purchases are made at supermarkets and larger retailers. As a way of boosting the nation's economy in times of recession, SNAP is a remarkably effective tool to stimulate jobs and growth.

In fact, because of the ongoing COVID-19 pandemic, in December 2020, Congress passed a relief bill that included increased SNAP and WIC benefits, amounting to approximately $100 in additional food assistance per month for a family of four. These increased benefits were set to expire by June 2021. In January 2021, the new Biden administration submitted a proposal to extend these provisions beyond their June expiration date and to ensure that SNAP and WIC benefits reach those most in need. One justification for this extension is that, when public school ends for the summer, children can no longer access free or reduced-price school meals. Although research on the impact of COVID-19 on food insecurity is still emerging, the most recent Census Bureau Survey, conducted in 2020 showed that 11 percent of U.S. adults did not get enough to eat on weekly basis. This is a significant increase from the 3.4 percent pre-pandemic estimate of food insecurity recorded in 2019. Families of color are twice as likely to experience food insecurity.

In addition to SNAP, WIC is specifically for women who are pregnant or breastfeeding and infants up to age 5. The benefits that WIC provides extend to various health care services including nutritional guidance and support. Families who are eligible receive an EBT card, as they do for SNAP, which allows them maximum flexibility. WIC is a short-term assistance program that applicants must reapply for if they exceed the time limit of approximately six months to one year. In addition to family status or pregnancy, eligibility is determined by residency, income, and health status.

Like SNAP, families receiving other forms of assistance may already qualify for WIC. The income requirements are set by states and can vary from 100 percent to 185 percent of the federal poverty level. This can mean a range of between $26,200 and $48,470 for a family of four. The five states with the lowest WIC coverage rates are Montana, Utah, Colorado, Idaho, and Illinois, where only about 50 percent of those eligible participate. The five states with the highest coverage rates are Vermont, the District of Columbia, California, Minnesota, and Maryland, which hover around 70–75 percent participation among eligible residents (Martinez-Schiferl 2012).

Until 2014, the Commodity Supplemental Food Program also focused on women and children. Today, it exclusively serves individuals who are 60 and older whose incomes are at or below 130 percent of the federal poverty line. For a single adult in 2020, this is an annual income of $16,588. Approximately 675,000 seniors participated in this program on a monthly basis in 2018. Unlike the EBT cards that SNAP and WIC recipients get, food for seniors can be delivered to individual homes or served in congregate food settings.

U.S. Department of Homeland Security (DHS): Federal Emergency Management Agency (FEMA)

FEMA administers the Emergency Food and Shelter Program (EFSP). EFSP was first authorized in 1983 by the Temporary Emergency Food Assistance Act and again in 1987 by what has since become known as the McKinney-Vento Homeless Assistance Act. It is the oldest federal program serving the entire homeless population, as opposed to specific subgroups. FEMA operates the EFSP through the Department of Homeland Security (DHS), which was created in 2002. FEMA is a USICH member agency that represents DHS. In a typical budget cycle, EFSP provides over $100 million in funding to approximately 2,500 jurisdictions and 10,000 local agencies. FEMA works closely with the USICH to align the goals of EFSP with the national strategic plan to end homelessness, *Home, Together*. FEMA coordinates with local CoC planning boards and utilizes systems of data collection, like HMIS, to document EFSP participation. EFSP funding supports existing resources in some communities and, particularly in rural areas, can be the only source of support for homeless people.

FEMA convenes a National Board that directs the EFSP. It includes representatives from the Salvation Army, the United Way Worldwide, the American Red Cross, Catholic Charities USA, United Jewish Communities, and the National Council of Churches of Christ in the USA. The National Board uses unemployment and poverty rates to determine which communities are eligible for funding. Local communities establish their own advisory boards and make funding decisions for local providers, who receive funding directly. The EFSP serves people who are hungry or homeless both during nonemergency times and when the president declares a national disaster. Both types of FEMA funding are discussed in this profile. Like many federal programs, EFSP is distributed to states and local communities to fund services that include providing shelter, groceries and food vouchers, hot food for shelters, transportation, and homeless prevention funds to cover rental or mortgage costs. A maximum of 3.5 percent of allocated funding is used for administrative costs, making this an efficient vehicle for the delivery of services.

FEMA uses baseline budget estimates to cover the costs of ongoing recovery efforts, as in the case of Hurricane Katrina, and to fund the nonemergency services discussed earlier. In 2021, because of the coronavirus, the CARES Act supplied $510 million in supplemental funding for local jurisdictions, with $400 million for the EFSP and the remainder for organizations that provide assistance to migrants at the U.S. southern border. With so many homeless people already living unsheltered or at risk, the coronavirus makes their housing and safety a national priority. Because of COVID-19, people living unsheltered or in congregate settings are seen as a public health risk. Eligible services funded by EFSP include congregate shelters like larger stadiums and convention centers and noncongregate shelters such as the tent cities used to facilitate social distancing. EFSP also funds evacuation costs, emergency supplies and personal protective equipment, and services like policing, security, and public communication.

FEMA estimates that since its beginning in 1983, EFSP has provided over 3 billion meals, 293.4 million nights of shelter, over $7 million in utility payments, and $5.3 million to keep families housed (FEMA 2020). In Mississippi alone, after Hurricane Katrina, FEMA spent over $1 billion on individual assistance, reaching a total of 274,000 people. Housing options pursued by FEMA included short- and long-term solutions, travel trailers, and mobile homes. The latter were eventually deemed unfit for permanent or long-term housing, and FEMA spent $400 million to determine better solutions. Although the focus on sustainable permanent housing was seen as the best option, the cost of its implementation and ongoing management made it hard to take to scale. In addition, as the COVID-19 pandemic demonstrates, finding quick and permanent solutions can often be hard to consider simultaneously.

National Organizations
National Law Center on Homelessness and Poverty (NLCHP)

The NLCHP was founded by lawyer Maria Foscarinis in 1989. The NLCHP is a nonprofit organization comprised of a national network of pro bono lawyers and advocates working at international, federal, state, and local levels. The primary goal of the NLCHP is to educate communities and to use the law to protect and serve people experiencing homelessness. Over time, the NLCHP has effectively raised public awareness by offering research-based evidence on related issues including youth and education, civil and human rights, housing, racial and economic equity, domestic violence, and the recent COVID-19 pandemic. The NLCHP also offers legal advocacy with a focus on at-risk populations within the homeless community, like women experiencing domestic violence, racial minorities, immigrants, and children and youth. It uses the legal system as a means of protection and defense and as a way of fulfilling the promise of equal treatment enshrined in the U.S. Constitution.

Before founding the NLCHP, Foscarinis was instrumental in crafting the Stewart B. McKinney Homeless Assistance Act (later renamed the McKinney-Vento Homeless Assistance Act), the first federal legislation to address the crisis of homelessness in the 1980s. The NLCHP remains dedicated to fulfilling the promise of McKinney-Vento by offering individualized state assistance in implementing its provisions. This includes ensuring equal access to primary education for students experiencing homelessness and assisting communities through the dispute and appeals process if access is denied. It also includes monitoring the use of vacant federal property by states, CoCs, and nonprofit organizations serving homeless people.

The NLCHP offers education and assistance about the negative effects of criminalization as a solution to homelessness. In so doing, it works to uphold the constitutional rights of homeless people, which criminalization ultimately threatens. Upholding these basic rights is an important part of the Housing Not Handcuffs Campaign, which fights criminalization by offering housing-based solutions to homelessness. Beginning in 2006, the NLCHP has provided communities with important resources for understanding the reach of criminalization by measuring its ongoing effects in 187 cities across the country. Through this report and ongoing advocacy work related to this campaign, the NLCHP has shown that criminalization leads to increased homelessness, reinforces cyclical poverty, and contributes to the overrepresentation of racial minorities experiencing homelessness. It is also costlier in terms of federal expenditures than providing permanent housing for homeless people.

The power of legal advocacy demonstrated through this campaign shows that documenting the negative effects of criminalization is a strategy that can garner federal support. In fact, beginning in 2015, communities demonstrating a reduction in criminalization, or efforts to manage or mitigate its effects, can gain valuable points on applications for federal funding administered through the HUD. This means significant financial rewards or penalties, and it ensures that addressing antihomeless criminalization is part of the federal funding and policy agenda. The NLCHP also warned that a shift back to criminalization as a tool for reducing homelessness, as suggested by the Trump administration, would lead to increased homelessness in the nation's cities and states.

The NLCHP views criminalization as a violation of international human rights law. Under the Universal Declaration of Human Rights (1948), which 192 nations, including the United States, have signed, the treatment of homeless people in the United States violates their human, constitutional, and civil rights. The reason for this is that without adequate housing, homeless people are often targeted by law enforcement for engaging in life-sustaining activities, like sleeping in public. NLCHP activists contend that this approach punishes the status of homelessness, rather than any illegal action, and amounts to cruel and unusual punishment. Rather than advocate for permissiveness regarding street sleeping, the NLCHP emphasizes that punishment without housing options is not a legally viable solution and only worsens the problem. This is part of the justification used by the organization to argue for a Homeless Bill of Rights based on emerging international law and adopted or proposed state legislation in the United States.

Interest in protecting the right to housing extends to tenant protection to avoid costly and traumatic evictions, a primary feeder into homelessness (Desmond 2016). The NLCHP also focuses on the legacy of racism and housing discrimination as factors leading people of color to experience higher rates of housing insecurity. In addition, they offer important state-by-state guidance in understanding the housing rights of survivors of domestic violence. In this sense, racial and economic equity are key underlying principles of the work of the NLCHP. This focus reflects the unfortunate fact that factors like race and gender influence susceptibility to homelessness and housing insecurity.

The resources available through the NLCHP for communities facing the dilemma of COVID-19 among homeless people demonstrate a rapid and coordinated response. The NLCHP marshals national experts focusing on the intersection of health concerns with congregate housing and social distancing, all amid a climate of criminalization and racial inequality. Among the main suggestions are that health and housing be seen as human rights, that communities do not enact criminalization measures without offering housing, that sanitary restrooms be made available continuously, and that shelters accept all clients and arrange temporary sites, as needed, to allow for social distancing. These recommendations are made using data showing that homeless people are twice as likely to be hospitalized, two to four times more likely to need critical care, and two to three times more likely to die of COVID-19 than the general population.

Criminalization also disproportionately affects black people, who represent only 13 percent of the general population but 40 percent of the homeless population, with black men comprising 34 percent of the prison population. A full 60 percent of the nation's homeless are people of color, and we know through the NLCHP that homelessness alone makes people eleven times more likely to go to prison. National estimates suggest that up to 15 percent of prison inmates experience homelessness in the year prior to incarceration, and formerly incarcerated people are ten times more likely to become homeless (Couloute 2018).

We also know, tragically through the COVID-19 pandemic, that racial, economic, and health equity go hand in hand, as people of color are more likely to be employed in frontline jobs and less likely to have access to quality health care. The COVID-19 data tracker, which offers state-by-state information, shows that black people who contract the virus are dying at over twice the rate of white people. Black people and people of color also make up a disproportionate number of the nation's incarcerated and homeless populations. Criminalization, in this sense, has contributed to the crisis and inequities leading to more people living in public or incarcerated and at heightened risk of succumbing to airborne illness. The NLCHP, which recently changed its name to the National Homelessness Law Center, has contributed to the nation's understanding of these important issues and to transformational policy changes and legislation. Foscarinis retired from her position as the organization's executive director at the end of 2020. She was succeeded by Antonia Fasanelli, who took over as executive director in April 2021. Despite the changes in name and leadership, the mission of the NLCHP remains the same—to use the law to help homeless people across the United States by upholding their civil, constitutional, and human rights.

National Alliance to End Homelessness (NAEH)

The NAEH was originally founded in 1983 to respond to and manage the emerging crisis of homelessness. Led by President and CEO Nan Roman, the NAEH's mission became focused on permanently ending homelessness in the United States. To accomplish this, the organization has developed an impressive team of researchers, policy makers, and experts in the fields of homelessness, poverty, and equity. The primary goals of the NAEH are supported through the work of the Homelessness Research Institute (HRI) and through ongoing efforts to influence federal policy. The NAEH is also supported through the work of the Center for Capacity Building, which offers training and assistance to community stakeholders. By working at federal, state, and local levels, the NAEH offers the tools and information needed to create a more coordinated and efficient way to serve and house people experiencing homelessness.

The NAEH was the first organization to challenge communities to work toward ending, rather than simply managing, the problem of homelessness. As detailed in the 2000 report, *A Plan, Not a Dream: How to End Homelessness in Ten Years,* the NAEH suggests that one way of reducing homelessness is to help people struggling with housing insecurity to keep their homes. It also suggests that to facilitate an end to homelessness, communities offer rapid rehousing and permanent supportive housing. Through building the knowledge and infrastructure necessary to advance these goals, the NAEH's vision and guidance have become important elements of the national conversation about homelessness.

In addition to following national trends in the homeless population, the NAEH tracks and reports on the current federal budget and legislation affecting homelessness. It also reports on the state of affordable housing in the nation. Through the HRI, the NAEH offers an annual *State of Homelessness* report using census data and data compiled through the annual PIT count and HIC. These data have been presented in graphic, webinar, and report form on an annual basis since 2007. This provides greater understanding of national homelessness trends, as well as those at the state and CoC levels. It tracks changes in overall numbers, regional and state issues, service and housing capacities, and persistent subpopulations.

Among the important findings in this report is that homelessness among single adult individuals remains the most difficult problem to solve, accounting for 70 percent of the overall homeless population. Although targeted funding and policy have reduced the number of veterans experiencing homelessness, by 50 percent, and resulted in a reduction in chronic homelessness by 10 percent, the problem among individuals remains significant. Homelessness is also concentrated within particular states and CoC regions. In fact, approximately one in three homeless people lives in one of twenty CoC regions that collectively bear a disproportionate share of the burden for addressing homelessness.

This information proved especially important as the nation prepared itself to face the COVID-19 pandemic. Areas with larger homeless populations have specific and ongoing challenges that they will need targeted funding to address. By emphasizing risk factors that heighten vulnerability to homelessness, like an unaffordable and inaccessible housing market, living temporarily with others, and paying over 50 percent of one's income on housing, the NAEH focuses on the immediacy and pervasiveness of the problem. The 2019 report, in fact, foreshadowed the issues these high-impact communities would face, including the threat of eviction, as the pandemic continues. This report reflects the NAEH strategy of offering information that holds the nation accountable, particularly at the federal level, to offer outcome-oriented solutions.

Another useful way of providing information and garnering support for ending homelessness through policy change is the NAEH annual conference. This event has hosted a number of high-profile presenters and keynote speakers, including former first lady Michelle Obama, *Evicted* author Matt Desmond, and actor Richard Gere. When held in Washington, DC, this event includes a Capitol Hill day designed to facilitate direct engagement with members of Congress in hopes of influencing policy. The NAEH also offers community resources including a portfolio of training courses offering guidance on critical issues facing homeless people, service providers, and policy makers throughout the nation. To address the COVID-19 pandemic, the NAEH rolled out a webinar series, publications, guidelines, and suggested policies and approaches for communities.

The primary overall solutions the NAEH advocates to end homelessness include greater coordination between homeless organizations and response systems. This means developing a planning process that is data driven and ongoing and works across agencies to assess needs and implement solutions quickly. While appreciating the continued need for emergency housing, the NAEH also lobbies for increasing housing subsidies and permanent supportive housing for the most vulnerable. Streamlining the process of intake and referral to match people with programs and services, and having multiple housing and shelter options available, ensures that homeless people do not get trapped in a revolving door of inadequate assistance and punishment. In addition, offering greater access to employment and education makes sustaining an exit from homelessness feasible. In conclusion, the NAEH's approach to ending homelessness through improving policy, building knowledge, and enhancing capacity has been a blueprint for the nation and a beacon during times of crisis.

National Coalition for the Homeless (NCH)

The NCH began in 1981 and is the oldest organization dedicated to ending homelessness in the United States. Like the NAEH and NLCHP, it is a nonprofit organization based in Washington, DC. Its proximity to lawmakers and close affiliation with other organizations working to end homelessness make the NCH an important national voice. Its foundation in grassroots advocacy is evident through its ongoing work to ensure the right to emergency shelter, to prevent the criminalization of homelessness, and to raise awareness. The NCH sees itself as building a movement to end homelessness beginning with people who have experienced it themselves and incorporating activists, advocates, service providers, and others dedicated to ending homelessness.

The NCH got its start in the 1980s, and its members included the late Michael Stoops, who served as NCH director from 2004 to 2015. Stoops worked with national advocate Mitch Snyder to protest the lack of shelter for homeless people in the nation's capital. Their activism, which included sleep outs and protests to bring attention to the problem of homelessness, helped gain support for the Stewart B. McKinney Homeless Assistance Act, which was passed by Congress and signed into law by President Reagan in 1987. Stoops also participated in social movement activities like Housing Now! and went on to found the North American Street Newspaper Association (NASNA) in 1997. This national organization includes papers like *Street Sense* in Washington, DC; *Street Sheet* in San Francisco; and over twenty additional publications throughout the United States. Altogether, more than forty publications around the world are associated with NASNA. These street newspapers are created and sold by people experiencing homelessness and are an important way of raising awareness, highlighting homeless voices, and providing a means of employment.

The signature goals of the NCH, established under Stoops' leadership, are ending homelessness, focusing on the immediate needs of homeless people, and upholding their civil rights. To reach these goals, the NCH offers direct assistance, research, action, and advocacy through a series of projects and campaigns related to the contemporary issues that homeless people face. The five ongoing projects that the NCH supports are the Faces of the Homeless Speaker's Bureau, Hunger and Homeless Awareness Week, the Homeless Challenge Project, Outreach Runs, and the Homeless Person's Memorial Day. All these projects have a common goal of highlighting the voices and direct experiences of homeless people and raising awareness among community members.

One of the distinguishing features of the NCH, in comparison with other organizations, is that its focus on foregrounding homeless voices extends to its administrative leadership, as well as the projects it supports. In fact, the current executive director of the NCH, Donald H. Whitehead Jr., personally experienced homelessness before working in a leadership capacity with the NCH. By serving in this role, as a formerly homeless person of color, Whitehead underscores the NCH's ongoing commitment to representative leadership, one of its most important founding principles. Related to this, one of the NCH's long-standing projects is the Faces of the Homeless Speaker's Bureau mentioned previously. This project trains, assists, and pays speakers who are currently or formerly homeless to share their experiences. Audiences for the Speaker's Bureau are wide ranging and offer speakers a chance to share their experience as experts. Not only is this an important way of building confidence and comfort interacting with others but it also highlights an experience that is often hidden and traumatic.

The additional projects that the NCH supports offer ways for community members to understand homelessness through simulations, commemorative activities, and organized events. Hunger and Homeless Awareness Week and the Homeless Person's Memorial Day are nationwide, annual activities that take place in November on the week before Thanksgiving and on or around December 21, respectively. These events are important ways of galvanizing community support to end homelessness. The resources that NCH offers for these events include a step-by-step training manual through which communities can organize and register their activities. Not only does this show tremendous community support, with over 700 locations registered for Hunger and Homeless Awareness activities alone, but it also raises awareness and money to support the cause.

In addition to these important projects, the main campaigns of the NCH orbit around such issues as Housing Now!, voting rights, hate crimes and violence, a homeless Bill of Rights, the criminalization of homelessness, and food access. Although these campaigns lend NCH support to other organizations, like the NLCHP and its Housing Not Handcuffs Campaign, the NCH is also a trailblazing organization because of its direct advocacy work. Particularly in the area of hate crimes against homeless people, the NCH is the only organization bringing this problem to the fore and tracking national instances of hate crimes over time. Defined as violent actions motivated by anti-homeless bias, hateful actions against homeless people can lead to injury or loss of life. Yet, the hidden nature of homelessness and the fear of antihomeless criminalization mean that most of these crimes go unreported.

Using NLCHP data to corroborate the harmful effects of criminalization, the NCH report on hate crimes against the homeless underscores just how vulnerable people are when living on the streets or in shelter. In addition, the NCH offers an array of publications including fact sheet summaries, as well as research papers, addressing hate crimes, criminalization, discrimination, and other issues of interest to homeless people, advocates, and supporters.

National Low-Income Housing Coalition (NLIHC)

The NLIHC is based in Washington, DC, and was established by Cushing N. Dolbeare in 1974. The sole focus of the non-profit NLIHC is on the housing needs of extremely low-income people. While it does not exclusively focus on the homeless population, the NLIHC addresses the risk factors that could lead to its dramatic increase. The primary goal of the NLIHC is to preserve existing affordable housing and expand housing options for those most in need. To do this, the organization offers resources that focus on education and awareness, resource mobilization, and influencing public opinion. It also provides important information on available affordable housing, existing tax credits, and how to understand and influence current federal housing policy priorities. Through its extensive research efforts and varied publications, the NLIHC contributes to a better understanding of the housing challenges and insecurities faced by low-income and extremely low-income households at risk of homelessness nationwide.

One of the early publications that illuminated these housing challenges was the report *Out of Reach*, which Dolbeare founded and authored in 1990. It used the American Community Survey (ACS) and aggregate data on median incomes and fair market rental prices to document the gap between wages and the price of housing. Known as the "housing wage," this measure calculates the hourly wage that a full-time worker would need to earn to be able to pay 30 percent of their income on rent, the standard measure of affordability. According to the 2019 report, this figure is $22.96 per hour, more than three times the minimum wage of $7.25, for a two-bedroom rental. For a one bedroom, it is $18.65. This means that in 2019, a minimum wage worker would need to work over 100 hours per week to afford basic housing. Without adequate child care or the time, training, and education needed to compete for higher wage jobs, people making minimum wage are trapped in a cycle of poverty. This is a pervasive national problem, as affordable rental housing is only available for minimum wage workers in 28 of over 3,000 counties in the United States.

Complementing the findings in *Out of Reach* on the lack of affordable housing for extremely low-income renters, *The Gap* is another important NLIHC publication that documents the shortage of affordable homes in the nation. This report also uses the ACS to show that while no state has sufficient, affordable, low-income housing, states like Hawaii, Massachusetts, and California have the most severe shortfalls, and urban environments are more seriously impacted. These are also states with large percentages of either individual or family homelessness. Reliance on low-wage work has only exacerbated the problem, as without additional assistance, a full-time minimum wage job does not cover the cost of basic housing. As a result, many people experience homelessness episodically rather than over long, sustained periods. Homeless people must also compete with other low-income and extremely low-income renters for available units, and the NLIHC estimates the shortage of affordable rental homes in the United States at 7 million in 2020.

The Gap also points out that the burdens of low-wage work, poverty, and the lack of available, affordable housing are unevenly distributed in U.S. society according to existing patterns of inequality. People of color, women, single parents, domestic violence survivors, children, the elderly, LGBTQ youth, and those with disabilities are all disproportionately at risk of homelessness. This vulnerability affects their physical and mental health, social ties, sense of stability, and ability to exit homelessness. It is also more expensive for communities to bear the cost of emergency services over housing. Homeless advocates thus emphasize that solving the problem of affordable housing would be a win-win solution for homeless people, low-income people, and communities as a whole.

In addition to raising awareness and providing data to assist advocates and renters in combatting these ongoing problems, the NLIHC offers tools for engaging in long-term advocacy. In its quarterly publication *Tenant Talk*, it emphasizes the concerns and voices of low-income renters. Its main focus areas include eviction prevention, voting rights, current issues of concern to renters, and pathways toward influencing policy. The NLIHC also produces an extensive advocates' guide to nationwide policies and programs related to affordable housing that affect low-income people. In addition, it updates constituents through a weekly newsletter offering the latest information on housing and related issues.

Throughout its history, the NLIHC has lobbied for additional housing and support for low-income and extremely low-income renters. In fact, Sheila Crowley, the former president of the NLIHC, was instrumental in securing funding for the Housing Trust Fund (HTF). Established in 2016, the HTF provides states with millions in essential funding for the production, preservation, rehabilitation, or operation of affordable rental housing. This key resource comes at no cost to the federal government, as funding comes from dedicated revenue streams and is not part of the appropriations process. This important resource remains part of the legacy of the NLIHC.

In addition to its signature publications, the NLIHC also offers extensive information on housing programs including the HTF, Section 8, rental housing through the HOME program, and existing tax credits. Its focus on current resources and issues of concern has made it an important resource for advocates, policy makers, and low-income renters, who may lack the resources for sustained community organizing. The NLIHC tracks how many affordable units are set to expire thirty years after the Low-Income Housing Tax Credit was established. The NLIHC estimates that the number of affordable units nationwide that will be up for price increases or demolition will reach approximately half a million between 2020 and 2029. Preparing for this is an important part of the NLIHC's planning and advocacy work.

National Association for the Education of Homeless Children and Youth (NAEHCY)

NAEHCY was founded in 1989, just after the passage of the Stewart B. McKinney Homeless Assistance Act in 1987. NAEHCY is a national nonprofit organization dedicated to making public education accessible to homeless and unaccompanied youth, at all educational levels. Early studies in the 1980s and 1990s showed that only about half of all homeless students were regularly attending school. By 2000, the number attending regularly jumped to over 75 percent, but this still left many homeless children without regular or stable schooling. NAEHCY estimated that over 1.2 million children under the age of 6 experienced homelessness in the United States in 2016—about one in nineteen children. In addition, many families are housing insecure. About one-third of all families experiencing homelessness with children under 18 pay more than 30 percent of their income on housing. The most heavily impacted states, with over 100,000 homeless children under age 6, are California, New York, and Texas, the country's three largest states by population. The states of Florida, Georgia, Illinois, Michigan, and Washington follow, with over 35,000 homeless children under the age of 6 in every state. NAEHCY collaborates with the Office of Early Childhood Education to smooth access to preschool and Head Start programs and offer information on child care and ESSA provisions.

NAEHCY programs directly serve approximately 1,750 unaccompanied youth and provide direct assistance to state and local homeless coordinators, school districts, and other educational stakeholders. Its programs offer information on current legislation, annual networking opportunities, and direct access to programs, scholarships, and trainings. Among the resources NAEHCY offers are easy-to-understand reports of frequently asked questions regarding government legislation. Its website provides detail on amendments to McKinney legislation that offer additional programs and supports for homeless students. A primary example is the ESSA in 2015, which expands federal provisions for equal access to a high-quality education. NAE-HCY also provides resources in the areas of early childhood education, special education, and higher education and offers state coordinator contact information.

In addition to providing resources to support early childhood education, NAEHCY also supports students with special needs and students accessing higher education. It does this in part by helping people understand the provisions of the Individuals with Disabilities Education Act (IDEA) of 1975. This legislation also pertains to youth in foster care or who are considered wards of the state. IDEA offers federal grants to states and localities to oversee the distribution of resources. Funding is intended to provide free and equal access to education for students in IDEA categories, including special needs students experiencing homelessness. Students accessing higher education can also receive assistance through the College Cost Reduction and Access Act (CCRAA) of 2007. This act allows unaccompanied homeless youth to report independent status on their application for financial aid (FAFSA) and gain additional assistance from federal and local sources.

NAEHCY understands that students experiencing homelessness can suffer from a lack of basic needs items that interfere with academic performance. For this reason, its website offers a host of housing and food and nutrition resources for families. These include the national school breakfast and lunch programs, SNAP and WIC benefits, and other federal resources. NAEHCY's national conference is an annual event that offers a wide range of focus areas and presents a unique opportunity for networking among stakeholders. NAEHCY also maintains a scholarship program that supports homeless students in their pursuit of secondary education. Overall, NAEHCY's reach is impressive, given its relatively small operating budget. Part of its influence is felt in the multiple trainings it offers at state and local levels, its direct collaboration with federal agencies, and detailed reports and information on various issues related to housing, poverty, and homelessness.

The Urban Institute

The Urban Institute was founded in 1968, when the war on poverty was in full swing, and the nation was coming to terms with systemic racism and blight in its inner cities. The Urban Institute was created to address issues of inequality in America and to evaluate policy solutions in urban areas in the United States as well as in developing nations. It is an independent research-based organization dedicated to racial equity and social justice. In over fifty years, the Urban Institute has tracked significant changes in federal policy related to affordable housing, welfare, tax cuts, and health care reform. It also has examined the nation's policy responses to such diverse crises as Hurricane Katrina, the 9/11 attacks, the subprime mortgage crisis, and the COVID-19 pandemic.

Located in Washington, DC, the Urban Institute is led by a team of over 400 researchers, lawyers, and policy makers. It has twenty-five research areas, all of which have dedicated researchers, ongoing initiatives, and current reports and publications. It hosts twelve policy centers, twenty-five cross-center initiatives, and a blog called Urban Wire. Urban Institute research is used to inform U.S. federal policy and evaluate federal programs and initiatives, as well as programs implemented in states and localities. It offers statistical models that can be applied to diverse social issues and pressing social problems. Its research examines innovative solutions to advance the nation's understanding of and ability to end homelessness. The Urban Institute measures the impact of policy changes, using its research capabilities to influence real-world issues facing people at risk.

The Urban Institute's research focuses on issues related to population and identity, including adolescents and youth, aging, children, families, gender and sexuality, immigrants and immigration, race, poverty, vulnerability, and gaps in the social safety net. All these are overlapping risk factors that lead to and perpetuate homelessness. The Urban Institute explores access to basic needs including food and nutrition, health and health policy, and areas of struggle for homeless and low-income populations. It also examines education and training, economic growth, and income and wealth as possible ways of preventing and ending homelessness. The Urban Institute evaluates the Pay for Success program, implemented through a partnership between HUD and the DOJ. It also examines the more general issue of crime and justice in urban areas. The research areas with the most obvious connection to homelessness are housing and poverty, vulnerability, and the social safety net.

The Urban Institute provides data and evaluation to address issues related to homelessness in specific communities. It examines solutions to end or reduce homelessness that include outreach and engagement, prevention, housing, tax cuts, and legislation. Institute research and publications related to homelessness include a focus on the following subgroups: unsheltered and chronically homeless people, homeless youth, LGBTQ, veterans, and families. Urban Institute research also examines alternatives to criminalization and recidivism as ways of breaking the cycle of homelessness and poverty.

Martha Burt has held several roles at the Urban Institute and remains a leading researcher in the field of homeless policy research. She is a renowned author and advocate for homeless rights and has contributed to McKinney-Vento legislation and its reauthorization. Burt pioneered one of the first and only annual counts to use rigorous statistical methods to sample the homeless population. Her books include *Over the Edge: The Growth of Homelessness in the 1980s*, *Repairing the US Social Safety Net*, and *Homelessness: Prevention, Strategies, and Effectiveness*. She has numerous other publications including books, articles, and reports on homelessness and has testified before Congress.

The Urban Institute is in the process of pursuing a new phase of research that will chart its focus for the next fifty years. Its stated goals are to advance equity, social mobility, and shared prosperity. Using the rigorous research that is its signature feature, the Urban Institute will continue to inform policy on multiple levels by providing innovative technological tools to enhance its problem-solving capacity. Its research in the next fifty years will reinforce its commitment to addressing structural racism and to working with and empowering states and local communities. Although homeless people are not its only focus, the Urban Institute has provided invaluable research and insights to serve this community.

Individual Profiles
Alice Solenberger

Alice Solenberger worked for the Central District of Chicago's Bureau of Charities in the early 1900s. At this time, Chicago was the epicenter of the nation's railroad travel. The city's large vice district surrounded the massive rail yards. Known as Skid Row, "West Madison Street," or simply "The Main Stem," this neighborhood occupied most of the West Loop neighborhood. The bureau was located about six blocks away, offering various forms of aid and employment to the immigrants, travelers, and itinerant laborers who settled in Skid Row lodging houses.

Solenberger collected data on homeless men seeking any kind of assistance from the bureau, from 1900 to 1903, and remained employed there until 1910. She recorded information on the men, detailing their personal histories, maladies, and the causes of their homelessness. She recorded extensive qualitative and quantitative data. Her job was to develop a treatment plan for the men and to reconnect them with work, family, and settled life. Although her writing reflects the language and social codes of the time, which viewed men as needing moral assistance, correction, or reform, her detailed data gathering helped broaden the nation's understanding of homelessness.

The categories Solenberger uses to describe homeless men are more detailed than the often-cited saying, "the hobo works and wanders, the tramp dreams and wanders and the bum drinks and wanders" (Anderson 1923). Solenberger (1911) focuses on mobility, over employment or drinking, as something that distinguishes homeless men from tramps, stating:

Almost all "tramps" are "homeless men," but by no means are all homeless men tramps. The homeless man may be an able-bodied workingman, without a family; he may be a runaway boy, a consumptive temporarily stranded on his way to a health resort, an irresponsible feeble-minded or insane man, a professional beggar, or a criminal,—but unless he is also a wanderer, he is not a tramp. (209)

Solenberger introduces a classification scheme that character-izes men's economic independence as key to their self-esteem and reintegration into the social mainstream. It is this sense of fitting into what was considered normal that informs her char-acterization of homeless men as those who are "self-supporting," "temporarily dependent" on others, "chronically dependent," and "parasitic," or criminal. Those who are self-supporting are closer to mainstream, "regular" men and easier to reintegrate, while those described as parasitic choose to be homeless and prey upon others. It is only this last group for whom she sug-gests dealing with along "corrective and repressive" lines.

After three years of extensive data collection, Solenberger followed up with detailed oral histories and interviews of the men, allowing her impressions and interpretations to change over time. Through this careful work, she offers generalizable patterns among groups and investigates the credibility of indi-vidual stories. Always an advocate for the men's return to set-tled society, Solenberger goes to great lengths to connect them with friends, family, safety, and employment. She does not, however, suggest treating homeless men as a class of people for whom one solution applies. She states, "The plea must be made for the consideration of the individual man upon the basis of his individual merits and needs as these shall be discovered through intelligent, thorough, and sympathetic investigation of his history" (188).

Although Solenberger offers extensive detail on the mobility, lifestyle, and unique life histories of the men on Skid Row, her untimely death in 1910, just before her book *One Thousand*

Homeless Men: A Study of Original Records (1911) was published, prevented her from offering summary conclusions.

Nels Anderson

As a young boy, Nels Anderson traveled with his family, while his father sought seasonal employment. Anderson was the youngest of nine children and began riding the rails in 1908, when he was 19. As Anderson tells the story, he was thrown off the train in Nevada and taken in by a family who saw his promise and nurtured his academic talent. With their support, he attended high school in 1912 and went on to study at Brigham Young University. He was enlisted briefly in the U.S. Army and arrived in Chicago in 1920, ready to begin his academic career. Flat broke and needing employment, Anderson worked at the Chicago Home for Incurables to support himself while he pursued the study of sociology at the University of Chicago. These institutions were not only close together but also a stone's throw away from the Skid Row area, which Anderson refers to as "Hobohemia."

Anderson's understanding of hobo life was part of his personal and family history, and making it part of his academic career was transformational. His interest in studying hobos and Skid Row was initially met with skepticism, because the University of Chicago feared that a study on hobos was "outside the zone of respectability." As a result, Anderson found financial support for his work through an associate of Benjamin Reitman, "King of the Hobos," whom he met at a lecture. Like Anderson's mentors Robert Park and Ernest Burgess, Reitman was taken with Anderson's unique, firsthand perspective. This, along with a tradition of white, male privilege in the academy, meant that Anderson was well on his way to a storied career. Reitman secured funding for him to conduct a full-scale study of hobo life, and mentors Park and Burgess assembled a committee to oversee his work.

This opportunity allowed Anderson to pursue research on Skid Row and to reside in Hobohemia while he conducted his study. His resulting book *The Hobo: The Sociology of the Homeless Man* informs a tradition of participant observation, still thriving in the field of sociology today. It is the first in a series of research monographs by the Chicago School Sociology Department. It includes a map of hobohemia and a description of the institutions designed to serve homeless men. In his view, hobos were in-between workers, "willing to go anywhere to take a job and equally willing to move on later" (Anderson 1923, xviii). Hobohemia catered to their highly mobile lifestyle, almost exclusively male culture, and reliance on seasonal labor. In fact, Anderson claims, "These conditions of work tend to require and to create the migratory worker" (1923, 62).

Despite his experience hoboing, Chicago was Anderson's first time living and working in an urban environment. He witnessed the seasonal fluctuations on Skid Row, as the population doubled during the winter months, when men who could afford to lived there for the winter. Anderson describes the specifics of lodging, employment, and entertainment on Skid Row, and he describes the hobo's rustic jungle camps, close to the railroads but outside of the urban center. This book also examines the problematic nature of the hobo lifestyle and its relationship with the law and with the civil society.

Anderson describes the causes of homelessness as lacking the ability or interest in industrial work, addiction to drugs or alcohol, suffering from "feeble-mindedness," pride or independence, personal crises, racial and national discrimination, "wanderlust," or a combination of these. His categorization of the men on Skid Row includes five types: "the seasonal worker, the transient or occasional worker or hobo, the tramp who 'dreams and wanders' and works only when it is convenient, the bum who seldom wanders and seldom works, and the home guard who lives in Hobohemia and does not leave town" (89).

As his academic career progressed, Anderson felt trapped by this characterization of the hobo and his own linkage to this marginal figure. To vent his frustration, he states, "I cleansed my soul by transferring all the old emotions of *The Hobo* to one

Dean Stiff, anonymous author of the parody." The book he is referring to, *The Milk and Honey Route*, is written as a handbook for hobos. Its title describes the railroad as a passage to plenty, harboring hidden dangers and lucrative opportunities. But, above all, this book is a lighthearted, playful rendition of hobo life.

By contrast, Anderson's book *Men on the Move* details the patterns of migration and work and offers a compilation of existing data and reports. It describes the changing nature of hobos and migration, who migrants were, their ages, characteristics, and reasons for migrancy. He examines what types of work they sought and how changes in the nation's industrial and agricultural labor made finding employment elusive. He also examines welfare and work opportunities but stops short of offering solutions that corroborate the prevailing view of migrancy as a problem. He merely suggests better coordination and control to calibrate migrancy with work opportunities.

Anderson received his PhD from New York University and taught at Columbia University from 1928 to 1934. He published books and articles on slum life, urban sociology, and his time in military service. Anderson became head of the UN Educational, Scientific, and Cultural Organization (UNESCO) Institute for Social Science at Cologne and eventually joined the University of New Brunswick's Department of Sociology, where he remained until 1977. Anderson died in 1986.

Cushing Dolbeare

Cushing Dolbeare founded the NLIHC in 1974. Dolbeare was a lifelong advocate for housing as a basic right, viewing it as integral to family, community, and the integrity of the nation. A graduate of Swarthmore College, she got her start in housing advocacy by working for the Citizens Planning and Housing Association of Baltimore and the Housing Association of Delaware Valley. Dolbeare went on to become a consultant for the U.S. Commission on Civil Rights. She created the NLIHC in response to the federal moratorium on public housing, implemented by the Nixon administration. Although the government promised that this action would eventually lead to better housing, early indications showed that it was having detrimental effects in several cities.

After founding the NLIHC, Dolbeare designed the methodology for the *Out of Reach* report and was its original author. *Out of Reach: The Gap between Housing Costs and Income of Poor People in the United States* was first published in 1989. It documents the national shortfall between income and housing costs. As Dolbeare writes, "My basic premise is that this 'affordability gap' is the underlying cause of homelessness and that significant progress in eliminating homelessness requires giving housing assistance to very low-income households to enable them to cover the gap" (1992, 151). *Out of Reach* remains one of the most important, annually updated sources of data on low-income housing to the present.

Dolbeare's research publications are also extensive, focusing on access to low-income housing, tenant rights, and the rights of underserved communities, including homeless people. She also examines the efficacy of various forms of assistance including federally funded housing and tax subsidies. Dolbeare's approach combines rigorous data analysis with a sound understanding of the problem of affordability, noting that "the 1991 Fair Market Rent for a one-bedroom unit is beyond the reach of at least one third of renter households in every single state" (1992, 155). The reason for this, as she describes, is a combination of more low-income renters, fewer available housing units, and the inadequacy of basic forms of assistance to cover rental costs. The proposed remedy is to support mainstream programs to offer subsidized housing to all homeless people and poor households.

Dolbeare was the NLIHC's executive director from 1977 to 1984 and again from 1993 to 1994, although she remained active in the organization throughout her life. When she received the Heinz Award for the Human Condition in 2002, in recognition of her work, the announcement read, in part, "she almost single-handedly put low-income housing on the national agenda and made the Coalition the pivotal player that it remains to this day." Despite this recognition, Dolbeare was frustrated with the pace of change, noting that affordable housing was still far from being a national reality.

Although Dolbeare's focus was not exclusively on homelessness, she published two papers on federal homeless social policies and on homelessness and the low-income housing crisis, in the early 1990s. These articles show a clear link between homelessness, housing affordability, and housing insecurity. Dolbeare died in 2005. Her obituary in the *Washington Post* offers an assessment of her work from colleague Sheila Crowley, NLIHC president, calling her the "conscience and the brains" of the U.S. affordable housing movement.

Martha R. Burt

Few people have made as significant an impact on how the nation understands and researches homelessness as Martha R. Burt. Her methodological precision and rigorous data collection provided one of the first nationwide estimates of the homeless population in 1987. Burt has published numerous books, articles, and reports throughout her career, as principal research associate for the Center on Labor, Human Services and Population in the Urban Institute. She has researched issues including hunger and homelessness, teen pregnancy, parenting and child care, welfare and welfare reform, domestic violence, and the impact of social services and polices to address them. The enduring legacy of Burt's work informs the debate about homelessness by providing an accurate, credible way of measuring population size and demographics and underscoring the necessity for specific definitions and accurate data. In so doing, her work urges advocates and policy makers to question basic assumptions about the causes of homelessness and to create informed solutions.

In the 1980s, and arguably to the present, social science research on homelessness tends to use either participant

observation or ethnographic work to highlight individual characteristics and risk factors or quantitative work or hypothesis
testing to focus on how structural forces impact changes in
the population. Neither approach fully defines the problem
or solves it, but both contribute to a better understanding of
the personal struggles and societal inequalities that homeless
people face and the interplay between the two. The problem
with developing a national sample of homeless people is that
the population is scattered, hidden, and highly mobile, so it is
often difficult to marshal the coordination needed to collect
data. Although the HMIS attempts to address this shortfall by
collecting intake information at all points of service delivery,
Burt's work was groundbreaking in terms of its methodology
and a focus on national trends.

Burt presented the results of the 1987 count, conducted
with colleague Barbara Cohen for the Urban Institute, in her
book *Over the Edge: The Growth of Homelessness in the 1980s*.
This study emerged in the context of the 1980s homeless crisis
and an ongoing debate about the size of the population and
the reasons for its increase. For this reason, Burt's book and the
study itself strive to present "correct numbers and true causes."
To do this, she offers a probability sample of homeless people
in twenty cities with populations over 100,000. This allowed
for generalizations about homelessness across the nation, something that had not yet been done reliably. It also allowed her to
control for individual variation across states and offer a sense of
trends and patterns across homeless groups. Overall, the report
measured the effects of changes in housing availability and
affordability, poverty and household income, income support
programs, and mental illness and addiction, on the size and
composition of the homeless population.

In 2001, the Urban Institute published Burt's co-authored
book, *Helping America's Homeless*, which examines the state of
homelessness in the 1990s. Initially understood as a short-term
crisis, set off by economic downturn, homelessness increased
in the 1990s, despite the economic prosperity enjoyed by the

nation overall. One of the book's main conclusions is that "as structural conditions worsen, even people without personal vulnerabilities other than poverty may experience crises that precipitate a homeless episode" (Burt et al. 2001, 8). Characteristic of Burt's research, this book weighs individual and structural risk factors against the efficacy of the U.S. social safety net in reducing or ending homelessness. It concludes that neither better services nor better planning has helped enough to end the problem, and they have become entrenched and costly. The solution, in Burt's estimation, is to offer housing, "through shelter plus care, vouchers, group homes, or any other mechanism."

By 2009, as the United States felt the effects of the great recession, Burt co-authored *Repairing the U.S. Safety Net*. This book describes how efficient various forms of assistance are in combatting homelessness and poverty. It offers a comprehensive overview of the successes and failures of specific kinds of assistance in reaching people in poverty and ultimately preventing homelessness. Burt's research and writing about homelessness continue to explore equal access to basic needs, including housing and supports for vulnerable populations. Her research offers communities important information and tools to evaluate their own success in streamlining the assistance and housing processes, and she remains a luminary in the field of homelessness and data collection, poverty, housing, and at-risk populations.

Maria Foscarinis

Throughout her career, Maria Foscarinis has challenged the exclusion of homeless people from the freedoms and protections that apply to everyone, under U.S. law. She has championed the fight to make access to basic needs, including housing, universal. Against all odds and at great personal sacrifice, she blazed a trail of legal advocacy that became the NLCHP, founded in 1989, and renamed the National Homelessness

Law Center in 2020. This nonprofit organization is the only one of its kind that uses the protections and provisions of federal and state law to address the unfair, unjust targeting of homeless people for minor, life-sustaining "offenses." The work of the Law Center spans all fifty states with a team of law firms that work pro bono to litigate on behalf of homeless people and to uphold their civil rights and protections afforded by the U.S. Constitution.

Foscarinis began homeless legal advocacy work in 1985, when she left a prestigious New York City law firm to join the NCH in Washington, DC. She became a central force in the creation and passing of the McKinney Vento Homeless Assistance Act, the only federal legislation specifically targeted to address U.S. homelessness. Foscarinis argued, among other provisions, for equal access to K–12 education and the use of federal properties to house homeless people. Since the passage of McKinney Vento, the Law Center has litigated cases of non-compliance, to ensure that students experiencing homelessness can access a public K–12 education and that federal properties do not sit empty, while people sleep on the streets. For Foscarinis, upholding these basic rights is a matter of human dignity.

Foscarinis' work involves holding the federal government, members of Congress, the USICH and its member organizations, and cities and states, accountable for the treatment of homeless people. Her work addresses the intersection of criminalization, basic needs, and human rights. Criminalization measures often target appearance, identity, and location, over crime, or they target homeless people for actions that others conduct regularly without punishment. When cities and communities enact ordinances and other restrictions that target homeless people; without legal protection, they run the risk of criminal justice involvement. Because the United States does not have adequate shelter or affordable housing, and because this is not equally accessible for everyone because of race, class, and other risk factors, homeless people often find themselves violating public space rules and norms, and they can be punished repeatedly.

Through detailed investigation and ongoing litigation, Foscarinis and Law Center colleagues demonstrate that the criminalization of homeless people is expensive for communities, prolongs time on the streets, causes stress and trauma, and increases rather than prevents or ends homelessness. The alternative, Foscarinis argues, is to provide housing as a basic human right. After thirty years under Foscarinis' direction, the Law Center has achieved several notable victories toward this end. Among them are the prioritization of reducing criminalization as a condition for HUD funding, preventing eviction for renters in foreclosed properties, protecting the right to housing for survivors of domestic violence, ongoing litigation to preserve the rights of homeless students and ensure equal access to K–12 education, and providing for low-income communities during times of crisis, including the COVID-19 pandemic.

Chapter 2 of this book offers a more comprehensive overview of the issue of criminalization, using the *Martin v. Boise* case that established protections for homeless people who are sleeping on the streets in the Ninth Circuit. By preventing the issuance of citations for sleeping in communities without adequate housing or shelter, this case protects the basic human rights of homeless people. Foscarinis discusses this important case and her own trajectory of involvement in the issue of homelessness and the creation of the NLCHP in Chapter 3. Related to this, Chapter 5 reviews the NLCHP publication *Housing Not Handcuffs* and its campaign to reduce criminalization. This groundbreaking report became a national litmus test of legal inclusion for homeless people. It called out good and bad practices, holding even the U.S. government accountable for criminalizing people experiencing the myriad factors of homelessness. Foscarinis' instrumental role in creating the NLCHP and in fighting criminalization through research, publications, and litigation, including testifying before Congress, makes her an enduring leader in the field of homelessness.

Rosanne Haggerty

Roseanne Haggerty founded the organization Common Ground in 1990 (later renamed Breaking Ground). She was inspired to do this after volunteering at Covenant House, a shelter for runaway children. She realized that services alone, even including shelter, were not enough to end homelessness. She also realized, as she commented in an interview, that "when there are not structures in place, you create them, even if it means starting from scratch and doing it yourself." Common Ground began with the premise that housing is a key to family and community stability and that it is a basic human right. Based in New York City, one of the first projects that Common Ground tackled was the renovation of the Times Square Hotel, the largest single room occupancy hotel in the city. This project housed roughly 650 formerly homeless people, but, as Haggerty notes, it did not end the problem.

Despite her success in creating several affordable, supportive housing projects in New York City, the lingering issue of how to take this solution to scale still remained. For this reason, Common Ground took the unique approach of stopping, midstream, to evaluate its goals, mission, and progress. Part of this included reaching out to homeless people themselves to search for solutions. In 2003, Common Ground launched its Street to Home initiative designed to reduce street homelessness. This approach used the vulnerability index as a tool to measure individual risk and prioritize people for housing on this basis. Haggerty's success in reducing street homelessness in the Times Square area earned her a MacArthur Fellowship, or "genius grant," in 2001. This award highlighted her work turning historical buildings into affordable homeless housing. Her innovation in this area did more than simply beautify city blocks but offered long-term housing that was less expensive than institutional or shelter care and benefited individuals and communities. For this reason, she also won the Jane Jacobs Medal in 2012. As a recognized social entrepreneur and innovator, Haggerty was in high demand, reflected by her numerous awards and accolades.

In 2010, she launched the 100,000 homes campaign, to focus on permanent supportive housing nationwide and to assist chronically homeless people and at-risk populations. Part of this approach included highlighting homeless voices and getting to know homeless people as individuals. Its success led Haggerty to leave Common Ground and create a new organization, Community Solutions, in 2011. Among the innovative approaches this organization takes is that communities should have a zero-tolerance policy for homelessness and that nothing short of ending it should be the ultimate goal. Community Solutions argues that homelessness is not only a symbol of our national character but is also symbolic of the racial inequality that is infused throughout American life and that permanent housing can help remedy. By 2014, the 100,000 homes campaign announced that it exceeded its original goal by at least 5,000 homes.

In 2015, Community Solutions launched the Build for Zero campaign to provide permanent housing for chronically homeless people and veterans in communities nationwide. This project involves a network of eighty-three cities and counties and a team of sixty-six people, using "a data driven, public health approach to reduce and end homelessness." Making homelessness rare and brief is what the campaign considers "functional zero." Campaign results include achieving functional zero for chronically homeless people or veterans in fifteen communities, with three achieving functional zero for both populations, and reducing homelessness in over half of the eighty-three participating locations. Keys to the campaign's success are monthly data collection and treating homeless people as individuals, knowing their names, and not giving up on them. The three-year report on this campaign also offers communities a recipe of essential ingredients needed to reach functional zero.

Lastly, in 2021, Community Solutions was awarded the #100AndChange grant from the MacArthur Foundation to

advance the goal of functional zero for seventy-five communities by 2026. The grant provided $100 million in funding,
distributed over three years, to advance an end to homelessness
in seventy-five communities nationwide and serve as a model
for the nation. Some of its core suggestions involve engaging elected officials to establish a community commitment
to ending homelessness and advancing racial equity. Overall,
throughout her work, Haggerty argues that solving the problem of homelessness is within reach for communities that make
a sustained commitment.

References

Anderson, Nels. 1923. *The Hobo: The Sociology of the Homeless Man*. Chicago: University of Chicago Press.

Baggett, Travis P., Stephen W. Hwang, James J. O'Connell, Bianca C. Porneala, Erin J. Stringfellow, E. John Orav, Daniel E. Singer, and Nancy A. Rigotti. 2013. "Mortality among Homeless Adults in Boston: Shifts in Causes of Death over a 15-year Period." *JAMA Internal Medicine* 173(3): 189–195.

Bamhill, Anne. 2011. "Impact and Ethics of Excluding Sweetened Beverages from the SNAP Program." *American Journal of Public Health* 101(11): 2037–2043.

Baumohl, James and Robert B. Huebner. 1991. "Alcohol and Other Drug Problems Among the Homeless: Research, Practice, and Future Directions." *Housing Policy Debate* 2(3): 837–866.

Burt, Martha R., Laudan Y. Aron, Toby Douglas, Jesse Valente, Edgar Lee, and Britta Iwen. 1999. "Homelessness: Programs and the People They Serve. Findings of the National Survey of Homeless Assistance Providers and Clients—Summary." Prepared for U.S. Interagency Council on Homelessness.

Burt, Martha, Laudan Y. Aron, and Edgar Lee *with* Jesse Valente. 2001. *Helping America's Homeless: Emergency Shelter or Affordable Housing?* Washington, DC: The Urban Institute Press.

Congressional Research Service. "Homelessness: Targeted Federal Programs," Report RL30442. https://crsreports .congress.gov.

Congressional Research Service. 2020. "The Emergency Food Assistance Program (TEFAP): Background and Funding," Report R45408, January 8. https://fas.org.

Couloute, Lucious. 2018. "Nowhere to Go: Homelessness among Formerly Incarcerated People." Prison Policy Initiative. https://www.prisonpolicy.org/reports /housing.html

Culhane, Dennis, Stephen Metraux, and Trevor Hadley. 2002. "Public Service Reductions Associated with Placement of Homeless Persons with Severe Mental Illness in Supportive Housing." *Housing Policy Debate* 13(1): 107–163.

Cunningham, Mary K., Sarah Gillespie, and Alexandra Tilsley. 2017. "Homelessness Is a Solvable Problem." The Urban Institute.

Desmond, Matthew. 2016. *Evicted.* New York: Broadway Books.

Dolbeare, Cushing N. 1992. "Homelessness and the Low Income Housing Crisis." *The Journal of Sociology & Social Welfare* (19)4: 151–175.

Doran, Kelly M., Neloufar Rahai, Ryan P. McCormack, Jacqueline Milian, Donna Shelley, John Rotrosen, and Lillian Gelberg. 2018. "Substance Use and Homelessness Among Emergency Department Patients." *Drug and Alcohol Dependence* (188)1: 328–335.

Federal Emergency Management Agency. 2020. "FEMA Disburses Emergency Food and Shelter Program Funding,"

news release no. HQ-20-159, June 8. fema.gov/news
-release/20200726/fema-disburses-emergency-food-and
-shelter-program-funding

Freudenberg, Nicholas, Sara Goldrick-Rab, and Janet
Poppendieck. 2019. "College Students and SNAP:
The New Face of Food Insecurity in the United States."
American Journal of Public Health. https://ajph
.aphapublications.org/doi/full/10.2105/AJPH.2019
.305332

Heilig, Markus, Kenneth R. Warren, George Kunos, Peter
B. Silverman, and Brenda G. Hewitt. 2010. "Addiction
Research Centres and the Nurturing of Creativity."
*The National Institute on Alcohol Abuse and Alcoholism:
Addiction Research Centres Series* 106: 1052–1060.

Heisler, Elayne J. 2017. *Federal Health Centers: An Overview.*
Congressional Research Service.

Huebner, Robert B., Harold I. Perl, Peggy M. Murray, Jack
E. Scott, and Beth Ann Tutunjian. 1993. "The NIAAA
Cooperative Agreement Program for Homeless Persons
with Alcohol and Other Drug Problems: An Overview."
Overview of NIAAA Cooperative Agreement Program:
The Haworth Press.

Jones, Marian M. 2015. "Creating a Science of Homelessness
during the Reagan Era." *The Milbank Quarterly*
93(1): 139–178.

Ku, Leighton, Erin Brantley, and Drishti Pillai. 2019.
"The Effects of SNAP Work Requirements in Reducing
Participation and Benefits from 2013 to 2017." *American
Journal of Public Health* 109(10): 1446–1451.

Levine, Irene S. and Debra J. Rog. 1990. "Mental Health
Services for Homeless Mentally Ill Persons." *American
Psychologist* 45(8): 963–968.

Lubran, Barbara G. 1989. "NIAAA's Homeless Initiative; an
Update." *Alcohol Health & Research World* 13(3): 281–285.

Maness, David L. and Muneeza Khan. 2014. "Care of the Homeless: An Overview." *American Family Physician* 89(8): 634–640.

Martinez-Schiferl, Michael. 2012. "WIC Participants and Their Growing Need for Coverage." The Urban Institute, April 25. https://www.urban.org/research/publication /wic-participants-and-their-growing-need-coverage

Nestle, Marion. 2019. "The Supplemental Nutrition Assistance Program (SNAP): History, Politics, and Public Health Implications." *American Journal of Public Health*. Published online November 6. https://ajph. aphapublications.org/doi/10.2105/AJPH.2019.305361

Orwin, Robert G., Howard H. Goldman, L. Joseph Sonnefeld, M. Susan Ridgely, Nancy Gray Smith, Roberta Garrison-Mogren, Ellen O'Neill, and Anne Sherman. 1994. "Alcohol and Drug Abuse Treatment of Homeless Persons: Results from the NIAAA Community Demonstration Program." *Journal of Health Care for the Poor and Underserved* 5(4): 326–352.

Rothstein, Richard. 2017. *The Color of Law: A Forgotten History of How Our Government Segregated America*. New York: W. W. Norton & Company, Ltd.

Shinn, Marybeth and Jill Khadduri. 2020. *In the Midst of Plenty: Homelessness and What to Do about It*. NJ: Wiley Blackwell.

Solenberger, Alice W. 1911. *One Thousand Homeless Men: A Study of Original Records (1911)*. New York: Russell Sage Foundation.

U.S. Department of Housing and Urban Development. 2015 "Homeless Emergency Assistance and Rapid Transition to Housing: Defining Chronic Homelessness." *Federal Register* 80(233). https://www.govinfo.gov/content/pkg/FR-2015 -12-04/pdf/2015-30473.pdf

U.S. Department of Justice, Office of Violence against Women. 2018. *The 2018 Biennial Report to Congress on the*

Effectiveness of Grant Programs under the Violence Against Women Act.

Wakin, Michele. 2020. *Hobo Jungle: A Homeless Community in Paradise*. Boulder, CO: Lynne Rienner Publishers.

Zerger, Suzanne. 2002. "Substance Abuse Treatment: What Works for Homeless People? A Review of the Literature." National Health Care for the Homeless Council. Prepared for Translating Research into Practice Subcommittee National HCH Council and HCH Clinicians Network Research Committee.

Zlotnick, Cheryl, Suzanne Zerger, and Phyllis B. Wolfe. 2013. "Health Care for the Homeless: What We Have Learned in the Past 20 Years and What's Next." *American Journal of Public Health* (103)2: 199–205.

Collecting accurate, representative, generalizable data is a key part of conducting social research. It also informs policies and programs to serve homeless people. This chapter presents the data and documents that best represent national efforts to understand homelessness, define and track changes in the population, and develop innovative policies, programs, and solutions. The data and documents included here illustrate structural challenges homeless people face, in terms of housing, education, employment, or criminal justice involvement. These structural barriers intersect with individual risk factors including race, gender, and class. In this sense, policy is a bridge that can take into account personal challenges and remove structural barriers to exit.

Homelessness is a heavily stigmatized condition, and homeless people often fear hate, violence, and criminalization from the wider society. This is one of many reasons they choose to stay hidden, but it makes counting the homeless population difficult. Communities seeking federal funding must tally their sheltered and unsheltered populations and collect demographic information on subpopulations of interest. They must also enter data on homeless clients into the Homeless Management Information System (HMIS), a tool used by the federal

Homeless tent cities proliferate in Los Angeles, California, the city with the nation's largest unsheltered homeless population. With the onset of COVID-19, tent cities are a temporary housing solution that offers social distancing. (Meinzahn/Dreamstime.com)

government since the late 1990s, to track demographics, service use, and progress toward ending homelessness.

Rigorous data collection allows the U.S. Interagency Council on Homelessness (USICH) to present an annual report to Congress, the Annual Homeless Assessment report (AHAR). The first part of the AHAR provides a one-night "snapshot" count of homelessness. The second part uses HMIS data to examine annual trends as a supplement to the one-time count. In addition, the AHAR offers a housing inventory count (HIC) of the number of homeless beds in all continuum of care (CoC) regions nationwide. This chapter begins with a summary of national- and state-level trends in homelessness and housing in the 2019 AHAR. It also presents brief results from part I of the 2020 AHAR, released in March 2021. This offers a profile of U.S. homelessness that corresponds with the outbreak of the COVID-19 pandemic and acts as a baseline measure of the population.

To further examine the federal response to homelessness, this chapter follows its review of the AHAR with a summary of the most recent federal strategic plan, entitled *Expanding the Toolbox: The Whole of Government Response to Homelessness*. This plan offers federal guidance that shapes the nation's approach to ending homelessness and drives policy and funding efforts. Government support of specific initiatives and subpopulations is spelled out in the federal plan. It also typically includes goals and benchmarks, an organizational structure, and timelines for ending homelessness. Because the federal plan reflects the current administration's priorities and because these shift over time, this review presents an overview of major changes in approach and thinking since the first plan was released in 2010.

Following the examination of the AHAR and the federal plan, this chapter focuses on housing. This is a crucial resource to examine because housing availability and affordability, above all else, determine homelessness. This chapter uses the document, *Out of Reach*, published by the National Low-Income

Housing Coalition (NLIHC) to summarize the current state of affordable housing in the United States. *Out of Reach* is an annual report that assesses how realistic it is for homeless and low-income people to access rental versus subsidized housing. Of course, housing affordability varies from state to state as well as within individual states. *Out of Reach* offers a comprehensive summary of national wage data and a breakdown by state and by county. It considers housing along with low-wage employment and rising inequality in U.S. society as factors that contribute to homelessness.

Following *Out of Reach*, this chapter turns to the *Housing Not Handcuffs* report by the National Law Center on Homelessness and Poverty (NLCHP). Released in 2019, *Housing Not Handcuffs* examines the legal risks that come with a life of homelessness. The report examines and defines various forms of criminalization, as law enforcement strategies and policies that reinforce rather than eliminate structural barriers to housing. Criminalization targets homeless people for citation and other punitive actions and delays their chances for exit. *Housing Not Handcuffs* is a key document to examine because of the recent rise in unsheltered homelessness and the fact that people living without shelter are the most frequent targets of criminalization. The title of the report demonstrates the data-informed belief in Housing First and policies that advocate for universal housing. The NLCHP has been central in the drive to stop criminalization because it worsens homelessness, it is costly to implement, and it violates homeless people's civil and constitutional rights.

The final document that this chapter examines is the Coronavirus Aid, Relief, and Economic Security (CARES) Act. Like other crises, including the ones discussed in Chapter 1, the COVID-19 pandemic demanded a strong federal response. Legislation to provide housing and services to homeless people during the pandemic is also an important test of our national character. While these data and the impact of the CARES Act and the COVID-19 pandemic are still emerging, this legislation defines the nation's response to its most vulnerable. Throughout American history, responses to homelessness have been more generous during times of crisis. Unfortunately, ameliorative responses to crises, like the CARES Act, often address immediate over long-term needs.

DOCUMENTS

The Annual Homeless Assessment Report (AHAR) to Congress

The first AHAR to Congress was released in 2007. This report is published by the Office of Community Planning and Development under the U.S. Department of Housing and Urban Development (HUD). The AHAR uses point-in-time (PIT) count data to provide a one-night snapshot count of homelessness at the national, state, and CoC levels. It also uses HMIS data to track homelessness over the twelve-month period the report covers. Finally, it uses data from the HIC to offer a national inventory of emergency, transitional, and permanent supportive housing (PSH) beds. Specific chapters on families with children, unaccompanied homeless youth, veterans, and chronically homeless individuals provide additional information on these subpopulations.

Since 2015, the AHAR includes a set of system performance measures designed to test the efficiency of the CoC planning process. The basic question addressed is: How efficient are CoCs in reducing, preventing, and ending homelessness? The first five measures, collected using the HMIS system, are reported at the national and CoC levels. They include:

Measure 1: The length of time individuals and people in families remain homeless. Results are from shelter, transitional housing, and safe haven stays.

Measure 2: The extent to which individuals and families who leave homelessness experience additional spells of homelessness.

Measure 3: Overall change in the number of homeless individuals and families, represented as counts of people in each year staying in emergency shelters, safe havens, and transitional housing.

Measure 4: Jobs and income growth for homeless individuals and families, represented as counts of people with increases in earned income and total income from project start to project exit (called system leavers).

Measure 5: Success at reducing the number of individuals and families who become homeless, represented as counts of people without a prior entry to the homeless system.

The report does not include a sixth measure but a three-part seventh, which reads as follows:

Measure 7a: Successful placement from street outreach to shelter, transitional housing, or safe haven.

Measure 7b1: Successful housing placement to a permanent housing destination from emergency shelter, transitional housing, safe haven, or rapid re-housing projects.

Measure 7b2: Successful housing placement to a permanent housing destination from permanent housing projects not including rapid re-housing, and also including people who stay in permanent housing projects longer than six months.

(U.S. Department of Housing and Urban Development 2020b)

Communities that report this information receive incentive points that may entitle them to additional resources, so they are motivated to reduce the length of shelter stays, and to encourage employment and sustained permanent housing. From 2015 to 2019, communities nationwide reported that the average length of time people spent homeless hovered consistently around 165 days. Once housed, few people returned to homelessness within six months. When this time period was lengthened to twenty-four months, however, about 20 percent returned to homelessness. This suggests the need for a longer assessment period to ensure sustained exit. Measure 3 reports PIT count data, discussed later in this chapter. Measure 4 shows that most people who participated in homeless service and shelter and then exited were more likely to experience greater earned and total income. This suggests that permanent housing has a positive effect on the ability to accumulate wealth and sustain housing in the long term. Prevention is also an important aspect of CoC planning. Measure 5 shows that the number of people newly homeless decreased by approximately 40,000 from 2015 to 2019.

Preventing people from entering homelessness is a strategy that must be combined with ending homelessness for those currently experiencing it. Measure 7 asks how many people were placed into permanent housing from several different locations: street, shelters, rapid rehousing, and permanent housing projects. The report found that over 95 percent of those placed in permanent housing from other permanent housing projects remained housed. This includes people who stayed in permanent housing for more than six months. Data indicates a lower success rate in moving people from street to shelter. This also declines over time, from over 47.1 percent moving from street to shelter in 2015 to just over 33 percent in 2019. Placement rates for people from shelter to housing are also modest but remain consistent over time at about 40 percent. These results show that placing homeless people in permanent housing is a successful strategy, particularly when combined with other resources. This is an important insight, as permanent supportive housing programs and Housing First, which prioritizes housing over service compliance, have been criticized as inefficient.

The 2019 AHAR begins with a message from HUD secretary Ben Carson. In it, he touts the nation's progress in reducing veteran homelessness. He explicitly connects the success of this initiative with HUD's use of the Housing First approach. Reductions in veteran homelessness are diminished only by the fact that overall homelessness increased by 3 percent between 2018 and 2019. California is specifically mentioned as contributing disproportionately to this increase. The report notes that half of all unsheltered people in the United States live in California and that the state has roughly one-third of the country's homeless population. The decline in transitional beds is seen as contributing to the increase in the number of unsheltered homeless people. PSH is also critiqued as a costly solution, although one that HUD supports, and the report urges that more emergency beds be made available for homeless populations.

The 2019 AHAR presents national estimates from 2007 to 2019 for all homeless people and for those living sheltered and unsheltered. Although the PIT count has undergone changes in methodology and guidelines for counting, there were 79,543 fewer homeless people counted in 2007 than in 2019 across subpopulations. This is about 1,590 fewer people, per state, over a twelve-year period, a 12 percent decrease overall. These results suggest that homelessness is a long-term feature of life in the United States, although slow and consistent progress has been made to reduce the population. But where does the decrease come from? The AHAR shows that the sheltered population decreased by over 34,000 people (9 percent) and the unsheltered population by over 44,000 people (17 percent) since 2007. In 2019, the average homeless person is a white male over the age of 25 living in or near a major city in a shelter.

Despite overall reductions in homelessness since 2007, disturbing trends emerge over time. Among these are the consistent overrepresentation of African Americans and people of color, recent increases in chronic homelessness, and the prevalence of unsheltered homeless youth. The AHAR distinguishes between CoC regions, separating them into those that comprise the fifty largest U.S. cities and those that are largely urban, largely suburban, or rural. Although most of the nation's CoCs are suburban, more than half of the country's homeless population resides in a major city. The report found that New York City and Los Angeles alone house 24 percent of the U.S. homeless population. California and Hawaii have the highest rates of individual homelessness and, along with Oregon, house most of the nation's unsheltered population. Pinpointing population changes, size, and demographics is one of the AHAR's notable strengths, as it allows for targeted policy changes.

Between 2018 and 2019, individual homeless populations (as opposed to homeless families) increased the most in major cities and drove a rise in the numbers of people unsheltered. It is important to point out that sheltered and unsheltered homeless people cluster in different areas in the country. States with the highest percentages of unsheltered people include California (72 percent), Oregon (64 percent), Hawaii (57 percent), Nevada (53 percent), and Arkansas (52 percent). The five states that house approximately 95 percent of sheltered people are North Dakota, New York, Massachusetts, Maine, and Nebraska. Whether states have large sheltered or unsheltered populations depends in part on weather, but other factors include the political and economic climate in the state and possible community hostility to hosting homeless services. This phenomenon, which may present itself on any number of development and regulatory issues, is sometimes known as "not in my backyard," or NIMBYism. States with major cities are also more likely to have higher numbers of homeless people.

The 2019 AHAR estimates that 30 percent of the total homeless population includes individuals in families, and 60 percent of them are children under 18. The vast majority of families are sheltered, a fact that has changed over time. Since 2007, the number of people in families experiencing homelessness declined by 27 percent, primarily among the unsheltered. These gains were undermined within the last year, with an increase of 27 percent in sheltered chronic family homelessness. This suggests that long-term sheltered families are not making a sustainable transition to self-sufficiency. Instead, they merely cycle between low-income housing and shelter. Homeless families, like other groups, are more prevalent in particular states. New York, California, and Massachusetts are high shelter states. They collectively account for half of the nation's homeless families with children who receive shelter/housing. California, Oregon, and Florida host most of the nation's unsheltered homeless families.

Like homeless individuals, families tend to cluster disproportionately in the nation's largest cities. This clustering is also race based, as most homeless families in major cities are African American or Latino. This trend reverses in rural areas where the homeless population is 63 percent white for families and 73 percent for individuals. White people make up half of all unsheltered homeless families, followed by African Americans at 21 percent and Latinos at 6 percent. The report also notes that although Native American families experience homelessness at a rate that equals their share of the U.S. population, approximately 2.2 percent, the unsheltered Native American homeless population saw a 28 percent increase from 2018.

In addition to race, parenting youth (families with parents under 25) are specifically mentioned as a vulnerable category. Unaccompanied youth, who are less likely to be white and more likely to be female, are also mentioned, as population decreases among this population remain small. Chronic homelessness saw the largest increase, as numbers rose for the third straight year in 2019. Since 2007, there has been only a 5 percent drop in chronic homelessness. By contrast, the number of veterans decreased dramatically during the 2010s, with modest decreases to the present. Overall, government support has fueled a 50 percent decrease in veteran homelessness since 2009. In the 2019 PIT count, California accounted for almost one-third of all veterans experiencing homelessness and over half of all unsheltered veterans. The state also hosts 40 percent of the nation's unsheltered chronically homeless individuals, with Los Angeles reporting the highest percentage of the national total for this population.

In addition to providing information on the PIT count, the AHAR also includes an inventory of beds available to people experiencing homelessness in the United States. The report distinguishes between the two general categories of "shelter" and "permanent housing." Sheltered housing includes emergency shelters, which are temporary or nightly, and transitional housing, which offers up to twenty-four months of shelter and supportive services. It also includes safe haven housing, which is for "hard to serve" homeless people, who are severely mentally ill and often unsheltered or with other overlapping conditions. Sheltered housing makes up 43 percent of the nation's 911,657 beds, with 75 percent emergency shelters, 25 percent transitional housing, and 6 percent safe havens.

Permanent housing includes three categories. The first two are rapid rehousing, which offers short-term assistance, and PSH, which is long-term and targets specific subgroups, like people with disabilities or chronically homeless. In addition, the AHAR includes "other" permanent housing that is not specifically for formerly homeless people or for particular subgroups and may or may not come with services. Most beds, 71 percent, are permanent housing beds, and 22 percent are for rapid rehousing programs. The AHAR notes that since 2007, the nation added 180,657 permanent housing beds, 80,386 emergency beds, and 93,114 rapid rehousing beds. Bed totals continued to rise from 2018 to 2019. At the same time, the nation lost 115,759 transitional housing beds and over 5,000 in the prior year. Despite a net gain of over 230,000 beds, it is clear that additional support and coordination are needed to effectively house homeless people.

Part of the difficulty in offering specific types of housing for specific subgroups of homeless people is supply and demand. It is difficult to calibrate which and how much housing to offer, according to changing population needs. Specific locales also come with specific challenges, including prohibitively costly housing markets. Limited resources compound the problem, as long-term housing is not only expensive but also involves a lengthy building and permit process and the provision of ongoing services. Most kinds of emergency housing beds are split between individuals and families or are targeted to specific subgroups. There is no guarantee, in other words, that enough emergency shelter or PSH beds will be available in communities with high needs. In addition, program beds are not interchangeable, so an emergency bed cannot easily be converted to a family bed. The AHAR notes that about half of the nation's PSH stock is reserved for chronically homeless people.

From 2007 to 2019, the number of PSH beds for chronically homeless people increased by 143,698. PSH is the most common type of permanent housing for formerly homeless people. This suggests that long-term support that comes with PSH is a key feature of its prevalence and success. It also suggests that the people served through PSH may face challenges that threaten their success in the mainstream rental market. PSH is more common in rural and suburban CoCs than in major cities. The same thing is true for rapid rehousing beds.

Table 5.1 presents data featured in the 2019 AHAR. It lists the ten states with the largest total number of homeless people. For each state, there is also breakdown of homelessness by families and individuals, unaccompanied homeless youth, veterans, chronically homeless people, and those sheltered and unsheltered. Unequivocally, the states with the largest numbers in every category are California, New York, and Texas, followed by Florida, Washington, and Oregon. Of course, these states vary in size and density, so it is hard to come to conclusions using state totals alone. Table 5.1 and this brief summary examine overall trends to see which states lead the nation in homelessness.

Table 5.1 States with the Largest Homeless Populations

State	Per 10K	Individuals	Families	Youth	Veterans	Chronic	Shelter	Unsheltered	Total
CA	38.3	128,777	22,501	11,993	10,980	39,275	42,846	108,432	151,278
NY	46.4	42,113	49,978	2,978	1,270	5,965	88,044	4,047	92,091
FL	13.5	21,265	7,063	1,450	2,472	5,181	15,852	12,476	28,328
TX	9.1	19,611	6,237	1,355	1,806	3,338	14,626	11,222	25,848
WA	29.1	15,985	5,592	1,911	1,585	4,446	12,020	9,557	21,577
MA	26.9	6,259	12,212	480	917	1,392	17,642	829	18,471
OR	38.3	12,354	3,522	1,590	1,438	4,609	5,734	10,142	15,876
PA	10.3	8,426	4,773	737	857	1,775	11,569	1,630	13,199
GA	10	7,913	2,530	596	801	1,081	6,563	3,880	10,443
OH	8.9	7,041	3,304	643	676	807	8,838	1,507	10,345

Source: U.S. Department of Housing and Urban Development (2020a)

States reporting over 10,000 homeless individuals in 2019 were California (128,777), New York (42,113), Florida (21,265), Texas (19,611), Washington (15,985), and Oregon (12,354). California, New York, Texas, and Washington also have the nation's highest numbers of families with children. States like Massachusetts and Florida have high numbers of one category and not the other. Florida, for example, has only 7,063 homeless families, which is about one-third of its individual population. Massachusetts is the opposite, with double the number of families with children versus individuals. Both Massachusetts and Florida are high shelter states, meaning that the number of people in shelter is higher than those living unsheltered. This is particularly true in Massachusetts, where fewer than 1,000 people were unsheltered during the 2019 PIT count. In contrast with this kind of variation, some states are leaders across categories, suggesting a more systemic problem.

At the time of this writing, the first part of the 2020 AHAR was released, in March 2021. It offers snapshot, PIT estimates of homeless people and estimates of housing and shelter bed use, collected in January 2020. It also reflects the Biden administration's renewed focus on Housing First as a cogent strategy for ending homelessness, yet it does not reflect the full impact of the COVID-19 pandemic. The 2020 AHAR shows increases in homelessness for the fourth consecutive year. The following information offers select summary points from the 2020 count and reflects specific increases for subpopulations.

National Estimates, 2020

- The number of people experiencing homelessness nationwide increased by two percent between 2019 and 2020, or 12,751 more people. This marks the fourth consecutive year that total homelessness has increased in the United States.
- The overall increase was driven by increases in the unsheltered homeless population. Between 2019 and 2020, the number

of people counted in unsheltered locations rose by seven percent or 14,787 people. The number of people staying in shelter remained largely unchanged between 2019 and 2020, declining by less than one percent (2,036 fewer people).

- Across both household and shelter types, nearly three-quarters of people experiencing homelessness were adults aged 25 or older (428,859 people), 18 percent were children under the age of 18 (106,364 children). Eight percent were young adults aged 18 to 24 (45,243 young adults).

- The gender characteristics of all people experiencing homelessness reflected the high percentage of men in the individual homeless population. Six of every 10 people experiencing homelessness were men or boys (61% or 352,211 men and boys), 39 percent were women or girls (223,578 women and girls), and less than one percent were transgender (3,161 people) or gender nonconforming (1,460 people).

- Almost 4 of every 10 people experiencing homelessness in January 2020 were black or African American (39% or 228,796 people). A higher percentage of people in shelter were black or African American (47% or 280,612 people) and white people made up somewhat more than half of the unsheltered population (57%).

- Almost a quarter of all people experiencing homelessness, 23 percent, were Hispanic or Latino (counting people of all races who identify as Hispanic or Latino). The proportion is similar for people staying in sheltered and unsheltered locations (22% and 24%).

- Between 2019 and 2020, the number of veterans experiencing homelessness increased by less than one percent (167 more people). The increase was entirely among veterans staying in unsheltered places (859 more veterans).

- Fewer veterans were found in both sheltered and unsheltered locations in 2020 than in 2009. Between 2009 and

2020, both sheltered and unsheltered veteran homelessness dropped by almost half (49%) a reduction of 21,361 sheltered veterans and 14,754 unsheltered veterans.

(U.S. Department of Housing and Urban
Development 2021, 7–8, 52)

State Estimates, 2020

- States with the largest absolute increases in homelessness between 2019 and 2020 were California (10,270 more people), Texas (1,381), and Washington (1,346).
- More than half of all people experiencing homelessness as individuals (52%) did so in a major city. Nearly one-quarter of individuals experiencing homelessness (23%) were in largely suburban areas.
- Los Angeles had the largest number of individuals experiencing homelessness 51,290 people, followed by New York City, 36,394. The order is reversed for all people experiencing homelessness, as New York City has large numbers of homeless people in families.

(U.S. Department of Housing and Urban
Development 2021, 12, 14, 26)

If any conclusions can be drawn from this summary of the national state of homelessness in January 2020, they all point toward a crisis that is worsening, even before the COVID-19 pandemic.

The Federal Strategic Plan to Prevent and End Homelessness

The first Federal Strategic Plan to Prevent and End Homelessness, Opening Doors, was released in 2010 by the Obama administration. It was written in response to a growing national cry for a plan that would put an end to homelessness and focus on vulnerable populations. The plan's four primary goals included:

(1) Finishing the job of ending chronic homelessness in five years;

(2) Preventing and ending homelessness among veterans in five years;

(3) Preventing and ending homelessness for families, youth, and children in ten years;

(4) Setting a path to ending all types of homelessness.

   (U.S. Interagency Council on Homelessness 2010, 26)

Opening Doors *officially endorsed the Housing First approach as a way of assisting the most-difficult-to-serve populations. It also focused on the idea of that securing housing for the homeless was a way of restoring dignity, community, and a sense of national character. The following first paragraph, written by former president Obama, expresses this sentiment:*

Since the founding of our country, "home" has been the center of the American dream. Stable housing is the foundation upon which everything else in a family's or individual's life is built—without a safe, affordable place to live, it is much tougher to maintain good health, get a good education or reach your full potential.

From years of practice and research, we have identified successful approaches to end homelessness. Evidence points to the role housing plays as an essential platform for human and community development. Stable housing is the foundation upon which people build their lives—absent a safe, decent, affordable place to live, it is next to impossible to achieve good health, positive educational outcomes, or reach one's economic potential. Indeed, for many persons living in poverty, the lack of stable housing leads to costly cycling through crisis-driven systems like foster care, emergency rooms, psychiatric hospitals, emergency domestic violence shelters, detox centers, and jails. By the same token, stable housing provides an ideal launching pad for the delivery of health care and other social services focused on improving life outcomes for individuals and families. More recently, researchers have focused on housing stability as an important ingredient for the success of children and youth in school. When children have a stable home, they are more likely to succeed socially, emotionally, and academically.

(U.S. Interagency Council on Homelessness 2010, 6, 8–9)

In Opening Doors, *Housing First was understood as a way of providing low-barrier housing and services and saving money on emergency expenses. The federal plan was amended in 2012 and again in 2015 and 2018, reaffirming the plan's original goals and approach, adjusting the timeline, and including or re-emphasizing a focus on families with children, unaccompanied youth, people with disabilities, and veterans.*

The plan's most recent version was released by the USICH, under the guidance of the Trump administration, in October 2020. Titled Expanding the Toolbox: The Whole of Government Response to Homelessness, *it was a departure from previous plans in form and substance. Far shorter than previous plans, this one was largely devoid of specific goals, objectives, funding sources, timelines, or a division of responsibilities. It reflects administrative and ideological changes in how the United States approaches its solution to the problem of homelessness. The 2020 plan rejected long-standing, data-driven approaches to ending homelessness, including Housing First, and the provision of government housing subsidies.*

Expanding the Toolbox *begins by drawing an important distinc-tion between the definition of homelessness used by the Department of Education (ED) and the one employed by HUD. The primary difference is that the former includes children and youth who are doubled up with others, living in shared or precarious housing. The plan noted dramatic increases in child and youth homelessness among those living unsheltered and in shelters, transitional hous-ing, and motels. It also reported a dramatic increase in the number of homeless children enrolled in public schools, up 122 percent from 2006–2007 to 2016–2017. Most of this increase came from those living doubled up. The plan noted that studies conducted in Los Angeles, Santa Cruz, San Francisco, and Seattle confirmed that youth homelessness is a feeder into adult homelessness, accounting for 15–20 percent of the adult homeless population.*

The plan's main focus was to address what it identified as the root causes of homelessness. The report also included a list of broad guiding principles for combating homelessness. They are:

The Importance and Power of the Dignity of Work

Mental Health and Trauma Informed Care

Affordable Construction Leads to Affordable Housing

Prevention Will Save Money by Reducing Trauma

The Need for Population Specific Programming

Renewed Focus on Racial Disparities

Promotion of Alternatives to Criminalizing People Experi-encing Homelessness

Importance of National Emergency Readiness

(U.S. Interagency Council on Homelessness 2020, 1)

The report also emphasized that increases in federal funding for programs and initiatives to help homeless populations have not done the job of ending homelessness. The plan used PIT count data to show that despite a 200 percent increase in federal funding over the previous ten years, unsheltered homelessness increased by

20.5 percent from 2014 to 2019. The plan observes that most of this increase came from the state of California and suggests that the implementation of Housing First is to blame.

> In California, from 2015 (the year before the State restricted state-funded projects to only housing first) to 2019, unsheltered homelessness in California rose 47.1 percent in four years and overall homelessness (as represented by all five AHAR categories) rose from 115,278 to 151,278, a 30.7 percent increase. It should be noted that beyond the shift to housing first only policies, California's high cost of housing has also contributed to these increases. California now boasts nearly one in four of America's homeless population, even though it contains only 12 percent of the United States population. California's state-wide prescriptive policy should be considered when understanding the state's significant rise in homelessness and its significant portion of the nation's homeless population.
>
> (U.S. Interagency Council on Homelessness 2020, 10)

The plan mistakenly summarizes Housing First as a "one-size-fits-all" approach that offers government-subsidized housing vouchers without conditions or requirements. The alternative solution endorsed by the report was to reduce government-subsidized housing and its concomitant costs and focus on providing affordable housing, gainful employment, and customized, trauma-informed wraparound services. How any of those resources would be delivered, however, was not included in the plan. Instead, housing is compared with means-tested federal poverty programs, like Pell Grants and Temporary Assistance for Needy Families (TANF), suggesting that program requirements should be crafted to increase self-sufficiency. This is the plan's idea of the "dignity of work." Expanding the Toolbox, though, was notably vague about how to provide sustainable employment for the homeless. Instead, it suggested that local communities work with local constituents to provide training and employment. Ongoing efforts in this direction, funding for new partnerships and opportunities, and a general plan for moving forward with this solution are not included in the plan. Ties to other mainstream forms of assistance or other federal agencies or departments are also not mentioned. These omissions are highlighted in the other reports from advocates for the homeless included in this chapter.

To address the lack of affordable housing, Expanding the Toolbox *suggested that local governments "critically evaluate their zoning, housing permitting, regulations, and building fees" and await further federal guidance. Informing this solution, in February 2020, the Council of Economic Advisers (CEA) released its annual* Economic Report of the President. *In it, the CEA targets eleven cities it sees as having overregulated housing markets, leading to high rental and purchase prices and contributing to homelessness. In 2019, the Trump administration established a council to explore deregulating housing in these areas and nationwide, but no additional guidelines were released before Trump's defeat in the 2020 presidential election.*

One main concern about claims that increased affordable housing can be decisive in reducing homelessness is that even if more of it becomes available, it is likely to be filled primarily by low- and middle-income renters rather than homeless people. Expanding the Toolbox *is confusing on this point because it suggests that any approach to homelessness must be trauma-informed and tailored to unique needs, key features of the Housing First approach that the plan critiques. At the same time, the plan suggests that homeless people need to be pushed into mainstream housing and employment markets.*

Many promote housing first as the only tool needed in the toolbox. They believe the provision of housing only solves homelessness and housing first provides housing. On December 20, 2013, a Notice of Funding Availability (NOFA) from the Department of Housing and Urban Development formally prioritized housing first and for the first time formally funded rapid rehousing while reducing funding of transitional housing, which in turn dramatically altered the way federal homelessness assistance is allocated.

Unfortunately, shortly following the policy shift towards no preconditions or service participation requirements in homeless assistance, unsheltered homelessness rose from 175,399 in 2014 to 211,293 in 2019, a 20.5 percent increase in five years. Simultaneously, during this exact timeframe, the number of individuals receiving subsidized Rapid Rehousing and Permanent Supportive Housing vouchers rose from 338,065 to 482,254, a 42.7 percent increase in five years.

The housing first approach has produced concerning results. Advocates for housing first argue that increasing the number of subsidized vouchers and permanent supportive housing units decreases unsheltered homelessness. Yet unsheltered homelessness increased 20.5 percent while subsidized housing vouchers increased by 42.7 percent. Taken together, these facts suggest that the provision of subsidized or dedicated housing has not led to reducing the total population of people experiencing homelessness.

One significant feature of the housing first approach is the elimination of participation requirements in order to receive housing and assistance. housing first proponents argue issues such as sobriety, participation requirements and program compliance should not be a barrier to continuing to receive subsidized housing. Yet participation requirements may well be a key element to improved health and increased self-sufficiency, thus reducing the number of people experiencing homelessness.

The welfare policy reforms enacted in 1996 required program participation to receive government assistance. Pell grants require recipients to make satisfactory academic progress, take a full class-load and maintain a certain grade point average (GPA). Unemployment benefits require program participation, including demonstrated participation in prescriptive job searches. Temporary Assistance for Needy Families (TANF), which provides benefits to families in poverty, requires beneficiaries to work or advance their education.

A one-size-fits-all approach can actually harm many populations experiencing homelessness that need and benefit from customized, trauma-informed wraparound services. The federal toolbox must include approaches that respect the unique circumstances of each individual and family experiencing homelessness.

Our aspirational goals should expand our thinking to move beyond the basic goal of providing subsidized housing assistance. As Congress has suggested, we must optimize self-sufficiency through the reduction of reliance on public assistance and implement policies that pursue this as an end goal. Communities should prioritize projects that increase self-sufficiency. Regulatory constraints should be removed, and innovation should be encouraged. Program quality should be measured by reductions in homelessness and by increases in exits from any kind of subsidized housing to unsubsidized market rate housing.
(U.S. Interagency Council on Homelessness 2020, 9–12)

In addition to the lack of action steps to provide homeless people with housing and employment, Expanding the Toolbox *also misunderstands the goals and program requirements of Housing First. Nevertheless, the federal government still requires adherence to Housing First principles as a condition of funding and both HUD and the USICH have endorsed Housing First, as have all other pre-Trump administrations. The Trump administration's strategic plan was the first to blame Housing First for increasing homelessness and confuse its basic premise.*

Critiques of Housing First say that it has offered little funding and guidance toward implementation, and that it has produced inconsistent results in many communities. It is important to note, however, that Housing First in practice *diverges from Housing*

First in principle, *as established by the Pathways to Housing First (PHF) program. The basic principles of PHF are its emphasis on consumer choice, the provision of community-based support services, permanent scatter-site housing, and harm reduction (Padgett et al. 2016). The Housing First approach also has documented success in reducing veteran homelessness, which* Expanding the Toolbox *ignores entirely. Instead, the plan proposes reducing federal housing subsidies, without providing an immediate housing alternative, or a plan for offering services.*

In addition to its critique of Housing First, the 2020 USICH report decried the loss of about 100,000 transitional shelter beds and the increase of 112,961 rapid rehousing beds. These beds often serve different populations, however, and transitional shelter has had mixed reviews from researchers and advocates. Expanding the Toolbox *overlooks these facts, using these numbers to justify the claim that housing subsidies have not reduced homelessness.*

In reality, the connection between homelessness, employment, and housing is clear. If homeless people can access housing and employment, they will exit homelessness. The connection between homelessness, mental illness, and substance use disorders is also clear, as these risk factors are often barriers to exiting homelessness. To address these barriers, Expanding the Toolbox *suggested greatly expanding services. It mentioned offering intensive case management, developing trauma-informed care, and including people with lived experience being homeless. None of these suggestions were new to people or organizations that work to help the homeless or to the Housing First initiative, and no new funding streams or action plans for these efforts were identified.*

The remaining solutions that Expanding the Toolbox *high-lighted were equally vague. They include prevention, population-specific solutions, increased attention to racial disparities, and alternatives to criminalization. Veterans, children, youth, and families and unaccompanied women were specifically mentioned as categories of homeless people deserving of help, but no new funding streams, specific goals, or timelines for measuring progress in reducing homelessness among these populations were included.*

Instead, the strategic action listed under unaccompanied women is "As with other targeted groups, use focused research to develop effective strategies and tactics." Without any funding or direction to implement this strategy, the plan simply notes that the desired outcome is to "reduce the number of unaccompanied women experiencing homelessness."

The burden of ending racial disparities in homelessness was placed on "local service agencies," who "should actively examine existing policies and practices." The service system, in other words, is both blamed for and tasked with solving systemic racism as a contributor to homelessness. This means challenging long-standing inequalities in the U.S. housing market, employment, education, and wealth accumulation. Local stakeholders were also tasked by the report's authors with reducing recidivism among homeless people involved in the criminal justice system. The plan suggested cultivating partnerships, offering training for law enforcement and behavioral health officials to better respond to homeless people. Of course, no new funding streams or other types of support were outlined for any of these new and costly partnerships. Critics of Expanding the Toolbox *asserted that by suggesting these solutions for an already overburdened service system without providing additional financial or structural resources, the Trump administration was not genuinely interested in meaningfully addressing the issue of homelessness.*

Finally, the plan emphasized the need for emergency readiness in managing the COVID-19 crisis, as well as other potential national emergencies. Service providers to the homeless were tasked with establishing connections with local governments and with public health and emergency organizations and offering their own staff emergency training. This is the one solution in which the plan referenced USICH collaborations with the Centers for Disease Control and Prevention (CDC), ED, Federal Emergency Management Agency (FEMA), Department of Health and Human Services (HHS), HUD, U.S. Department of Agriculture (USDA), and other federal agencies. Despite these important partnerships, providing housing and shelter solutions to allow social distancing and stop the spread of COVID takes substantial funding. With the passage of the CARES Act in 2020, Congress and the Trump administration contributed millions to make emergency assistance a reality. Yet without ongoing funding and coordination across solutions and programs, they have little chance of success beyond the immediate crisis.

Out of Reach: National Low-Income Housing Coalition

The NLIHC report Out of Reach is released annually. The 2020 report was written in the context of the COVID-19 pandemic. It documents the significant and decades-long gap between average renter wages and the cost of housing in the United States. It acknowledges that systemic racism has locked many people of color out of affordable housing opportunities and their attendant resources, like quality education and health care. This inhibits their ability to live comfortably and to accumulate wealth. It also accounts for the overrepresentation of people of color in the homeless population and in low-paying, frontline jobs, primarily in customer service roles. In fact, across all income categories, wages for black and Latino workers are 24 percent to 25 percent below wages for white workers.

When businesses across the United States began to close in the early spring of 2020 because of COVID-19, about half of all lost jobs came from food- and travel-related services, retail, health care, and social assistance industries. Other low-paying jobs were deemed "essential," and these workers were expected to risk their lives for poverty wages. As the following excerpt indicates, existing inequity made these problems worse with the onset of COVID-19.

Even before the pandemic, more than 211,000 people in the U.S. were experiencing homelessness on sidewalks or other unsheltered locations (HUD, 2020). They face a considerably higher risk of becoming ill, and they have nowhere to self-quarantine and recover if they do.

Another 356,000 people were experiencing homelessness in emergency shelters, with limited ability to self-isolate. In addition, more than 2.7 million renters were living in overcrowded housing conditions, making social distancing from an ill housemate difficult.

As is true in almost every aspect of American life, the greatest risks are borne by people of color. Early research and reporting on COVID-19 shows people of color face greater mortality risks from the pandemic (Gross et al., 2020; Thebault, Tran, & Williams, 2020). Pre-existing structural injustices, including unequal access to health care, greater exposure through low-wage and frontline jobs, and limited housing options, contribute to these risks. Black Americans accounted for 13% of the U.S. population in 2019 but 40% of all people experiencing homelessness. People identifying as Hispanic or Latino were 18% of the overall population but 22% of the population experiencing homelessness (HUD, 2020). Similar disparities exist with overcrowding. Latino households accounted for 12% of all households (excluding interracial couples) but 43% of overcrowded households; Asian households accounted for 4% of all households but 10% of overcrowded households; and American Indian or Alaska Native households accounted for 0.5% of all households but 1% of overcrowded households. Such disproportionate rates of homelessness and overcrowding mean those groups are less able to self-isolate when needed.

The economic downturn spurred by the virus further increases the risk of housing instability for millions of low-wage renters at a time when stable housing is vital. Prior to the pandemic, more than 7.7 million extremely low-income renters were spending more than half of their limited incomes on housing costs, sacrificing other necessities to do so (NLIHC, 2020b). Millions of renters were one financial shock away from housing instability, and for many the pandemic and economic fallout is that shock. (National Low-Income Housing Coalition 2020, 1)

The report's title and contents emphasize the fact that housing in the United States is not affordable for most renters. The report illustrates a significant gap between what low-wage earners make, a renter's wage, and the actual cost of rental housing, a housing wage. Housing wages are the amount needed to rent a two-bedroom apartment, paying 30 percent of one's total income on rent and utilities. In twenty-one states and Puerto Rico, renter's wages lag behind housing wages. Workers in occupations that do not pay enough for rental housing make up 38 percent of the total U.S. workforce.

To afford rental housing, workers work longer hours, double up, or pay more than 30 percent of their income on rent. This is particularly true for black and Latino households, which are more likely to be renters. In times of crisis, low-wage workers are less able to weather financial setbacks like unemployment, which in turn heightens vulnerability to eviction. Both unemployment and eviction are leading contributors to homelessness. With over half a million people experiencing homelessness and 7.7 million renters spending over 50 percent of their income on housing costs, the United States was facing a major housing crisis even before COVID-19.

The Out of Reach *report found the nationwide average fair market rent for a one-bedroom apartment to be $1,017, while $1,246 was the average fair market rent for a two-bedroom apartment. People making minimum wage or relying on Supplemental Security Income (SSI) can afford $377 or $235, respectively, as individuals or sole wage earners in households. People receiving unemployment insurance, families of four making poverty level wages, and full-time workers earning the average rental wage of $18.22 also find themselves priced out of "average" rental housing. This means that over 40 percent of wage earners in the United States cannot afford a one-bedroom rental by themselves, and over 60 percent cannot afford a two-bedroom rental. Homeless people* *are often in the same boat with low-wage earners because of the overall lack of affordable rental housing. Moreover, given the additional challenges that homeless people may face, including trauma, mental illness, addiction, disability, inconsistent work history, and a lack of a permanent address, they are often last in line for available rentals.*

The report uses fair market rental prices to show the states with the largest shortfall between renter's wages and housing costs. The eight states with the largest shortfall are Hawaii, Maryland, California, New Jersey, Vermont, Massachusetts, Washington, and Connecticut. Of these states, only California, Washington, and Massachusetts also have large total homeless populations. Pictured in Table 5.2, these "high homeless" states, in bold, also have high housing costs. The income needed to secure stable rental housing, in other words, is simply out of reach for homeless people.

Using Out of Reach *data, Table 5.2 lists average wages for renters in each state and the wage needed to afford a fair market, two-bedroom rental. None of the high homeless states show average renters being able to afford a two-bedroom apartment if they spend only 30 percent of their income on housing and utilities. As a result, many renters pay more than 30 percent, go without paying other bills, or double up with others to afford basic housing. In four of ten states, there is a surplus difference between affordable rent and fair market rent (FMR) one-bedroom rentals. This means that in Texas, Pennsylvania, Georgia, and Ohio, renters have a better chance at affordable housing in some areas.* Out of Reach *also notes that there is considerable variation within and across states that is difficult to reflect in the report.*

For homeless people, as well as low-income and very low-income renters, available jobs don't always pay enough to afford fair market rental housing. To further complicate matters, there is no private market incentive to produce affordable housing, as higher rents allow for greater profits for property owners. The report concludes that additional government assistance is necessary to increase the nation's affordable housing stock, as most of the current HUD budget goes to funding existing housing renewal projects. It also suggests

Table 5.2 Affordability Data for Basic Housing

State	2BRM Wage	Renter's Wage	1BRM FMR	2BRM FMR	Affordable Rent	Monthly Shortfall 1BRM/2BRM	
California	$36.96	$23.96	$1,522	$1,922	$1,246	-$276	-$676
New York	$32.53	$25.68	$1,457	$1,691	$1,335	-$122	-$637
Florida	$24.43	$17.28	$1,027	$1,270	$898	-$129	-$372
Texas	$20.90	$19.56	$892	$1,087	$1,017	+$125	-$70
Washington	$30.46	$21.90	$1,286	$1,584	$1,139	-$147	-$445
Massachusetts	$35.52	$21.74	$1,498	$1,847	$1,131	-$367	-$716
Oregon	$24.37	$21.90	$1,046	$1,267	$872	-$174	-$395
Pennsylvania	$19.23	$15.90	$811	$1,000	$827	+$16	-$173
Georgia	$19.11	$21.74	$858	$994	$911	+$53	-$83
Ohio	$15.99	$14.42	$656	$832	$750	+$94	-$82

Source: National Low-Income Housing Coalition. 2020. Out of Reach: The High Cost of Housing.

fully funding the Housing Choice Voucher Program, known as Section 8, expanding the national Housing Trust Fund (HTF) to preserve and expand rental housing for extremely low-income renters and a federal investment in public housing. Additional solutions include support for Project-Based Rental Assistance (PBRA) for subsidized housing that is privately owned and reforming the Low-Income Housing Tax Credit to bolster the production of affordable housing. The final solution that the report suggests is developing a housing stabilization fund to weather the long-term effects of COVID-19 beyond the eviction moratorium.

Housing is a basic necessity—an essential ingredient of individual and public health, stability, and dignity. The COVID-19 crisis has demonstrated the recklessness of letting people's access to basic necessities like housing depend on the contingencies of the economy.

While the COVID-19 public health crisis and explosive growth in unemployment has triggered some immediate protections for some renters, far more must be accomplished to secure emergency rental assistance and to realize longer-term housing solutions. The federal eviction moratoriums for renters in federally-supported rental properties included in the CARES Act and other state and local moratoriums are important protections for renters during this crisis, but they provide a patchwork of temporary protections that exclude many renters. Many of these moratoriums are coming to an end. We need a uniform, national moratorium that would cover all renters.

Evictions moratoriums do not relieve renters of accrued debt from missed rental payments. Emergency rental assistance is needed to ensure renters can afford to remain stably housed at least until the economy begins to recover.

In the long run, Congress should create a permanent National Housing Stabilization Fund to provide emergency assistance to families who experience a sudden and temporary shock to their finances. Many low-wage workers live one financial emergency—like the sudden loss of income or unexpected medical expenses—away from housing instability. Temporary assistance would prevent evictions, housing instability, and, in the worse cases, homelessness by helping households stay in their homes during and after those unexpected events.

Addressing the roots of the housing affordability problem, however, requires a significant and sustained commitment to rental housing programs that provide long-term rental assistance to low-income renters, increase the affordable housing supply, and preserve the affordable rental homes that already exist. (National Low-Income Housing Coalition 2020, 9–10)

Out of Reach *embraces housing as a basic human right. The previous excerpt emphasizes the fact that CARES Act funding offers only temporary assistance, and the report cites studies indicating that at least twenty-four months of assistance are needed to keep low-income renters stably housed. The report underscores that the shortage of affordable housing is a well-documented, long-term crisis that existed before the pandemic. A longer-term solution is therefore needed to address it.* Out of Reach *also mentions several pending congressional initiatives designed to shore up long-term assistance and create funding streams to keep households stably housed during crisis times. Despite these productive actions, the report emphasizes that COVID-19 has exposed dramatic inequality within the U.S. economy that is directly tied to housing and shows no signs of abating.*

Housing Not Handcuffs: National Law Center on Homelessness and Poverty

Since 2006, the NLCHP has released a report titled Housing Not Handcuffs *on the state of criminalization laws targeting homeless people. The report uses municipal code data from 187 representative cities across the United States to examine the form and frequency of criminalization. Its central finding is that criminalization practices exacerbate cyclical poverty. They are destructive for people experiencing homelessness, illegal and costly for communities to enforce, and make surviving and exiting homelessness that much more difficult. Criminalization also perpetuates harmful stereotypes about homelessness that affect public opinion and advocacy efforts.*

Housing Not Handcuffs *identifies a variety of harmful practices that some communities engage in, from aggressive policing and sweeps on encampments to harsh regulations on food sharing. What is or is not permissible on city sidewalks, public parks, plazas, beaches, and other public spaces and facilities is determined by a sense of public order. Spelled out in cities' municipal codes, criminalization includes laws related to sleeping and camping, sitting, lying down, loafing, scavenging, and panhandling. People living without shelter are the most frequent recipients of citations related to such activities. Citations for these offenses have risen dramatically since 2006, the year of the first report. When tent cities are established in public parks, or homeless people panhandle on city streets, local communities often step up enforcement measures to reclaim those city spaces.*

Criminalization practices have risen since 2006 and, from 2016 to 2019, when the most recent reports were released. This increase coincides with the national increase in unsheltered homelessness. Table 5.3 represents the most common categories of offenses that homeless people are routinely cited for, as reported in Housing Not Handcuffs. *It shows the prevalence of these offenses in the 187 survey cities in 2019 and increases since the prior reports in 2016 and 2006. In addition to the offenses listed in Table 5.3, other common forms of criminalization documented in sample cities include illegal storing of personal property, rummaging/scavenging/dumpster diving, and public urination/defecation. The report notes that without access to basic needs facilities or access to private space or shelter, homeless people are at heightened risk of running afoul of these criminalization laws and doing so repeatedly.*

Table 5.3 Common Homeless Offenses: Laws Enacted in Sample Cities

Offenses in 187 Sample Cities	Frequency of Laws in 2019	Increase since 2006	Increase since 2016
Camping	72%	70%	15%
Sleeping (citywide)/ Particular places	51%	50%/29%	18%/44%
Sitting/Lying down	55%	78%	17%
Loitering/Loafing/ Vagrancy	35–60%	103%	10%
Begging	83%	103%	42%
Vehicles	50%	213%	31%

Source: National Law Center on Homelessness and Poverty. 2019. *Housing Not Handcuffs: Ending the Criminalization of Homelessness in US Cities.*

Some of the behaviors listed in Table 5.3, like sleeping, are biological necessities. Others, like sitting and lying down, are routine needs of sheltered and unsheltered alike. Part of the rationale for increasing criminalization is punishing homelessness as a lifestyle choice or a symbol of bad behavior, but the report notes the lack of shelter and housing opportunities for homeless people in many cities and towns as the reason for their presence in the first place. It also notes that in some cities, when shelters require participation in religious service or pose physical or mental health risks, homeless people avoid them. They do this for reasons of safety or personal autonomy, but they can be criminalized in the process. This is an important point, as it relates to the question of choice. If living unsheltered is the safer of two alternatives, is doing so truly a free choice or simply the lesser of two evils?

Housing Not Handcuffs *notes that common indicators of homelessness, such as surrounding oneself with all one's worldly possessions, are often used to justify the issuance of citations. Because few homeless people are able to safely store their possessions, they are often forced to take them wherever they go or store them in unauthorized encampments. In addition, when homeless camps are targeted for "sweeps" that remove them from specific city areas, people living in these camps can lose everything. Without documentation or identification, they are further at risk and less likely to be able to prove their identity, access benefits, or exit homelessness. The report notes that any legal involvement, civil or criminal, places homeless people at risk of further instability and can cause long-term problems accessing public benefits.*

Housing Not Handcuffs demonstrates that criminalization perpetuates the problem of homelessness instead of solving it. The report's main conclusions, excerpted next, also emphasize the multiple risk factors and forms of inequality that criminalization exacerbates.

Laws criminalizing homelessness are rooted in prejudice, fear, and misunderstanding, and serve businesses and housed neighbors over the needs of unhoused neighbors. It is critical for lawmakers, policy advocates, and other key stakeholders to understand the fundamental roots of laws criminalizing homelessness: ignorance of the causes of homelessness and deep-seated prejudice against and fear of people experiencing it. The inaccurate belief that homelessness is a result of poor life choices, mental illness, and/or drug addiction motivates public calls for punitive approaches to homelessness. Businesses and commercial entities also drive criminalization policies by lobbying for such laws and even by enforcing them with private security personnel.

The effects of criminalization are devastating to people and communities. Criminalization of homelessness contributes to mass incarceration and racial inequality, as homelessness is a risk factor for incarceration, and incarceration makes it more likely that a person will experience homelessness. Over-policing of homeless people, who are disproportionately people of color, also exacerbates racial inequality in our criminal justice system. Indeed, unhoused people of color are more likely to be cited, searched, and have property taken than white people experiencing homelessness. Those with multiple marginalized identities, like LGBTQ+ people of color, are even more vulnerable to homelessness and laws criminalizing homelessness.

Criminalization of homelessness results in fines and fees that perpetuate the cycle of poverty. Financial obligations, such as from fines for using a tent or vehicle to shelter oneself, can prolong the amount of time that a person will experience homelessness, and can also leave homeless people less able to pay for food, transportation, medication, or other necessities. Civil and court-imposed fines and fees can also prevent a person from being accepted into housing, or even result in their incarceration for failure to pay them.

Criminalization of homelessness harms public safety. Criminalization policies divert law enforcement resources from true street crime, clog our criminal justice system with unnecessary arrests, and fill already overcrowded jails. They also erode trust between homeless people and police, heightening the risk of violent confrontations between police and unhoused people, and leaving homeless people more vulnerable to private acts of violence without police protection. This is why the federal Department of Justice has filed statement of interest briefs and issued guidance arguing against the enforcement of criminalization ordinances in the absence of adequate alternatives.

Criminalization of homelessness and encampment evictions harm public health. City officials frequently cite concerns for public health as reason to enforce criminalization laws and/or to evict homeless encampments, a practice often referred to as a "sweep." But such practices threaten public health by dispersing people who have nowhere to discard food waste and trash, to expel bodily waste, or to clean themselves and their belongings to more areas of the city, but with no new services to meet their basic sanitation and waste disposal needs. Moreover, sweeps often result in the destruction of homeless people's tents and other belongings used to provide some shelter from the elements, cause stress, and cause loss of sleep, contributing to worsened physical and mental health among an already vulnerable population. Due to these harms, the American Medical Association and American Public Health Association have both condemned criminalization and sweeps in policy resolutions.

(National Law Center on Homelessness and Poverty 2019, 15)

The NLCHP identifies cities that are egregious in their pursuit of criminalization strategies and includes them in the report's "Hall of Shame." These cities include Ocala, Florida; Sacramento, California; Wilmington, Delaware; Kansas City, Missouri; and Redding, California. Many of the top offending counties are in California, which also has the largest number of unsheltered homeless people in the nation and the least affordable housing market. The report also notably calls out both the state of Texas and the U.S. government for adopting a punitive approach to homelessness. As the next excerpt indicates, the NLCHP charges that inadequate or punitive government policies have long caused and perpetuated the homeless crisis.

Dramatic cuts to federal funding for subsidized housing led to the modern homeless crisis, and today funding is so inadequate that only 1 in 4 people who are eligible for housing supports actually receives it. In September 2019, the Trump Administration's Council of Economic Advisers released a white paper claiming that homeless people remain so because they are "too comfortable" living on the streets, and calling for policing as a tool, "to help move people off the street and into shelter or housing . . ." Most worrisome is that this white paper appears to lay a policy basis for what Trump is reportedly considering—razing encampments and forcibly removing unhoused people off the streets to vacant federal properties . . . The federal government's disinvestment in subsidized housing, its reported plan to "crack down" on homelessness, and its failure to use the real property assets at its disposal to constructively address the homeless crisis earn the U.S. Government a place on our Hall of Shame.

(National Law Center on Homelessness and Poverty 2019, 59)

The 2019 report by the CEA, critiqued previously, is used in the Federal Strategic Plan, to justify a rejection of Housing First initiatives and federally subsidized housing. In contrast, Housing Not Handcuffs *contends that it is the inadequacy of federally funded subsidized housing, combined with deep socioeconomic inequality and systemic racism, that has led to the current crisis.*

In addition to harmful criminalization practices, the report contributes a summary of best practices that communities can adopt to end homelessness. Some of these are immediate solutions to address emergencies, and some are long-term policy approaches. They are designed to be "sensible, cost-effective, and humane," in contrast with criminalization, which the report describes as "cruel and unusual punishment." The first long-term approach that Housing Not Handcuffs *endorses is Housing First, or PSH. It notes that seventy-eight communities and three states have ended veteran homelessness using this approach. Several additional communities have used it to reduce chronic homelessness and save money on emergency services.*

A growing body of research comparing the cost of homelessness—including the cost of criminalization—with the cost of providing housing to homeless people shows that ending homelessness through housing is the most affordable option over the long run. Indeed, the provision of housing using a Housing First model, which focuses on providing people with quick access to housing and any needed services to maintain housing stability, is cheaper and achieves better outcomes than all other strategies for addressing homelessness. Each person housed is one less who needs to make their home on the streets, reducing the visible impacts of homelessness that housed residents and business owners complain to their elected officials about. Housing is a win for housed and unhoused persons alike.

(National Law Center on Homelessness and Poverty 2019, 72)

Other long-term approaches include expanding access to and funding for permanent affordable housing subsidies. The report also suggests maximizing the use of federal property to house and provide emergency services for homeless people through the Title V program of the McKinney-Vento Homeless Assistance Act. In addition, several local governments have effectively dedicated funding for housing and services through tax-based initiatives. The report suggests innovative approaches including so-called tiny homes, temporary encampments, and safe parking lots as intermediate, harm-reduction strategies for providing assistance to the homeless. Homeless prevention strategies to keep low-income renters from becoming homeless are also mentioned. In conclusion, the report's most important contribution is that it provides evidence of the inefficiency, cruelty, costliness, and inhumanity of criminalization practices as a strategy for reducing homelessness in the United States and suggests positive alternatives.

The Violence Against Women Act

The Violence Against Women Act (VAWA) was signed into law in 1994 by President Clinton. It is the first federal legislation to address various forms of domestic violence and violence against women. Before VAWA's passage, domestic violence was not taken seriously as a criminal justice issue, and rape victims lacked adequate protection; in some cases, rape victims were themselves subjected to more legal scrutiny than their attackers. In addition, perpetrators of violent crimes could often cross state lines to avoid legal prosecution.

Victims were also routinely discriminated against in the search for safe housing, leading to eviction and eventually homelessness.

To address these issues, VAWA held perpetrators accountable by increasing arrest rates and strengthening federal penalties for repeat sex offenders. It also included a federal "rape shield law," prohibiting questions about a victim's prior sexual history during rape trials. Today, programs made possible through VAWA focus on community and criminal justice responses to domestic violence, dating violence, sexual assault, and stalking. Occasionally, they also address prevention. Overall, VAWA changed the nation's view of violence against women and girls and various forms of domestic violence and expanded the tools available to law enforcement to prevent and punish these crimes.

Like other federal programs, VAWA distributes funding to states, tribal and local governments, nonprofit organizations, and universities. The Department of Justice oversees the Office on Violence against Women, which was created in 1995 to implement VAWA and to administer its grant program. Close to $4 billion has been awarded since then, with an additional $225 million awarded through the American Recovery and Reinvestment Act in 2009. Grant expenditures for FY2018 totaled $269 million. VAWA has been reauthorized three times, in 2000, 2005, and 2013, and its programs have expanded to include sexual assault and stalking and a focus on underserved populations. The primary data sources that inform VAWA are national data sets; the health-focused National Intimate Partner and Sexual Violence Survey (NISVS) and the criminal justice–focused National Crime Victimization Survey (NCVS).

This review of VAWA describes its evolution and explores how it affects people experiencing homelessness. Although responses to homelessness in the United States tend to dwell on alleged individual failings, it is important to note that many people are homeless as a direct result of the consequences of being victims of trauma and violence, not to mention systemic inequality and racism. As the 2018 report indicates next, housing insecurity also places victims at greater risk of domestic and sexual violence, trauma, and homelessness.

Women and men who have experienced housing insecurity are at higher risk for rape, physical violence, or stalking. NISVS found that 10% of women and 8% of men who faced housing insecurity were victims of intimate partner violence, as compared with 2.3% of women and 3.1% of men who did not face housing insecurity (Breiding, Chen, & Black, 2014). Housing instability is a strong predictor of poor health outcomes for those in abusive relationships, exacerbating PTSD, depression, substance abuse, medical noncompliance, absences from work and/or school, and hospital/emergency room use (Daoud et al., 2016; Rollins et al., 2012).

Shelter and transitional housing programs that support victims in escaping abuse can help remove barriers to long-term housing security. They may also provide follow-up support, counseling and advocacy, legal assistance, financial literacy education and employment counseling, and referrals to other sources of help. In fact, helping victims find stable housing requires addressing interconnected issues related to trauma, poverty, disabilities, and discrimination, and an advocate may spend up to 10 hours or more per week with each victim (Sullivan, López-Zerón, Bomsta, & Menard, 2018). Women who reside in a shelter tend to receive a broader range of support services for a longer period of time, compared to women who never enter a shelter (Grossman & Lundy, 2011; Sullivan & Virden, 2017b). A recent study found that the amount of help received in a shelter positively influenced victims' ability to advocate for themselves and their hopefulness for the future (Sullivan & Virden, 2017a).

VAWA-funded transitional housing bridges the gap between emergency and permanent housing. Programs offer a wide range of services (e.g., case management, child care, financial assistance, therapy, job and education development, parenting groups, etc.) to help victims establish self-sufficiency. Housing units are either owned or rented by the programs, from local housing authorities or private landlords. Programs may provide housing at no cost to the victim or provide subsidies to offset rental costs, and may pay all or portions of required deposits, utilities, and phone services. Residents are generally permitted to remain in transitional housing units from six months to two years and are typically required to establish goals to work toward economic stability.

(U.S. Department of Justice 2018, 35)

To examine how VAWA serves homeless people, it is important to note that domestic violence is commonly understood to be a direct cause of homelessness. On a given night in 2019, approximately 48,000 homeless service beds were set aside for survivors of domestic violence across the United States. One study found that 38 percent of all domestic violence victims become homeless at some point in their lives (Baker et al. 2003). Women experiencing domestic violence are often unable to return to their homes or find affordable housing. They are more likely to be evicted or to be turned away from housing because landlords discriminate against them and fear perpetrators. The National Center for Children in Poverty estimates that over 80 percent of homeless mothers with children previously experienced domestic violence. Women seeking shelter are also often being pursued and harassed by their abusers, making confidentiality paramount.

VAWA created the National Domestic Violence Hotline in 1996, for anyone affected by domestic and intimate partner violence. It operates 24/7, is completely confidential, and works to empower victims, assist perpetrators in finding treatment for their abusive conduct, and keep people safe. The hotline receives over 20,000 calls per month, with increases during times of crisis. Like the hotline, women's shelters must also adhere to strict protocols to ensure safety and confidentiality. But without an adequate supply of beds, survivors and their children are often at risk of ongoing violence and trauma. Women of color, immigrants, and indigenous women all face additional risks of violence that VAWA attempts to address. In so doing, VAWA acknowledges the systemic inequality and racism that have pervaded both patterns of abuse and policy responses.

Women are the most frequent victims of domestic violence, although the law has expanded to protect other categories. When VAWA was reauthorized in 2000 and 2005, it expanded protections for victims of dating violence. Communities of color, immigrant women, LGBTQ people, and tribal and native communities all received additional protections. There are approximately 23 million immigrant girls and women in the United States. Under VAWA, victims of domestic violence who are immigrants are able to petition for legal status. In 2005, additional provisions were added to VAWA to help combat cyberstalking.

In 2013, VAWA was reauthorized again, with changes that expand protections against domestic violence to include "intimate partners" as well as spouses. VAWA's reach was also expanded to provide protections to people who had suffered violence or harassment as a result of their religion, sexual orientation, or gender identity. VAWA reaffirmed its commitment to respecting cultural competence as well. For example, the 2013 VAWA reauthorization granted American Indian tribes authority to issue and enforce their own personal protection orders, called "special domestic violence criminal jurisdiction" (SDVCJ). Finally, among the 2013 changes most relevant to homeless people is the addition of housing provisions. VAWA extended eviction protection measures for female tenants, required the provision of safe transfer emergency housing units, and added employment assistance to the possible list of services.

A 2018 report on grants received through VAWA shows that although communities identify ongoing challenges, the reach and scope of VAWA are impressive.

Between July 1, 2015, and June 30, 2017, VAWA discretionary grant programs funded more than 2,000 grantees and technical assistance providers. Over one million services were provided to victims and their families as they coped with the immediate and long-term impact of violence in their lives, helping victims remain safe and establish independence after leaving an abusive relationship, and connecting victims with resources to support their recovery. During each six-month reporting period, on average, VAWA-funded grantees provided 112,302 individuals with supportive services such as shelter, crisis intervention, and advocacy.

VAWA-funded grantees used funds to train 714,768 service providers, criminal justice personnel, and other professionals to improve their response to victims. More than 1.2 million individuals participated in VAWA-funded education, awareness, or prevention activities. Law enforcement made 48,413 arrests, and courts disposed of 3,139 criminal cases, of which 38% resulted in convictions.

(U.S. Department of Justice 2018, 67)

As this report shows, the criminal justice response to domestic violence has been positively influenced by VAWA. More police officers and people at all levels of the criminal justice system have been offered domestic and sexual violence training. This has resulted in greater rates of prosecutions and convictions and longer sentences for violent crimes against women, girls, and other groups protected by the law.

VAWA was reauthorized in 2021, after a brief lapse in 2018. It reaffirms the nation's commitment to addressing various forms of domestic violence and expanding protections to underserved communities. It also acknowledges the direct connection between homelessness, housing and economic insecurity, and domestic violence.

Studies find that 60 percent of single women lack economic security and 81 percent of households with single mothers live in economic insecurity. Significant barriers that survivors confront include access to housing, transportation, and child care. Ninety-two percent of homeless women have experienced domestic violence, and more than 50 percent of such women cite domestic violence as the direct cause for homelessness. Survivors are deprived of their autonomy, liberty, and security, and face tremendous threats to their health and safety.

(Violence Against Women Act Reauthorization Act of 2021)

The Coronavirus Aid, Relief, and Economic Security Act

The CARES Act was signed into law in March 2020 (H. R. 748, Public Law 116–136). It allocated $2.2 trillion in economic stimulus funding to offset the economic effects of the pandemic. The CARES Act provided $12 billion in funding for programs and services related to homelessness, just over one-fourth of the total amount for homeless services in 2019. CARES Act funding paid for direct services, shelter, and housing for people currently experiencing homelessness. It also provided assistance for families and individuals facing unemployment and eviction because of the crisis.

The drive to provide assistance during crisis times illustrates an unfortunate irony about homeless assistance in the United States: there is a way but not the will. Providing a universal basic income or a guaranteed right to housing is possible. Achieving this level of social stability for the entire population is undermined only by the lack of a will to do so. The current pandemic shows that when the entire population is at risk, change is possible. But more often in the United States, only certain groups are considered worthy of an investment of resources. Others must submit to complicated means tests or receive only temporary assistance. In the latter case, assistance comes only when there is a threat to the general population or when money can be saved by offering housing over shelter. The CARES Act, like many economic stimulus plans or solutions developed while in crisis, offers temporary assistance. What happens to homeless people when the economy bounces back?

Understanding the impact of the CARES Act on homeless people is difficult because it is primarily designed for the general population. It must, therefore, encompass people at risk of homelessness as well as those already experiencing it. It must address the precipitant crises of inadequate housing, unemployment, systemic racism, and risks to public health. Funding for homelessness is distributed through several forms of existing federal assistance. Community Development Block Grants (CDBG) fund programs that bolster support services as well as permanent and transitional housing. CDBG money also funds public improvement programs. The CARES Act authorized an additional $5 billion in CDBG funding for a wide range of activities. As the Urban Institute reports, "Exactly how CDBG funds will be used for COVID-19 is unclear. Slightly more than half of CDBG expenditures in 2019 went toward public improvements, public services, and economic development activities, and communities may fund those activities first" (Gerken and Boshart 2020, 4).

The CARES Act also includes $4 billion in additional funding for emergency shelters through the Emergency Shelter Grant (ESG) Program. Of this amount, $40 million goes to technical assistance, and the remaining money is allocated based on a formula that attempts to determine risk and need. Communities with large homeless populations and unaffordable housing markets could see the largest amounts. Although there is no data yet on how CARES funding has actually been distributed, the amount for ESG funding exceeds the 2019 allotment roughly fourteen times over (Gerken and Boshart 2020). Although this is a significant expenditure, it is being spent on homeless people because they are seen as personally at risk and as a risk to public health.

The emergency food and shelter program also received $200 million in CARES Act funding. This program is administered by the FEMA. Funding is distributed to states prioritized by rates of unemployment. Eligible costs include medical care, noncongregate shelter expenses, food distribution, and communication and safety *measures including personal protective equipment (PPE). Like the ESG Program described previously, this funding is intended to manage a short-term emergency. Once the immediate crisis is averted, funding will return to pre-pandemic levels. This is an important point to consider, as this book has discussed the dangers of neglecting long-term planning. Unsheltered homelessness and unaffordable housing were already reaching crisis levels before the pandemic. After COVID-19, the need will be even greater for permanent solutions to ensure these basic provisions for all.*

The coronavirus poses a threat to many renters, who may not be able to afford rental payments. Federal housing programs that serve homeless people include tenant- and project-based rental assistance and public housing. The CARES Act offers $2.25 billion for project- and tenant-based rental assistance and $685 million for public housing. These costs are split among the various administrative functions associated with preparing for the pandemic. They may also cover rental income for households that are unemployed during the pandemic. Because of the dramatic risk posed to current and future unemployment, increased assistance will be needed to cover these programs for a longer period of time. Other solutions include a universal voucher program or the suspension of rental payments. These solutions are costlier to implement but would address both the emergency and the long-term nature of the problem.

Some of the provisions outlined in the CARES Act were extended through the American Rescue Plan Act (ARP), signed into law on March 11, 2021. The plan includes approximately $50 billion in resources to address homelessness, including housing. As the NLIHC reports, $27 billion in rental and utility assistance will eliminate some of the debt accumulated by renters unable to cover these costs because of COVID-19. Since the beginning of the pandemic through March 2021, roughly $85 million has been allocated for homeless assistance and emergency housing. At the time of this writing, FEMA reports that only three states, California, Connecticut, and North Carolina, received approval to support noncongregate sheltering. Under the ARP, FEMA reimburses states for 100 percent of these expenses. As data on funding and outcomes *emerges, it will be important to consider the levels and demographics of inequality, which already put the nation's low-income people, homeless people, and people of color at risk.*

References

Baker, Charlene K., Sarah L. Cook, and Fran H. Norris. 2003. "Domestic Violence and Housing Problems." *Violence Against Women* 9(7): 754–783.

Council of Economic Advisers. 2019. "The State of Homelessness in America." Executive Office of the President of the United States.

Gerken, Matthew and Abby Boshart. 2020. "The CARES Act Supports Key Programs, but More Is Needed Soon." The Urban Institute: Metropolitan Housing and Communities Policy Center.

National Law Center on Homelessness and Poverty. 2019. *Housing Not Handcuffs: Ending the Criminalization of Homelessness in US Cities*. Washington, DC: National Law Center on Homelessness and Poverty.

National Low-Income Housing Coalition. 2020. *Out of Reach: The High Cost of Housing*. Washington, DC: National Low-Income Housing Coalition.

Padgett, Donald K., Bruce F. Henwood, and Sam J. Tsemberis. 2016. *Housing First: Ending Homelessness, Transforming Systems, and Changing Lives*. New York: Oxford University Press.

U.S. Congress, Senate, Committee on Small Business and Entrepreneurship. 2020. *Coronavirus Aid, Relief, and Economic Security Act*. 116th Cong., 2d sess., March 19.

U.S. Department of Housing and Urban Development. 2020a. *Annual Homeless Assessment Report to Congress*. Washington, DC: Office of Community Planning and Development.

U.S. Department of Housing and Urban Development. 2020b. *National Summary of Homeless System Performance 2015–2019*. Washington, DC: U.S. Department of Housing and Urban Development.

U.S. Department of Housing and Urban Development. 2021. *Annual Homeless Assessment Report to Congress*. Washington, DC: Office of Community Planning and Development.

U.S. Department of Justice. 2018. *2018 Biennial Report: The 2018 Biennial Report to Congress on the Effectiveness of Grant Programs under the Violence Against Women Act*. Washington, DC: Office of Violence Against Women.

U.S. Interagency Council on Homelessness. 2010. *Opening Doors: Federal Strategic Plan to Prevent and End Homelessness*. Washington, DC: U.S. Interagency Council on Homelessness.

U.S. Interagency Council on Homelessness. 2020. *Expanding the Toolbox: The Whole-of-Government Response to Homelessness*. Washington, DC: U.S. Interagency Council on Homelessness.

Violence Against Women Act Reauthorization Act of 2021, H.R. 1620 – 117th Congress (2021–2022).

This chapter includes resources about homelessness that roughly correspond with the crisis points discussed in the first chapter. It offers important avenues for further research on the controversies reviewed in Chapter 2 and perspectives outlined in Chapter 3. It also includes websites with additional resources from government and national sources that correspond with the profiles included in Chapter 4. The most common sources are research books and articles from sociological and historical perspectives. Other fields within the humanities and social sciences are also represented.

Although this book focuses in the most detail on the overall homeless population, this chapter includes sources that focus on specific subpopulations. It offers avenues for further research on the risks and challenges of homelessness that unique subpopulations face and explores innovative solutions. For authors or organizations with multiple works on a specific topic, the most important or seminal works are included as a starting point for further research.

This chapter begins with an overview of sources written about hoboing and itinerant labor. It includes research on women, people of color, and boy and girl tramps. It features historical sources that detail the emergence of the hobo as a social category and sociological sources that examine the hobo's place in

Homeless people line up to receive food. Providing food for homeless people is one of the most generous and long-standing forms of assistance in the United States. (Wieslaw Jarek/Dreamstime.com)

the world. These books and articles examine the work and leisure patterns of hobos and their urban and jungle homes. Some
sociological sources use participant observation to explore the
meaning of hobo life, along with those experiencing it. Including diverse sources, time periods, and populations, this section
provides avenues for additional understanding of homelessness
in the early 1900s.

As public awareness of homelessness surged in the 1980s,
a fast-growing body of literature emerged to examine why it
became a crisis and what could be done to solve it. The sources
included here outline the distinction between "old" and "new"
homelessness that defined the era. New homelessness can be
distinguished from old because of differences in population size
and demographics, occupation of city spaces, and public perception of homelessness. Sources in this section focus on structural, societal-level causes of the crisis. They include works on
individual subpopulations and the unique circumstances they
face, as well as the challenges involved in establishing a reliable,
national estimate of the number of homeless people. Finally,
this section describes several proposals to end homelessness,
including Housing First programs and trauma-informed care.
These solutions have their roots in this era but remain viable to
the present.

Although this chapter is grouped into sections that correspond with specific time periods, they are loose groupings.
Sources that are published outside of a specific time frame are,
in some cases, included because of their importance or coverage of a particular subject. Sources can also be published in
retrospect but cover an earlier time period of interest. Current
sources included in this chapter are those published after 2000
and more often after 2010. They offer general reference materi-
als and outline current approaches in the field. Although there
is consensus on many of these issues in policy, advocacy, and
research circles, this chapter includes differing perspectives on
what can be done to solve the crisis. This chapter concludes
with brief profiles of the federal organizations and national
nonprofit agencies presented in Chapter 4. It offers links to

each agency's website and outlines specific resources and publications of interest, for further research.

Homelessness in the Early 1900s

Anderson, Nels. 1923. *The Hobo: The Sociology of the Homeless Man*. Chicago: University of Chicago Press.
> Nels Anderson was part of the early Chicago School of Sociology. In *The Hobo*, he uses participant observation to understand the lifestyle of the hobo in the early 1900s. His study details life on Skid Row as well as in the more rugged hobo jungles. Other publications by Anderson include *Men on the Move* and *The Milk and Honey Route* (as Dean Stiff). Those sources focus on the hobo's employment patterns and social life.

Berry, Chad. 2000. *Southern Migrants, Northern Exiles*. Chicago: University of Illinois Press.
> This historical account describes the out-migration of white workers from southern states during the Great Depression. Calling it the "great white migration," Berry uses the firsthand accounts of workers describing their struggle to survive and prosper in the north. This is an important companion to sources on hobos as it describes the plight of white, working-class, southern families and seasonal workers.

Bruns, Roger A. 1980. *Knights of the Road: A Hobo History*. New York: Methuen.
> This book uses newspapers, interviews, and a variety of archival material to illustrate hobo life. It chronicles the dangers and adventures of life riding the rails from the late 1800s to the Great Depression. In addition, it documents life on Skid Row and the opportunities and amenities available to hobos during the aforementioned era of American history. It also includes a glossary of hobo terms.

Caplow, Theodore. 1940. "Transiency as a Cultural Pattern." *American Sociological Review* 5(5): 731–739.

This article examines the reasons for hoboing, or what the author calls "transiency." It relies on the author's experience riding the rails in 1939, including 1,200 contacts with hobos. A prominent sociologist, Caplow examines the position of the hobo in society, as well as the socio-economic conditions that created the hobo. Hobos are categorized as a social group according to their work, mobility, and public perception of them in society.

Chambliss, William. 1964. "A Sociological Analysis of the Law of Vagrancy." *Social Problems* 12(1): 67–77.

This article provides a brief history of vagrancy law. Chambliss' main contention is that laws are responsive to vagrants as social types. He suggests that vagrancy law is at least partially dependent on economic interests. The law is either enforced or dormant, on this basis. This article makes an early contribution to literature on the criminalization of homelessness.

Cresswell, Tim. 2001. *The Tramp in America*. London: Reaktion Books.

This book explores the nation's understanding of the hobo as a unique social type. It describes the range of public responses to hobos, ranging from fear to sympathy. Cresswell examines how hobos were portrayed as both comic and tragic figures. He also describes how the nation's view of hoboing changed over time as hobo populations dwindled.

DePastino, Todd. 2003. *Citizen Hobo: How a Century of Homelessness Shaped America*. Chicago: University of Chicago Press.

This book offers a meticulously detailed historical account of the early heyday of the American hobo, from the late 1800s to the 1980s. It tracks the rise of Skid Row and hobohemia and examines the positive and negative aspects of hobo life and culture. DePastino also shows how stereotypes about hoboing and changes in the American economy led to the crisis of homelessness in the 1980s.

Flynt, Josiah. 1972 [1899]. *Tramping with Tramps: Studies and Sketches of Vagabond Life.* Patterson, NJ: Smith Publishing.
Flynt is a sociologist who traveled with tramps in the late 1800s. This source offers early historical detail and is an important precursor to hobo literature during the Great Depression. It helps situate the 1930s hobo within a tradition of transiency that included both children and European immigrants. Flynt provides detail on the appearance, travel, culture, and language of early tramps and hobos.

Garon, Paul and Gene Tomko. 2006. *What's the Use of Walking if There's a Freight Train Going Your Way? Black Hoboes and Their Songs.* Chicago: Charles H. Kerr Publishing.
Garon and Tomko provide an eloquent description of the lives of black hobos in the early 1900s. Using letters, stories, and song lyrics, this book explores their struggles and triumphs through the emergence of the blues, among other musical genres. It describes the unique and threatening conditions black hobos faced and situates them within the overall context of hobo life.

Gravelle, Randal. 2015. *Hooverville and the Unemployed: Seattle during the Great Depression.* Randal Gravelle.
This book provides a firsthand look at people who lost their jobs and their homes during the Great Depression. It offers an overview of the structure and hierarchy of the Depression-era shanty towns, known as Hoovervilles. The book is primarily situated in Seattle, the birthplace of the term "skid row." Gravelle describes how people who found themselves trapped without employment prospects often ended up in Hooverville. This book champions the

spirit of the newly unemployed as they struggled to regain a foothold in the Depression-era economy.

Gregory, James N. 1989. *American Exodus: The Dust Bowl Migration and Okie Culture in California*. New York: Oxford University Press.

This source examines migration out of the Dust Bowl in the 1930s. Gregory describes the economic crisis that hit midwestern agricultural families and their search for employment in California. Its focus on poverty among families illustrates the pervasiveness of poverty and want that characterized this era.

Hall, Joanne. 2010. "'Sisters of the Road?' The Construction of Female Hobo Identity in the Autobiographies of Ethel Lynn, Barbara Starke, and 'Box-Car' Bertha Thompson." *Women's Studies* 39: 215–237.

This article examines the world of female hobos through three famous accounts, one of them written by Benjamin Reitman, the "hobo doctor." Hall's review of the books by Lynn and Starke, which are firsthand accounts of their experiences hoboing, shows how these authors protected themselves from charges of immorality while portraying the dangers of the road. By contrast, Hall found that Reitman's reading of Boxcar Bertha emphasizes her sexuality, presenting a deviant and sensationalized image of female hobos from a man's perspective. Hall's overview situates the female hobo within societal understandings of women in the early 1900s.

Higbie, Frank T. 2003. *Indispensable Outcasts: Hobo Workers and Community in the American Midwest, 1880–1930*. Chicago: University of Illinois Press.

This source examines the lifestyle and work patterns of hobos in the Midwest. It offers an overview of the tenuous position of the hobo in society as both indispensable worker and feared menace. Higbie describes labor organizing among hobos and their association with the Industrial Workers of the World. The emphasis on labor organizing and resistance makes this work an important contribution to the literature on hobo life.

Johnson, Roberta A. 2010. "African Americans and Homelessness: Moving through History." *Journal of Black Studies* 40(4): 583–605.

This article provides a history of the experience of hoboing and homelessness for African Americans. It covers a vast time period, from colonial times to the 1980s. Johnson's book is an important contribution to the literature, as the African American experience is often left out, minimized, or misunderstood.

Kerr, Daniel R. 2011. *Derelict Paradise: Homelessness and Urban Development in Cleveland, Ohio*. Amherst: University of Massachusetts Press.

Set in Cleveland, Ohio, this book traces the origins and development of the modern homeless shelter system. Kerr compares early responses to homelessness and hoboing, from the late 1800s through the post–World War II era while also examining Cleveland's struggle to make itself attractive to tourists and businesses. This article shows how homeless people and advocates organize to resist marginalization.

Kusmer, Kenneth L. 2002. *Down and Out, On the Road*. New York: Oxford University Press.

Kusmer offers a social history of homelessness in American society. Beginning with the emergence of tramps and hobos in the mid- to late 1800s, this book explains their life and work patterns. It also details changes in the composition of the homeless population over time and explores the causes and consequences of homelessness.

Above all, Kusmer sees homeless people as sharing main-stream societal goals and suggests that viewing them as deviant is a barrier to their inclusion in American life.

Lennon, John. 2014. *Boxcar Politics: The Hobo in U.S. Culture and Literature, 1869–1956*. Amherst: University of Massachusetts Press.

Lennon describes the evolution of the hobo, from a feared menace to a nostalgic figure. He examines how the mobility of the hobo was a political act, symbolic of the critique of capitalism and wage labor. Viewing railroad cars as political spaces, Lennon describes the eventual demise of what he calls boxcar politics.

Minehan, Thomas. 1934. *Boy and Girl Tramps of America*. Philadelphia: Holt, Rinehart, and Winston, Inc.

Minehan's book is a sociological study of the lives of girls and boys who traveled as hobos in the early 1900s. He relies on over 500 case histories and thousands of contacts with children and youth that he collected while traveling through six states, spending over two years in the field. He describes the brutal reality of the dangers children faced. Minehan sees these children as a product of industrial development and economic hardship. Ultimately, he advocates for strategies that can return them to their homes and to a life of future prosperity.

Monkkonen, Eric H., ed. 1984. *Walking to Work: Tramps in America, 1790–1935*. Lincoln: University of Nebraska Press.

This book offers a collection of essays that describe the lives of tramps and industrial workers from the late eighteenth century through the heart of the Great Depression. It details the various trade professions associated with tramping and explores union organizing among tramps. It also examines regional variations in tramping, the mobility of this lifestyle, and the benefits and risks of transient labor.

Park, Robert E. 1967. "The Mind of the Hobo: Reflections upon the Relation between Mentality and Locomotion." In *The City*, eds. Robert E. Park and Ernest W. Burgess, 156–160. Chicago: University of Chicago Press.

In this article, prominent sociologist Robert Park examines hobo mobility. He evaluates whether or not the condition known as "wanderlust" is, in fact, a pathology. He notes that traveling and movement are usually associated with intelligence and creativity, but that despite this, the hobo has not contributed to society and lacks specific goals, other than temporary employment.

Reed, E. and E. Potter. 1934. *Federal Transient Program: An Evaluative Survey, May to July, 1934*. New York: The Committee on Care of Transient and Homeless.

This book offers a review of the Federal Transient Program, a social welfare program designed to assist itinerant people during the Great Depression. This program addressed widespread unemployment and people drifting in search of work. It provided assistance for people who resided in a particular state for less than twelve months. It also offered jobs and resources for unskilled workers, in an attempt to reintegrate them into community life. This book examines the structure and efficacy of the Federal Transient Program and makes recommendations for its continuance.

Reitman, Ben. 2002 [1937]. *Sister of the Road: The Autobiography of Boxcar Bertha*. Oakland, CA: AK Press/NABAT.

This book examines the life of a female hobo known as "Boxcar Bertha." It is a controversial book because it is an imagined account written by Reitman, based on his knowledge of female hobos. Reitman was an anarchist who began a Hobo College in Chicago and was known for a time as "King of the Hobos," or "the hobo doctor" because of the medical assistance he provided to the poor. In this book, he delves into the underworld that women on the road often experienced. He describes Bertha's radical upbringing and her life on America's margins, including her work in brothels.

Shaw, Clifford. 1930. *The Jack-Roller: A Delinquent Boy's Own Story*. Chicago: University of Chicago Press.
Shaw offers a unique, firsthand account of a young boy who lived life on the road in the 1920s. This book describes what attracts him to Skid Row and his immersion in the lifestyle he encountered there. It examines his family life, his experience with correctional institutions, and why he chose an itinerant lifestyle over other alternatives.

Starke, Barbara. 1931. *Touch and Go*. London: Jonathan Cape Ltd.
Barbara Starke offers a firsthand account of her journey across the country in the 1920s. She leaves her home in New England, escaping the constraints of her upbringing, and she is innocent to the dangers of the road. As a result, although she sees the seedier side of hobo life, she does not become a part of it. Rather, Starke's account suggests that there is more to female hoboing than sexuality. Her ability to survive depends on how she interacts with the world, demonstrating a kind of agency rarely discussed in the literature on female hobos.

Tapley, Heather. 2014. "The Making of Hobo Masculinities." *Canadian Review of American Studies* 44 (1): 25–43.
In this article, Tapley describes the perceived threat to white masculinity that occurs with the economic depressions in the late 1800s and early 1900s. It views hobos as a symbolic challenge to prevailing ideas of successful manhood. Hobos are also seen as struggling to counter the idea that they are deviant or unproductive. In so doing, they end up reproducing exclusion by pushing out women and men of color. This source is an important challenge to the claim that hobo culture was ultimately more inclusive than mainstream society.

Uys, Erroll L. 1999. *Riding the Rails: Teenagers on the Move during the Great Depression*. New York: TV Books.

> This book uses thousands of letters, questionnaires, and detailed interviews to describe the experience of riding the rails during the Great Depression. It includes descriptions of Skid Row, catching trains, and the dangers and freedoms of hobo life. It also details the experiences of young girls as well as boys, African American as well as white hobos, making a needed contribution to the literature.

Wyman, Mark. 2010. *Hoboes, Bindlestiffs, Fruit Tramps, and the Harvesting of the West*. New York: Hill and Wang.

> In this detailed history, Wyman describes the journey of hobos engaged in transient labor throughout the Pacific Northwest, Texas, and California in the early 1900s. He discusses the crops they picked and the conditions of their labor. He includes the experiences of men, women, and children and includes maps to illustrate the routes they traveled.

Homelessness in the 1980s and 1990s

Bahr, Howard. 1973. *Skid Row: An Introduction to Disaffiliation*. New York: Oxford University Press.

> One of three books Bahr released on disaffiliation in the 1970s, this one describes how men on Skid Row become alienated from society. Bahr's other books include the edited volume *Disaffiliated Man: Essays and Bibliography on Skid Row, Vagrancy, and Outsiders* and *Old Men Drunk and Sober*, authored with Theodore Caplow.

Baumohl, Jim, ed. For the National Coalition for the Homeless. 1996. *Homelessness in America*. Phoenix, AZ: Oryx Press.

> This edited volume offers a comprehensive overview of the causes of homelessness and its history in U.S. society. Experts in the field examine the evolving definition of homelessness and promising solutions. Many articles

examine the emerging field of homeless advocacy, as well as policy changes, that occurred in the 1980s.

Baxter, Ellen and Kim Hopper. 1981. *Private Lives/Public Spaces: Homeless Adults on the Streets of New York City*. New York: Community Service Society.

This book offers a portrayal of homeless men and women in New York City. Based on fifteen months of research, it explores the survival strategies that homeless adults use to survive. It examines pathways into homelessness and challenges stereotypical ideas about homeless people. One of the first books to present the realities of shelter life, this book is an important contribution to a tradition of advocacy research.

Burt, Martha. 1992. *Over the Edge: The Growth of Homelessness in the 1980s*. New York: Russell Sage Foundation.

Burt provides one of the most important and well-researched accounts of homelessness in the 1980s. Through extensive review of socioeconomic conditions in 147 cities, Burt critically examines the causes of homelessness. She shows that increases in homelessness signify larger changes in U.S. society. For this reason, homelessness persists, as wealth at the top continues to accumulate.

Cress, Daniel M. and David A. Snow. 1996. "Mobilization at the Margins: Resources, Benefactors, and the Viability of Homeless Social Movement Organizations." *American Sociological Review* 61: 1089–1109.

This article examines the resources needed to begin and sustain social movements among homeless people. Using ethnographic data from eight cities and fifteen different social movement organizations, this research looks at their long-term viability. It examines specific resources that facilitate and sustain homeless social movements. It also examines issues of voice and control, noting the frequency with which homeless people are marginalized in organizations and movements that purport to help them.

Dear, Michael and Jennifer Wolch. 1987. *Landscapes of Despair.* Princeton, NJ: Princeton University Press.

In this groundbreaking book, Dear and Wolch examine the idea of service-dependent ghettos for homeless people. They examine the consequences of deinstitutionalization, as it contributed to homelessness among people experiencing mental illness. This book suggests that the poor and marginalized often become trapped in urban spaces, in settings that reaffirm their marginality and dependence.

DeHavenon, Anna L., ed. 1999. *There's No Place Like Home: Anthropological Perspectives on Housing and Homelessness in the United States.* Westport, CT: Bergin & Garvey.

This book examines various forms of urban and rural housing for homeless people that emerged in the 1980s. Through detailed anthropological research, the authors examine the use of huts as housing, doubling up as a way of avoiding homelessness and shelter, and how various communities respond to their homeless populations. The authors examine the structural causes that led to homelessness and suggest a greater focus on health and employment to assist the population. This book proves the need for strategies that support emergency shelter options as well as long-term affordable housing.

Dordick, G. 1997. *Something Left to Lose: Personal Relations and Survival among New York's Homeless.* Philadelphia: Temple University Press.

Dordick uses participant observation to examine the resources and risks associated with various forms of homeless housing in New York City. She discovers the inner workings of a range of shelter types, from train stations and shanty towns to emergency and private shelters. She also examines the social relationships, survival strategies, and power dynamics that exist in each setting.

Erickson, John and Charles Wilhelm, eds. 1986. *Housing the Homeless*. New Jersey: Center for Urban Policy Research.

This book is a collection of articles that examine prevalent images of homeless people in the 1980s. It explores the causes of homelessness, particularly in New York City, emphasizing the impact of structural changes in urban areas. Experts on homelessness are included as authors throughout, offering solutions to the current issues and an outline of the federal response.

Failer, Judith L. 2002. *Who Qualifies for Rights? Homelessness, Mental Illness, and Civil Commitment*. Ithaca, NY: Cornell University Press.

This book explores the controversial case of Joyce Brown, a woman fighting involuntary commitment because of mental illness. Failer examines the intricacies of mental illness and civil rights and explores notions of moral personhood to examine how decisions of capability and commitment are rendered. Ultimately, she concludes with a call for more research to better manage the complex intersection of mental illness and human rights in the wake of deinstitutionalization.

Gabbard, W., C. Snyder, M. Lin, J. Chadha, J. D. May, and J. Jaggers. 2007. "Methodological Issues in Enumerating Homeless Individuals." *Journal of Social Distress and the Homeless* 16(2): 90–103.

This article points out the methodological challenges involved in documenting the size of the homeless population. It also notes that obtaining an accurate count is an essential part of funding for services and shelter. Using the 1984 U.S. Department of Housing and Urban Development (HUD) study, an early attempt to enumerate the nation's homeless population, this article examines the issues involved in data collection on homelessness.

Grigsby, Charles, Donald Baumann, Steven E. Gregorich, and Cynthia Roberts-Gray. 1990. "Disaffiliation to Entrenchment: A Model for Understanding Homelessness." *Journal of Social Issues* 46(4): 141–156.
    The authors of this article use survey data from over 150 homeless people in Austin, Texas, to explore how different groups of homeless people experience social isolation. They examine four groups of homeless people, ranging from recently to chronically homeless. The different adaptation strategies they discover offer important information on how to more effectively tailor outreach and services.

Hoch, Charles and Robert Slayton. 1989. *New Homelessness and Old*. Philadelphia: Temple University Press.
    In this book Hoch and Slayton offer an important and detailed examination of the kinds of housing that existed on Skid Row. They examine the role of single rent occupancy (SRO) housing in providing affordable shelter. They also distinguish between "old" and "new" homeless, the former defined in relationship to Skid Row housing and a sense of community. By contrast, today's new homeless are more diverse and are more frequently living on the streets or in shelters. The drive for profit that fueled the redevelopment of Skid Row is blamed for the rise in homelessness and its continuance.

Hopper, Kim. 2003. *Reckoning with Homelessness*. Ithaca, NY: Cornell University Press.
    Through a combination of research and social policy, Hopper offers an anthropological account of the emergence of homelessness in New York City in the 1980s and beyond. This book uses the concepts of liminality and

abeyance to describe the elusive, in-between, transitory nature of homelessness as a social category. Hopper brings together years of experience exploring the issue of homelessness, how to understand and frame it, and how to balance advocacy and engagement.

Hopper, Kim, Ezra Susser, and Sarah Conover. 1985. "Economies of Makeshift: Deindustrialization and Homelessness in New York City." *Urban Anthropology* 14 (1–3): 183–236.

This article takes on the important question: What caused the present homeless crisis? The authors detail the rise of homelessness in New York City as a result of changes in the urban economy. Instead of attributing homelessness to individual weakness or failure, this research describes it as a result of systemic forces. "Economies of makeshift" is used to describe the various strategies that homeless people use to acquire basic goods, services, and shelter. This article ultimately challenges the reader to think about the root causes of homelessness.

Katz, Michael B. 1989. *The Undeserving Poor: From the War on Poverty to the War on Welfare.* New York: Pantheon Books.

In this book, Katz describes how Americans have understood poverty and welfare over time. He shows that from the 1960s to the 1980s, punitive attempts to manage poverty have not ended the problem. Other books by Katz on this subject include *In the Shadow of the Poorhouse: A Social History of Welfare in America* and *The Price of Citizenship: Redefining the American Welfare State.*

Lamb, Richard H., ed. 1984. *The Homeless Mentally Ill: A Task Force Report of the American Psychiatric Association.* Washington, DC: American Psychiatric Association.

This edited volume offers fourteen articles by experts on homelessness and mental illness. It provides an exploration of early attempts to define, categorize, and serve people who are homeless and experiencing mental illness. The authors suggest a focus on wraparound services to prevent incarceration and ensure long-term housing.

Liebow, Elliot. 1993. *Tell Them Who I Am: The Lives of Homeless Women*. New York: Penguin Books.

In this book, noted anthropologist Elliot Liebow uses participant observation to explore the lives of homeless women. He describes their everyday frustrations and challenges. He examines their interactions with staff and with one another, presenting a human face to an inhuman problem. It is Liebow's description of homeless women's desire to be recognized and to have voice that makes this work profound.

Passaro, Joanne. 1996. *The Unequal Homeless: Men on the Streets, Women in Their Place*. New York: Routledge.

Using field research, Passaro examines reasons for the overrepresentation of black men among New York City's homeless. She also explores what leads people to become homeless in the long term. Her central finding is that a fragmented approach to homelessness leaves men on the streets. At the same time, it leaves women struggling to fit into traditional ideas of home and home making to gain housing and services.

Piven, Francis F., and Richard A. Cloward. 1993. *Regulating the Poor: The Functions of Public Welfare*. New York: Vintage Books.

Although this source is not only about homelessness or the 1980s, it is included here because of its insights about welfare. Piven and Cloward explore the early foundations of the American welfare system. They examine the role of welfare in preventing sustained economic downturn and in regulating poor people. This is an important source in setting the scene for welfare reform in the 1980s.

Rossi, Peter H. 1989. *Down and Out in America: The Origins of Homelessness.* Chicago: University of Chicago Press.

This book offers a sociological perspective on the primary causes of homelessness in the 1980s. It uses ethnographic research, counts of homeless people, and individual profiles to describe the main causes of homelessness. It also echoes other sources from this decade in viewing "new" homelessness as defined by a younger and more diverse population. It suggests several solutions that treat homelessness as both an emergency and a long-term problem.

Ruddick, Susan M. 1996. *Young and Homeless in Hollywood: Mapping Social Identities.* New York: Routledge.

Research for this book spans from 1975 to 1992. Ruddick examines the rise of street youth culture in Los Angeles and the contested nature of urban space. She examines how homeless youth are characterized versus how they see themselves. What emerges is a unique portrayal of the territorial wins and losses for homeless youth and how services can emerge to meet them where they are.

Seager, Stephen B. 1998. *Street Crazy: The Tragedy of the Homeless Mentally Ill.* Redondo Beach, CA: Westcom Press.

Of all of the sources on homelessness and mental illness, this is one of the most vividly detailed. During his time as a psychiatrist serving this population, Seager exposes the reader to the conditions experienced by the nation's most vulnerable. He illustrates the quandary of treating mental illness among a highly mobile, stigmatized population and examines their interactions with the criminal justice system. Seager also suggests several concrete solutions to better understand and house people with severe mental illness who are experiencing homelessness.

Snow, David and Leon Anderson. 1993. *Down on Their Luck: A Study of Homeless Street People.* Berkeley: University of California Press.

This book offers a profile of the lives of homeless people in Austin, Texas. It employs a combination of ethnographic interviews, participant observation, and data from homeless service agencies to describe life on the street. The authors view homelessness as characterized by flexibility, hard work, struggle, and comradery. They explore the toll that homelessness takes on identity and self-esteem and how survival strategies vary for the newly and long-term homeless. Snow and Anderson describe homeless people as down on their luck but not completely out of options.

Toth, Jennifer. 1993. *The Mole People*. Chicago: Chicago Review Press.

Toth offers a rare profile of a group of people living in abandoned subway tunnels in New York City. She details the dangers, intricacies, and surprising orderliness of this lifestyle. This book inspired research on this community, including the documentary film *Dark Days* (2000). A journalist, Toth personally encountered the dangers of tunnel life and eventually abandoned her study. This book remains an eye-opening account of a marginal lifestyle.

Underwood, Jackson. 1993. *The Bridge People: Daily Life in a Camp of the Homeless*. Lanham, MD: University Press of America.

This anthropological work examines the everyday lives of homeless people living under a bridge in Los Angeles. The author follows their routines and survival strategies, examining positive and negative aspects of living life unsheltered.

Wagner, David. 1993. *Checkerboard Square: Culture and Resistance in a Homeless Community*. Boulder, CO: Westview Press.

Set in a New England community called "North City," this book explores the everyday lives and struggles of homeless people. A social worker, Wagner offers a combination of structured interviews and participant observation to examine ideas of community and resistance. He characterizes the refusal of some homeless people to use emergency shelters as logical, given the risks encountered there. He also explores resistance activities as a counter to the idea that the proper place for homeless people is the emergency shelter.

Wolch, Jennifer and Michael Dear. 1993. *Malign Neglect: Homelessness in an American City.* New York: Jossey-Bass.

This book examines the ease with which American society discards homeless people. Using data from Los Angeles, this book shows how the sheer size of the homeless population is a result of policy changes and structural forces. This book examines survival strategies, including attempts to access social and supportive services, noting that their inadequacy has contributed to the problem.

Wright, Talmadge. 1997. *Out of Place: Homeless Mobilizations, Subcities, and Contested Landscapes.* Albany, NY: State University of New York Press.

This book examines how homeless people are excluded and marginalized in everyday life. Using research from Chicago and San Jose, this book takes a detailed look at how marginalization happens. It examines how city spaces and symbolic spaces shut down homeless voices and participation. It also explores modes of resistance and self-preservation among homeless people.

Homelessness in the Twenty-First Century

Amster, Ralph. 2008. *Lost in Space: The Criminalization, Globalization, and Urban Ecology of Homelessness.* New York: LFB Scholarly Publishing.

In this book, Amster examines the intersection of homeless people and urban space. He takes on the issue of criminalization to show the process by which homeless people are marginalized and excluded. Using examples from the United States and countries around the world,

Amster shows that criminalization is a global problem, made worse with advanced globalization.

Arnold, Kathleen R. 2004. *Homelessness, Citizenship, and Identity: The Uncanniness of Late Modernity*. New York: SUNY Press.
In this book, Arnold examines connections between homelessness and traditional notions of citizenship. She explores how the post–9/11 era led to the increased surveillance of urban spaces and the people who live there. In this sense, her book is about how homelessness intersects with other marginalized and surveyed groups. Her primary argument uses social theory to argue for an end to exclusionary social policy.

Borchard, Kurt. 2005. *The Word on the Street: Homeless Men in Las Vegas*. Reno: University of Nevada Press.
The title of this book shows an emphasis on how homeless men describe their own circumstances. Borchard offers a qualitative profile of the struggles of homeless men in Las Vegas. He examines why they are homeless, how they subsist on the streets, and the policies that threaten their survival. By focusing on homeless voices, Borchard avoids trying to save or blame homeless men. Instead, he explores the logic of their actions and circumstances from their perspective.

Burnes, Donald W. and David L. DiLeo, eds. 2016. *Ending Homelessness: Why We Haven't, How We Can*. Boulder: Lynne Rienner Publishers.
This edited volume offers a collection of articles that examine the current state of homelessness, as well as possibilities for eradicating homelessness in the future. It reviews some of the most important resources for exiting homelessness, namely, housing and supportive services. Featuring noted experts including Martha R. Burt, Sam Tsemberis, Jill Khadduri, and Sheila Crowley, this

book offers solutions that would change the nation's focus to eliminate structural barriers to basic needs services, including housing.

Burt, Martha, Laudan Y. Aron, and Edgar Lee, with Jesse Valente. 2001. *Helping America's Homeless: Emergency Shelter or Affordable Housing?* Washington, DC: The Urban Institute Press.

Martha Burt is one of the most highly regarded scholars researching homelessness. In this wonderfully documented book, Burt and her co-authors evaluate the nation's attempts to help homeless people. Using sources including a national survey of homeless providers, this book argues that without a sustained national attempt to provide affordable housing, homelessness will continue. Although the shelter and service industries offer myriad services, these are often directed toward managing rather than ending this pressing social problem.

Center for Social Innovation. 2018. *SPARC: Supporting Partnerships for Anti-Racist Communities.* Phase I Study Findings.

This source examines findings from six target communities across the nation. All are committed to studying how race and homelessness intersect. The SPARC project is impressive in scope and uses Homeless Management Information System (HMIS) data, surveys, and oral histories to examine how to advance racial equity. Findings show that people of color are overrepresented in the homeless population and face multiple barriers to exit. This report offers policy solutions, organizational changes, and new directions for research.

Crowley, Sheila. 2003. "The Affordable Housing Crisis: Residential Mobility of Poor Families and School Mobility of Poor Children." *Journal of Negro Education* 72(1): 22–38.

In this article, Crowley examines what happens to students whose families experience frequent mobility. Crowley details the academic delays that come with periods of homelessness and housing instability. While this article champions existing school-based assistance strategies, it also argues for increased federal funding. Crowley argues that the drop-off in federal assistance for the lowest-income households has caused their continued instability and increased homelessness. To remedy this, she argues for an investment in affordable housing and a focus on family stabilization.

Culhane, Dennis P., Jung Min Park, and Stephen Metraux. 2011. "The Patterns and Costs of Services Use among Homeless Families." *Journal of Community Psychology* 39(7): 815–825.

Dennis Culhane is a noted researcher who focuses on veteran homelessness and linkages between homelessness and housing policy. He was one of the first experts to show that permanent housing is less costly than emergency services. In this article, Culhane and co-authors describe how families access services before, during, and after they experience homelessness. They suggest that sheltered homelessness interrupts service use and that the corrective is ongoing, community-based services for families, whether or not they are in shelter.

DeVerteuil, Geoffrey. 2003. "Homeless Mobility, Institutional Settings, and the New Poverty Management." *Environment and Planning* 35: 361–379.

This study uses a sample of twenty-five women at a shelter in Los Angeles to examine institutional cycling as a form of poverty management. DeVerteuil describes poverty management as including various strategies to contain or disperse homeless people. This article examines mobility and institutional access as forcing homeless people to cycle within but not out of service dependency. This article is an important contribution to the literature on homeless women and on the spatial management of poor populations.

DiFazio, William. 2006. *Ordinary Poverty: A Little Food and Cold Storage*. Philadelphia: Temple University Press.

DiFazio presents an analysis of the American shelter system, as a bare-bones approach to addressing homelessness. It critiques the inefficient management of welfare assistance and suggests rethinking our approach to homelessness and poverty. Situating the United States within a global context of increased economic competition, DiFazio argues that people experiencing homelessness have become resigned to their own marginality. To remedy this, he suggests that the introduction of universal resources, like basic income, would make poverty extraordinary.

Donley, Amy M. and James D. Wright. 2012. "Safer Outside: A Qualitative Exploration of Homeless People's Resistance to Homeless Shelters." *Journal of Forensic Psychology Practice* 12: 288–306.

This article documents the lives of thirty-nine unsheltered homeless people camping in central Florida. The authors document the importance of basic needs services to assist this hidden population. They explain how a lack of access to long-term assistance is the result of overly complicated requirements that make the delivery of homeless services problematic. Reducing barriers to assistance and offering tailored services for those living unsheltered are among the suggested solutions.

Ellen, Ingrid G. and Brendan O'Flaherty, eds. 2010. *How to House the Homeless*. New York: Russell Sage Foundation.

In this important book, editors Ellen and O'Flaherty enlist experts in the field to examine how housing policies affect homeless and low-income people. From Housing First principles to rental subsidies, the policies and approaches evaluated in this volume offer important tools for thinking about the most effective strategies for ending homelessness.

Feldman, Leonard C. 2004. *Citizens without Shelter: Homelessness, Democracy, and Political Exclusion.* Ithaca, NY: Cornell University Press.

> This book examines how many approaches to homelessness reflect the idea that homeless people are fundamentally different and less than full citizens. Feldman critiques the criminalization of the homeless and offering bare-bones service assistance. He argues instead for a reconceptualization of the ideas of inclusion and democratic pluralism as a way of better serving and housing homeless people.

Gibson, Kristina E. 2011. *Street Kids: Homeless Youth, Outreach, and Policing New York's Streets.* New York: New York University Press.

> This source offers firsthand accounts from homeless youth in New York City. Gibson describes how criminalization strategies force youth to stay in motion. This makes outreach more challenging, as homeless youth are an increasingly marginalized, hidden population.

Gomez, Rebecca J. and Tiffany N. Ryan. 2016. "Speaking Out: Youth Led Research as a Methodology Used with Homeless Youth." *Child Adolescent Social Work Journal* 33: 185–193.

> This article documents the use of participatory action research as a way of connecting with homeless youth. The authors show how youth-led research fosters better data collection and eventually leads to better services and policy to assist this vulnerable population. In addition, youth-led participatory action research was found to support appropriate youth-adult relationships as well as self-esteem and self-efficacy.

Goodman, Lisa, A., Katya Fels, and Catherine Glenn, with contributions from Judy Benitez. 2006. "No Safe Place: Sexual Assault in the Lives of Homeless Women." *VAWnet: The National Online*

Resource Center on Violence against Women. https://vawnet.org/
material/no-safe-place-sexual-assault-lives-homeless-women.

This article details the prevalence of sexual assault as a threat to homeless women. It focuses on the emotional and physical toll of abuse and how it affects women differently, depending on the array of issues they face. The primary suggestion is an overhaul of homeless services to ensure that they do not reproduce trauma or perpetuate long-term homelessness.

Gowan, Teresa. 2010. *Hobos, Hustlers, and Backsliders: Homeless in San Francisco.* Minneapolis: University of Minnesota Press.

This book offers a unique combination of urban ethnography and discursive analysis. A sociologist, Gowan outlines basic constructions of poverty as a result of moral failing, disease, or systemic barriers and inequities. These ways of thinking about homelessness, described as "sick talk," "sin talk," and "systems talk," de-emphasize a sense of agency or control. In detailing the survival strategies of homeless people in San Francisco, Gowan explores the idea of agency. She discovers both intelligence and resilience amid criminalization and other challenges.

Heben, Andrew. 2014. *Tent City Urbanism: From Self-Organized Camps to Tiny House Villages.* Eugene, OR: The Village Collaborative.

Heben examines the use of tiny houses and tents as housing. He focuses on the reasons that homeless people prefer these settings over other alternatives. Heben describes camps and villages in Nashville, Tennessee; Ann Arbor, Michigan; Seattle, Washington; St. Petersburg, Florida; Portland, Oregon; Olympia, Washington; and Eugene, Oregon. He distinguishes between camps that are self-managed and those run by outside organizations. Overall, he advocates for the use of tent cities and tiny houses as alternatives to homelessness.

Kerr, Daniel R. 2016. "Almost Like I Am in Jail: Homelessness and the Sense of Immobility in Cleveland, Ohio." *Cultural Studies* 30(3): 401–420.

In this study of unhoused people, Kerr focuses on the idea of mobility. Using data from the Cleveland Oral History Project, spanning from 1999 to 2005, he explores people's feelings of being trapped. This is ironic, because homeless people are often highly mobile, just confined to cyclical motion in marginal and institutional spaces. In this context, occupying public spaces is seen as an act of resistance.

Kim, Mimi M., Julian D. Ford, Daniel L. Howard, and Daniel W. Bradford. 2010. "Assessing Trauma, Substance Abuse, and Mental Health in a Sample of Homeless Men." *Health and Social Work* 35(1): 39–48.

This article focuses on the effects of sexual trauma on a sample of 239 homeless men. The authors examine whether or not early experiences of sexual trauma result in addiction and/or mental and physical health problems. Their results show a greater prevalence of mental illness as a result of early trauma. This suggests the need for tailored care and outreach to address this population and the specific issues they face.

Lyon-Callo, Vincent. 2008. *Inequality, Poverty, and Neoliberal Governance: Activist Ethnography in the Homeless Sheltering Industry*. Toronto: University of Toronto Press.

This book presents a groundbreaking anthropological study that the author describes as "activist ethnography." Lyon-Callo's main argument is that neoliberal policy is in part to blame for the nation's failure to end homelessness. He describes the political and economic framework within which homelessness has flourished, even during prosperous times. Using fieldwork conducted at a shelter in Northampton, Massachusetts, he describes the shelter industry as managing, not ending, homelessness.

Marr, Matthew D. 2015. *Better Must Come: Exiting Homelessness in Two Global Cities*. Ithaca, NY: Cornell University Press.
In an innovative attempt to focus on exiting homelessness, Marr explores the process in Los Angeles and Tokyo. He examines the conditions leading to increased homelessness in these global cities and examines the limited pathways out. Marr documents how homeless people attempt to access various forms of housing and welfare and resist the stigma of homelessness. Ultimately, this book calls for greater equality and access to basic needs, to end homelessness in global cities.

Mitchell, Don. 2003. *The Right to the City: Social Justice and the Fight for Public Space*. New York: The Guilford Press.
In this book, Mitchell describes the drive to remove homeless people from public space. Seen as noncontributors in a global economy, homeless people are criminalized for their very survival in public. Mitchell asks the important questions: What does it mean to outlaw a group of people? What does it mean to outlaw public space? Using several examples of antihomeless criminalization in U.S. cities, Mitchell shows that these practices undermine our notions of citizenship and inclusion. He views public space as a venue for advancing both social justice and homeless rights.

Molina-Jackson, Edna. 2008. *Homeless Not Hopeless: The Survival Networks of Latino and African American Men*. Lanham, MD: University Press of America, Inc.
This book describes the social networks of Latino and African American men experiencing homelessness. It describes the work that goes into these relationships as driven by a combination of necessity and strategy. It also suggests that these social networks help integrate men into the culture of living on the street and address immediate and long-term survival needs.

Murphy, Joseph and Kerri Tobin. 2011. *Homelessness Comes to School.* Thousand Oaks, CA: Corwin Press.

This book examines the challenges that face school-aged children in homeless families and unaccompanied youth. It examines the history of homelessness in the United States and offers an overview of demographics, as well as causes and solutions. It assesses current services and barriers to accessing them. This book also offers suggestions for how parents and schools can partner with supportive agencies to protect and support the right to education.

National Academies of Sciences, Engineering, Medicine. 2018. *Evaluating the Evidence for Improving Health Outcomes among People Experiencing Homelessness.* Washington, DC: The National Academies Press.

This book evaluates the success of permanent supportive housing in reducing medical risk and improving health outcomes for homeless people. Although it uses limited data, the main finding is that permanent housing does not improve health, except for people with HIV/AIDS. The report interprets this finding cautiously, calling for additional research to prove the widely held belief that permanent supportive housing improves overall well-being and general health.

O'Connell, James J. 2015. *Stories from the Shadows: Reflections of a Street Doctor.* Boston, MA : BHCHP Press.

For over thirty years, Dr. James O'Connell has served as the founding physician of the Health Care for the Homeless Program in Boston, Massachusetts. In that time, he has transformed the city's understanding of the medical risks faced by homeless people on the streets and in shelters. He is also the pioneer of the vulnerability index, which prioritizes homeless people for housing based on these risks. In this book, he describes the events he witnessed and people he met in his quest to serve the homeless.

Ozawa, Martha N. and Hong-Sik Yoon. 2005. " 'Leavers' from TANF and AFDC: How Do They Fare Economically?" *Social Work* 50(3): 239–249.

Ozawa and Yoon use the 1993 and 1996 Survey of Income and Program Participation (SIPP) to compare outcomes for families on Aid to Families with Dependent Children (AFDC) versus Temporary Assistance for Needy Families (TANF). Given the stringent requirements of TANF, including lifetime limits on assistance, it is not surprising that leavers' economic status often declined as a result. With less scrutiny and longer-term assistance, AFDC leavers fared better.

Padgett, Deborah K., Benjamin F. Henwood, and Sam J. Tsemberis. 2016. *Housing First: Ending Homelessness, Transforming Systems, and Changing Lives*. New York: Oxford University Press.

Housing First is a common approach to ending homelessness in policy and advocacy circles. This book presents a view of Housing First through the eyes of its first architect, psychiatrist Sam Tsemberis. Along with co-authors Padgett and Henwood, Tsemberis describes the Housing First paradigm and its origins in New York City's Pathways to Housing. It summarizes the central tenets of Housing First and the pitfalls that have accompanied its implementation in the United States. It also offers evidence of the efficacy of this approach in Canada, Europe, and Australia.

Purser, Gregory L., Orion P. Mowbray, and Jay O'Shields. 2017. "The Relationship between Length and Number of Homeless Episodes and Engagement in Survival Sex." *Journal of Social Service Research* 43(2): 262–269.

This article discusses the many health risks associated with survival sex, or using sex to meet basic needs, including food and housing, for people experiencing homelessness.

Using data from Washington, DC's Metropolitan Area Drug Study, the authors examine what factors increase the likelihood of engaging in survival sex. These include length of time homeless or frequent homelessness, age, and experiences with drug use, depression, and institutionalization. Authors suggest a harm-reduction, Housing First model to address these multiple issues and ensure safety.

Roschelle, Anne. 2019. *Struggling in the Land of Plenty: Race, Class, and Gender in the Lives of Homeless Families*. New York: Lexington Books.

In this book, Roschelle conducts a four-year ethnographic study that explores the lives of homeless families in San Francisco. She uses intersectionality theory to understand the many challenges that homeless women face, as they embody several marginalized statuses at once. Even within the welfare system designed to assist them, women of color in particular are treated as guilty, dishonest, and fundamentally flawed. Roschelle takes a candid, unapologetic look at the survival strategies that homeless women use to manage multiple forms of challenge and risk.

Schwartz, Alex F. 2010. *Housing Policy in the United States*, Second Edition. New York: Routledge.

This source reviews the complex structure of housing policy in the United States. Schwartz provides a detailed, comprehensive overview of the various kinds of housing available. This book shows how tax policy and the housing finance structure lock extremely low income people out of affordable housing. It examines the role of the federal government in making affordable housing a priority and looks at state and local policies that reinforce this. Examining the various kinds of housing for the most vulnerable shows the need for increased housing subsidies to meet the nation's needs.

Schweid, Richard. 2016. *Invisible Nation: Homeless Families in America*. Oakland: University of California Press.

This is a journalistic account of how homeless families struggle to survive in major cities in the United States. It uses a diverse set of data from homeless families in cities including Nashville, Tennessee; Boston, Massachusetts; Fairfax, Virginia; Portland, Oregon; and Trenton, New Jersey. Overall, this book emphasizes the localized nature of solutions to family homelessness.

Shinn, Marybeth and Jill Khadduri. 2020. *In the Midst of Plenty: Homelessness and What to Do about It*. Hoboken, NJ: Wiley Blackwell.

This recent book examines the important questions: What causes homelessness, and what can be done to end it permanently? Noted experts in the field, Shinn and Khadduri offer an overview of the causes of homelessness, underscoring structural barriers to affordable housing. They evaluate the nation's ongoing effort to end homelessness and suggest increasing support for housing choice vouchers to house the most vulnerable.

Smith, Curtis, Ernesto Castañeda, and Josiah Heyman. 2012. "The Homeless and Occupy El Paso: Creating Community among the 99 Percent." *Social Movement Studies* 11(3–4): 356–366.

This article takes a critical look at homeless people and social movement activities. Focusing on the Occupy movement in El Paso, Texas, the authors discuss the movement's initial impulse to exclude homeless people. Once some protesters argued for homeless inclusion, everything changed, and their input and assistance were valued. Ultimately, this article underscores the importance of recognizing that homeless people have an organized role to play and expertise to share and that their inclusion can be transformative.

Von Mahs, Jurgen. 2013. *Down and Out in Los Angeles and Berlin: The Sociospatial Exclusion of Homeless People.* Philadelphia: Temple University Press.

Von Mahs offers a comparison between homelessness in Los Angeles and Berlin. He describes how different welfare regimes have similar outcomes, as both cities are home to large homeless populations. Overall, Von Mahs argues for a greater investment in assisting homeless people in accessing the means to exit homelessness.

Wardhaugh, Julia. 1999. "The Unaccommodated Woman: Home, Homelessness and Identity." *Sociological Review* 47(1): 91–110.

This article offers an overview of ideas of home and homelessness for women. It describes the unaccommodated, homeless woman as anomalous to the very idea of home. For this, she is rejected, castigated, and physically placed at risk. Wardhaugh describes the accepted meaning of home as a symbol of identity and social stability. Women who maintain homes are seen as good women. Homeless women, lacking the home as a symbol of goodness and protection, are seen as deviant.

Wasserman, Jason A. and Jeffrey M. Clair. 2010. *At Home on the Street: People, Poverty and a Hidden Culture of Homelessness.* Boulder, CO: Lynne Rienner Publishers.

This exploratory ethnography examines relationships and survival strategies among homeless people in Birmingham, Alabama. Rather than present homeless people as caricatures or offer overarching solutions, this book foregrounds homeless voices, needs, and concerns. It presents a poignant portrayal of people struggling for friendship and safety amid an alienating array of inadequate services, dangers, and risks.

Willse, Craig. 2015. *The Value of Homelessness: Managing Surplus Life in the United States.* Minneapolis: University of Minnesota Press.

Referring to homeless people as "surplus life," Willse describes their treatment within the homeless service industry. In a critique of shelters, social services programs, and social scientific approaches to homelessness, Willse argues that they manage rather than end the problem. The term "surplus life" also underscores the relationship between housing, economy, and social identity. Gradually, over time, U.S. society has locked people out of its opportunity structure and then created industries to manage them. This means engineering their continued homelessness and benefiting from it.

Government and Policy Websites

Federal Emergency Management Agency (FEMA): https://www.fema.gov/
FEMA offers guidance and assistance for the nation in times of emergency, including natural disasters like Hurricane Katrina, and public health crises like the COVID-19 pandemic. The Emergency Food and Shelter Program is its main program focusing on homeless people. This program is outlined in a fact sheet that discusses eligibility as well as the structure and format of the program.

National Institute on Alcohol Abuse and Alcoholism (NIAAA): https://www.niaaa.nih.gov/
The NIAAA offers important, data-driven studies on alcohol addiction in the general population. Its website also includes resources that examine the effects of alcohol on special populations, including people experiencing homelessness. Its current research focuses in the most detail on the general population and issues like the opioid crisis. It also examines co-occurring issues, like mental illness, along with drug and alcohol addiction.

National Institute on Drug Abuse (NIDA): https://www.drugabuse.gov/

Similar to NIAAA, NIDA offers important resources for understanding how addiction affects the general community. It offers information on particular drugs of abuse and emerging national trends. Because homeless people are not seen as more susceptible to either alcohol or drug addiction, they are not singled out for specific programs or interventions. Instead, NIDA offers information on addiction and the co-occurring issues that homeless people often face.

National Institute of Mental Health (NIMH): https://www.nimh.nih.gov/index.shtml
NIMH is the nation's leader on issues of mental health, both illness and wellness. Its website provides general resources and information. While homelessness is not a specific focus area, the NIMH website includes information on identifying and treating conditions, like depression and schizophrenia, that disproportionately affect the homeless population.

Substance Abuse and Mental Health Services Administration (SAMHSA): https://www.samhsa.gov/
SAMHSA provides services for the general population and includes homelessness as one of its signature program areas. SAMHSA's website offers information on programs for people experiencing homelessness and a combination of substance abuse and mental health issues. It provides access to annual reports that track the service population, services offered, and specific outcomes. SAMHSA also offers trainings and tools for providers working on these issues in local communities.

U.S. Department of Agriculture (USDA): https://www.usda.gov/
The USDA oversees the distribution of emergency food to food banks, shelters, and service organizations nationwide. It administers the food assistance programs including Supplemental Nutrition Assistance Program (SNAP) and Nutrition Program for Women, Infants, and Children (WIC),

as well as those targeting seniors. The USDA website offers reports and information that define current allocations and programs for homeless people. It also offers guidance in determining eligibility for individuals and localities and training in understanding its various provisions.

U.S. Department of Education (ED): www2.ed.gov/programs /homeless

The ED offers provisions for students experiencing homelessness, as legislated through the McKinney-Vento Homeless Assistance Act. Its website provides information on the ED programs that serve homeless students. It offers specific information on the Education for Homeless Children and Youth program, including eligibility requirements, funding levels, and performance measures. There is also an overview of the legislation and regulations associated with ED programs.

U.S. Department of Housing and Urban Development (HUD): https://www.hudexchange.info/

HUD offers resources for communities to access funding for housing and homeless services through the Community Development Block Grant (CDBG) program. HUD also oversees the continuum of care (CoC) process and coordinates the annual point-in-time (PIT) count. Its website offers count results, beginning with 2007. HUD manages the emergency solutions grants program, public housing program, and housing programs for specific populations. HUD also offers tools, support, and guidance for communities. In addition to PIT count results, HUD's website also provides program and funding information and information on partnership programs with other agencies, such as the Pay for Success program with the Department of Justice.

U.S. Department of Justice (DOJ): https://www.justice.gov/

The DOJ website offers information on specific partnerships and programs to address homelessness. In addition to officially denouncing the criminalization of homeless people, the DOJ focuses on diversion and re-entry. Realizing the direct linkage between homelessness and criminal justice involvement, the DOJ partners to address specific populations and issues faced by this population.

U.S. Department of Veterans Affairs (VA): https://www.va.gov/homeless/

The VA provides services and information for veterans experiencing homelessness. Its website offers resources that include accessing basic health care and mental health services and housing and employment assistance. Homeless programs under the VA are supported by the federal government. The VA website documents the significant progress that many communities have made toward ending homelessness among veterans.

U.S. Interagency Council on Homelessness (USICH): https://www.usich.gov/

The USICH coordinates the federal response to homelessness. It authors the annual federal strategic plan to end homelessness. The federal plan outlines the nation's goals in preventing and ending homelessness in general as well as for specific populations. The USICH website provides tools for communities to manage current issues and move toward the goal of ending homelessness. It also hosts an archive of previous federal plans and reports.

National Organizations

The National Alliance to End Homelessness (NAEH): https://endhomelessness.org/

The NAEH website offers an interactive "State of Homelessness" map where visitors can easily access detailed information on their state's homeless population. It also includes information on every CoC region within the state. Data is broken down by subpopulation and changes over time since 2007. Its educational resources for communities include toolkits for action, organized courses, and policy solutions. Notably, the NAEH site also provides information on accessing COVID-19 resources and on ensuring racial equity.

The National Coalition for the Homeless (NCH): https://nationalhomeless.org/

This site is primarily focused on the three goals of providing access to sources of direct assistance, research on homelessness, and resources for action. Its publications include reports and fact sheets on topics including hate crimes against homeless people, criminalization, and sweeps of tent cities. The NCH approach is advocacy based. It includes resources for communities to host homeless awareness and memorial events and a forum for formerly homeless speakers to discuss their experiences.

The National Law Center on Homelessness and Poverty (NLCHP): https://nlchp.org/

This website provides access to the NLCHP's groundbreaking work toward equal justice for homeless people, including publications like *Housing Not Handcuffs* and *Tent City USA*. These publications outline the criminalization of homelessness and explore the challenges facing unsheltered homeless people. The site includes resources and publications in the following focus areas: civil rights, criminalization, domestic violence, housing, human rights, and youth and education. It provides information on events, focus areas, and ways of becoming involved in the fight against criminalization. The NLCHP was recently renamed the National Homelessness Law Center.

National Low-Income Housing Coalition (NLICH): https://nlihc.org/

The NLICH provides up-to-date information on the nation's affordable housing for low-income renters. The website includes information on the federal eviction moratorium, provided through the COVID relief bill. It also offers access to the reports *Out of Reach* and *The Gap*, which provide comprehensive overviews of how unaffordable housing is for many Americans given prevailing wages. Complimenting these reports, the site provides easy access to state-level information on housing affordability. It also includes information on housing programs for homeless people, resources like the housing trust fund, and ways of getting involved in the fight for affordable housing.

This chronology identifies the agents, decisions, policies, and perspectives that have most affected homelessness in the United States over time, and particularly during the crisis points and controversies that this book identifies. This chronology also highlights the important role that advocacy and service communities have played in developing population estimates and creating innovative, data-driven solutions. This timeline includes benchmarks that chart major changes in the nation's approach to homelessness.

Some of the events included in this chronology are not directly or obviously about homelessness. They are included because they signaled changes in the U.S. economy that caused or perpetuated inequality or because they reflected innovative approaches to combating poverty. In this sense, a focus on government events and legislation emphasizes the systemic nature of homelessness and solutions to end it. This chronology also includes legal decisions that affect homeless people and those at risk of homelessness and housing insecurity.

1929   (October 24–29) The stock market crashes, over several dramatic days, and the Dow Jones Industrial average drops a full 24.8 percent.

A woman sits on her bed in a homeless shelter. Over time, the homeless service industry has attempted to better serve women and people of color facing homelessness. (Monkey Business Images/Dreamstime.com)

1930   Makeshift communities of Depression-era singles and families build shantytowns on the edges of cities nationwide. These "Hoovervilles," named after President Hoover, are extensive, organized communities. Seattle's Hooverville documents 639 residents in 1934, and 1,687 shacks still scattered throughout several Hooverville areas in 1941.

1930   (January–October) The bank failures in early 1930 are one of the first symbols of national economic instability. In the first ten months of the year, 744 banks fail, with 9,000 more failing throughout the decade.

1930   (July 21) President Herbert Hoover establishes the Veterans Administration (VA), under Executive Order 5398. Doing so consolidates benefits, specifically homes and pensions, and manages and expands various services.

1931   Massive dust storms begin to appear with frequency and voracity in the Great Plains area. The Agriculture College of Oklahoma reports that 13 out of 16 million acres in the state are seriously eroded. Dust storms and severe drought persist throughout the 1930s.

1932   (May 29) A group of between 15,000 and 40,000 World War I veterans and supporters march on Washington and set up a tent city to demand early pension or "bonus" payments. Calling themselves the "Bonus Army," they establish a tent city, and President Hoover eventually calls in federal troops to oust them.

1932   (July 21) The Emergency Relief and Construction Act is signed to provide funding for public works projects, including housing for low-income families.

1933   (March 4) Franklin Delano Roosevelt is inaugurated, becoming the thirty-second president of the United States. In his inaugural address, he tells the American people that they "have nothing to fear but fear itself."

1933   (March 9) The Emergency Banking Act by Congress proclaims a four-day national bank holiday to stabilize the banking system. During this time, all transactions are suspended and banks close their doors.

1933   (April 5) The Civilian Conservation Corps is established and remains in operation until 1942. This voluntary work relief program employs approximately 3 million young men on a range of public works projects including reforestation, irrigation, and habitat preservation across the United States. Segregated camps were provided for African and Native American men.

1933   (May 12) The Agricultural Adjustment Act is a federal law that attempts to protect farmers by refinancing their mortgages at lower rates and reducing surplus crops and livestock. Farmers are offered subsidies for not planting or for selling their animals for slaughter.

1933   (May 12) The Federal Emergency Relief Act offers employment assistance to states, to the tune of over $3 billion.

1933   (May 12) The Agricultural Adjustment Administration is established to raise prices by eliminating surplus products and offering subsidies to farmers.

1933   (May 18) The Tennessee Valley Authority is established to control floods, manage forests, and bring electricity to the following states: Kentucky, Mississippi, Alabama, Georgia, North Carolina, Tennessee, and Virginia.

1933   (May 27) President Roosevelt signs the Securities Act. This makes information about securities transparent for buyers, ideally eliminating fraud.

1933   (June 13) The Home-Owners Loan Act is signed into law to bolster home ownership and support mortgage lending institutions.

1933   (June 16) The National Industrial Recovery Act (NIRA) is signed into law. NIRA regulates industry by establishing standard pricing and working conditions including maximum weekly hours and a minimum wage. It also includes a ban on child labor. NIRA creates the Public Works Administration (PWA) to stimulate social and economic recovery. Among its initiatives, the PWA funds low-cost housing, in place of slum dwellings.

1933   (June 16) The widely debated Glass Steagall Act is signed into law by President Roosevelt. It establishes the Federal Deposit Insurance Corporation (FDIC), to protect bank deposits in case of economic downturn. It also separates commercial from investment banking.

1934   (January 30) The Gold Reserve Act is signed into law. It makes gold a commodity instead of an equivalent for currency. It also allows the president to set, by proclamation, the gold value of the dollar. Citizens were asked to return all monetary gold to the U.S. Treasury.

1934   (June 6) Franklin Delano Roosevelt signs the Securities and Exchange Act, a companion to the Securities Act of 1933, which regulated the securities industry. This act establishes the Securities and Exchange Commission (SEC) to ensure market growth and protect everyday investors.

1934   (June 28) Franklin Delano Roosevelt signs the National Housing Act, which establishes the Federal Housing Administration (FHA). The FHA provides federally guaranteed mortgages with longer, more flexible terms. Redlining is still legal, however, and this practice excludes African Americans from FHA benefits, affecting their overall ability to accumulate wealth and weather future economic downturns.

1935   (April 8) The Emergency Relief Appropriations Act is established to offer relief to millions experiencing unemployment, primarily those unable to work. It also established the Works Progress Administration (WPA) detailed later.

1935   (April 27) The Soil Conservation Service created within the U.S. Department of Agriculture is established as a permanent agency to mitigate the effects of various kinds of erosion, including water and wind, to the nation's soil.

1935   (April 30) The Resettlement Administration was established to allow poor families to relocate to areas with more productive farmland or employment opportunities.

1935 (May 6) The WPA employed 8.5 million people throughout the nation until 1943, to restore public infrastructure and to develop the nation's artistic and literary talent. Many recipients went on to become American icons, and their work endures to the present.

1935 (July 5) The Wagner Act establishes the National Labor Relations Board (NLRB) and ensures rights to collective bargaining for union employees.

1935 (August 14) The Social Security Act is signed into law. It establishes benefits for workers; the elderly; and people who are blind, disabled, unemployed, or are victims of industrial accidents. Benefits are not payable until 1941, and people working in agricultural and domestic jobs are ineligible for benefits.

1936 (November 3) Franklin Delano Roosevelt wins reelection to his second term in office.

1938 (June 25) The Fair Labor Standards Act establishes a federal minimum wage, maximum work hours, overtime eligibility, and standards regarding child labor applicable to both full- and part-time workers.

1939 (July 1) The Federal Works Agency is established to consolidate existing agencies overseeing housing, public roads, and public works projects.

1940 (November 5) Franklin Delano Roosevelt wins reelection to his third term in office. The Twenty-Second Amendment, signed into law in 1951, prevents a third term for any future president.

1941 (June) Executive Order 8802 is signed to reduce discrimination within the defense industry by allowing black Americans better access to employment and training opportunities. It also establishes the Fair Employment Practices Division.

1941 (December 7) The United States enters World War II.

1945 (April 12) Franklin Delano Roosevelt dies, mere months after being elected to his fourth term as president.

1946   (July 3) The National Mental Health Act (P.L. 79–487) is signed into law. It establishes the National Institute of Mental Health (NIMH) and makes mental illness a national concern.

1948   (July 26) Executive Order 9981 is signed. Despite strong opposition from senators representing southern states, President Truman signs this order to desegregate the armed forces.

1948   (December 10) The Universal Declaration of Human Rights is adopted by the UN General Assembly. It is intended as a global document. It recognizes basic human rights, which include "the inalienable entitlements of all people, at all times, and in all places."

1949   The American Housing Act is passed (amended in 1954, 1956, 1965, 1968). This act promises "a decent home and suitable living environment for every American." It expands the Federal Housing Administration's involvement in mortgage insurance, offers funding for urban renewal and slum clearance, and initiates new public housing construction.

1954   (May 17) The landmark Supreme Court case *Brown v. Board of Education* ends legal segregation in public schools. Economic segregation continues however, preventing full and equal access to education for African Americans.

1955   This year marks the beginning of the closure of mental hospitals, known as deinstitutionalization. State institutions for the mentally ill are closed, and community-based care facilities to replace them never materialize. This is a significant feeder into homelessness. Current sources estimate that approximately three-quarters of a million people who would have been hospitalized years ago are living in the communities and on the streets of today.

1956   (June 29) The Federal Aid Highway Act (officially the National Interstate and Defense Highway Act) is signed into law by Dwight D. Eisenhower. It bolsters the Interstate Highway System and is billed as a way of connecting the nation in case of military need. Many low-income communities of color were destroyed in the name of highway development.

1957   (September 9) The Civil Rights Act is signed into law by President Eisenhower. It establishes a commission on civil rights and permits legal action on behalf of African Americans who are denied the right to vote.

1963   (August 28) The March on Washington draws a quarter of a million people to fight for equal access to civil rights and economic opportunity. Dr. Martin Luther King's "I Have a Dream" speech argues for peaceful, dignified protest but does not retreat from the ideal of true equality. In response to the question, When will black people be satisfied? he explains, "We can never be satisfied as long as the Negro is the victim of the unspeakable horrors of police brutality; we can never be satisfied as long as our bodies, heavy with the fatigue of travel, cannot gain lodging in the motels of the highways and the hotels of the cities."

1963   (October 31) The Community Mental Health Centers Act is passed to bolster the development of community mental health facilities to replace larger hospitals. Prior to this, and even after its passage, communities are uneven in the establishment of centers and the delivery of services.

1964   (July 2) The Civil Rights Act is signed into law by Lyndon B. Johnson. This act legally prevents discrimination in employment and because of sex, race, color, or national origin.

1965   (August 10) The Housing and Urban Development Act is signed into law by Lyndon B. Johnson. It creates the U.S. Department of Housing and Urban Development (HUD) and ends the construction of high-rise "projects." It provides federal funding for new construction and rehabilitation for existing units and includes a rental subsidy program targeting the elderly and disabled. This act eases the path to home ownership for veterans. It also allows families qualifying for public housing to move into vacant units in the private market.

1968 The law against public intoxication is legally challenged in *Powell v. Texas*, for purportedly violating the Eight Amendment, against cruel and unusual punishment. The law is eventually upheld, although public intoxication laws vary from state to state.

Lyndon B. Johnson founds the Urban Institute. Its detailed research agenda focuses on identifying the outcomes of federal policy for a wide range of governmental initiatives to address underserved communities.

1972 In *Papachristou v. Jacksonville*, 405 U.S. 156, U.S. vagrancy law is challenged as unconstitutional and vague. Similar to criminalization laws that target homeless status, vagrancy law punishes vagrants for who they are rather than what they are doing. This gives police wide discretion leading to unnecessary or unfounded arrests and is eventually struck down.

1974 The Housing and Community Development Act consolidates existing programs into the Community Development Block Grant (CDBG) program. This includes the Housing Choice Voucher Program known as Section 8.

1974 (October 28) The Equal Credit Opportunity Act is signed into law to prevent discrimination in lending on the basis of factors not related to creditworthiness, like race and gender. It makes it legal for women to obtain their own credit cards, separate from their husbands.

1977 The Community Reinvestment Act is designed to encourage lenders to meet the credit needs of their communities. It is a direct response to disinvestment in low- and moderate-income areas.

1978 The National Low-Income Housing Coalition is formed to focus exclusively on the housing needs of low-income people. It merges previous initiatives including the Ad Hoc Low-Income Housing Coalition and the Low-Income Housing Information Service.

1980 President Carter signs an amendment to the Social Security Act. It imposes more stringent eligibility rules and greater work incentives. It applies to Supplemental Security Income (SSI) and Social Security Disability Insurance (SSDI) beneficiaries. In October, prisoners become ineligible for these benefits.

1981 (January 20) Ronald Reagan is sworn in as the fortieth president of the United States.

1981 (August 13) The Omnibus Budget Reconciliation Act is passed. It focuses on the Old-Age, Survivor, Disability Insurance Program and Medicare. It makes eligibility requirements more stringent and cuts back on benefits seen as less essential. It is part of Reagan's Program for Economic Recovery.

1982 The National Coalition for the Homeless (NCH) is formed as a non-profit organization based in Washington, DC. The NCH focuses on initiatives designed to end homelessness, and its widely disseminated reports and advocacy directly inform federal policy.

1983 The first Federal Task Force on Homelessness is created to allow states to make temporary claims on unused federal property, for the creation of makeshift shelters.

The National Alliance to End Homelessness is formed. It begins with an emergency focus and moves toward addressing systemic solutions, including the development of ten-year plans.

1984 (October 9) The Social Security Disability Benefits Reform Act is passed. It changes eligibility determinations and results in more people receiving SSDI.

HUD estimates the homeless population in shelters at 69,000 with 15,000 in families and 197,000 people unsheltered. Researchers consider these underestimates.

1986 The Homeless Person's Survival Act is passed in both houses of Congress. It is a precursor for the Stewart B. McKinney Homeless Assistance Act (P.L. 100-77).

The Homeless Housing Act is created, authorizing the Emergency Shelter Grant Program and transitional housing demonstration program, both administered by HUD.

The Homeless Eligibility Clarification Act removes barriers to voting, including the permanent address requirement. Removing this requirement also makes homeless people able to access programs including SSI, veterans' benefits, Aid to Families with Dependent Children (AFDC), food stamps, and Medicaid.

1987   The Urgent Relief for the Homeless Act includes emergency provisions for homeless individuals and families. It was later renamed the Stewart B. McKinney Homeless Assistance Act, after Representative Stewart McKinney, who died of pneumonia contracted during a homeless protest sleep out.

The Stewart B. McKinney Homeless Assistance Act (P.L. 100–77) (amended in 1988, 1990, 1992, and 1994) establishes a federal definition of homelessness. It establishes the U.S. Interagency Council on Homelessness and authorizes the emergency food and shelter programs administered by HUD and Federal Emergency Management Agency (FEMA). This act includes using surplus federal property as homeless housing and several programs under the Department of Health and Human Services. It expands the food stamp program and authorizes four additional programs to address education for children, youth, and adults.

The Urban Institute, under the direction of Martha Burt and Barbara Cohen, estimates double the number of homeless people reported by HUD. They use a stratified random sample of homeless users of shelters and soup kitchens for their estimate.

The Low-Income Housing Tax Credit is signed into law to compensate developers for units they acquire, build, or rehabilitate for low- and moderate-income renters.

1989   The National Law Center on Homelessness and Poverty is founded by Maria Foscarinis. This national-level organization focuses on legal advocacy and ultimately an end to homelessness in the United States.

1990   The Office of HIV/AIDS Housing is created to manage housing for people with HIV/AIDS under Housing Opportunities for People with Aids (HOPWA) program.

The National Affordable Housing Act reaffirms the nation's commitment to providing adequate and affordable housing for families. It does not mean a commitment to housing or shelter for all citizens but reiterates the national goal of partnering with states to make affordable housing accessible.

The Census Bureau conducts a "shelter and street" or S-Night count of the number of homeless people. It finds 179,000 people in shelters and 50,000 on the street.

The Hate Crimes Statistics Act (28 U.S.C. § 534) (HCSA) is passed. It requires data collection on hate crimes that are motivated by bias on the basis of race and ethnicity, disability, sexual orientation, religion, and other categories.

The Cranston-Gonzalez National Affordable Housing Act (42 U.S. Code § 12703) is passed. It includes the HOME Program and is designed to help families and individuals achieve the goal of affordable housing and home ownership.

McKinney-Vento is reauthorized to reduce barriers to a free and equal education for homeless youth and children. Money is distributed to states for direct educational services.

1994   The Violence Against Women Act (VAWA) is passed. It offers guidance on and support to prevent rape and physical assault. It makes battery a criminal offense and requires states to cooperate in enforcing orders of protection. VAWA is reauthorized in 2000 and 2005, increasing legal protection for victims and available services and resources.

McKinney-Vento is reauthorized again to increase educational services and better collaboration between states and localities.

1999   The Glass Steagall Act is repealed. This means that investment and retail banks can be consolidated into financial holding companies. These new entities are supervised by the Federal Reserve. Many banks did not want federal oversight and requirements. Those that did submit to increased regulation became giants, considered "too big to fail," necessitating their bailout during the Great Recession.

2000 The Developmental Disabilities Assistance and Bill of Rights Act (P.L. 106–402, 106th Congress) is passed. It provides specific ways for families and individuals with disabilities to have greater influence over the policies that serve them.

President Clinton passes legislation to rename the Stewart B. McKinney Homeless Assistance Act in honor of Representative Bruce Vento. It officially becomes the McKinney-Vento Homeless Assistance Act.

2001 The Homeless Veterans Comprehensive Assistance Act (H.R. 2716) is signed into law. It expands support and benefits, with the overall goal of ending chronic homelessness among veterans in ten years.

Congress reauthorizes the McKinney Vento Act through the No Child Left Behind Act of 2001. It expands provisions to ensure equal access to education for homeless children and youth.

2002 The U.S. Interagency Council on Homelessness begins the Chronic Homelessness Initiative, requiring states to develop ten-year plans to end chronic homelessness.

Philip Mangano is hired to lead the White House Interagency Council on Homelessness under George W. Bush. He garners widespread national support for the development of ten-year plans, a focus on Housing First, and programs that minimize cost while reducing or ending homelessness.

2003 Chronic homelessness is officially defined by HUD as "an unaccompanied homeless individual with a disabling condition who has either been continuously homeless for a year or more or has had at least four episodes of homelessness in the past three years." (HUD 2010). Ending chronic homelessness in ten years also becomes an official national goal.

2005 (January) The nation's first point-in-time count of homeless people is conducted. It is an annual requirement for all regions receiving federal assistance and includes sheltered and unsheltered people, subpopulations, and an inventory of available housing and shelter beds.

2007 Housing prices begin a precipitous fall, a sign of the impending subprime mortgage crisis.

2008 (October) The Troubled Asset Relief Program (TARP) is approved by Congress. It is part of the Emergency Economic Stabilization Act. Through this act, the federal government invests $475 billion on a range of initiatives. The most controversial are those that bail out big business, including $245 billion for eight of the nation's most prominent banks, $80 billion goes for auto giants GM and Chrysler, and $68 billion to the insurance giant AIG. In comparison, a mere $46 billion goes to foreclosure prevention for individuals and families.

Barack Obama is elected President. He is the first African American President and goes on to serve two terms and oversee the nation's effort to end veteran homelessness.

The Emergency Economic Stabilization Act (P.L. 110–343) is signed into law as a response to the subprime mortgage crisis. It is designed to restore financial stability and liquidity but bails out big business and, for that reason, remains controversial.

The Housing and Economic Recovery Act (HERA) is signed into law. It provides support for subprime borrowers by offering $300 billion in fixed-rate mortgages. Additional tax credits and mortgage and loan provisions are included. This act establishes the National Housing Trust Fund to support the creation and maintenance of rental housing for low-income and very low-income renters.

The Second Chance Act is signed into law. It is overseen by the Department of Justice, offering funding to government agencies and local organizations to prevent recidivism. As of 2017, over 160,000 people who were incarcerated participated in these programs and returned to their communities.

2009   (May 20) The Homeless Emergency Assistance and Rapid Transition to Housing (HEARTH) Act is signed into law through a reauthorization of McKinney-Vento. It focuses on rapid rehousing for individuals and families and better federal coordination of efforts to track and end homelessness including the use of systems performance measures as part of the PIT count.

2010   The first federal plan to end homelessness, *Opening Doors: A Federal Strategic Plan*, is released. Its goals are to end veteran homelessness in five years, chronic homelessness in seven years, and homelessness for families, youth, and children in ten years. It also suggests creating a path to end all types of homelessness.

2015   The Every Student Succeeds Act (ESSA) is signed into law in December, replacing the No Child Left Behind Act. ESSA increased the scope of assistance to focus on birth through higher education and a focus on college and career readiness.

2019   H.R. 1856, the Ending Homelessness Act is introduced to Congress as a bill to provide over $13 billion in emergency relief funding for key programs and initiatives related to homeless housing, services, and technical assistance.

2020   (March) The Coronavirus Aid, Relief, and Economic Security (CARES) Act is signed into law, offering emergency funding for states to implement social distancing measures, in place of congregate shelter. The CARES Act also offers unemployment assistance and a moratorium on evictions, as a result of the pandemic.

2021   The American Rescue Plan Act of 2021 is passed, under the Biden-Harris administration. It offers a series of measures designed to preserve existing housing, serve rural and under-served communities, and prevent renters and owners from becoming homeless.

Reference

U.S. Department of Housing and Urban Development. 2010. *The 2009 Annual Homeless Assessment Report to Congress.* Washington, DC: Office of Community Planning and Development.

This glossary includes terms and acronyms related to homeless services, policies, and legislation. It offers definitions that organize the nation's understanding of homelessness in general and for specific subpopulations. Most of the terms included are not only featured in this book but are also common in homeless policy, research, and advocacy arenas. This glossary highlights the crises and controversies included in earlier chapters and focuses on causes and solutions.

Affordable housing   The U.S. Department of Housing and Urban Development (HUD) defines affordable housing as that which costs no more than 30 percent of a family or individual's gross income, including utilities. Housing affordability is based on the area mean income (AMI), which can vary from state to state.

AHAR   Annual Homeless Assessment Report to Congress. This report is based on the annual point-in-time (PIT) count and the housing inventory count (HIC). It uses snapshot counts done on a single night in January and annual data collected through the Homeless Management Information System (HMIS).

Aid to Families with Dependent Children (AFDC)   AFDC was authorized by the Social Security Act in 1935. Popularly known as "welfare," AFDC became controversial in the 1970s and 1980s because of increasing costs. The 1996 Personal Responsibility and Work Opportunity Reconciliation Act (PRWORA) replaced AFDC with Temporary Assistance for Needy Families (TANF).

Authorization   This is the first part of the federal funding process. Authorization is the approval or continuation of a specific program or activity and often specifies appropriations or funding as well.

Chronic homelessness   Chronic homelessness is defined as someone with a disabling condition and long-term or frequent episodes of homelessness. HUD's official definition specifies the length of time of homeless episodes to include four distinct episodes totaling twelve months in a three-year period and spaced at least seven days apart. If living at an institution, upon exit, up to ninety days of their stay counts toward their time homeless. Homeless service providers are responsible for verifying chronic homelessness using this definition.

Community Development Block Grants (CDBG)   These are federal grants distributed by HUD to states, cities, and communities to fund programs related to economic opportunity and community improvement. They apply to the entire community, with a specific focus on low- and moderate-income households.

Continuum of care (CoC)   A CoC region is an area that coordinates federal funding and homeless services and housing. CoC regions can include cities, states, towns, or rural areas. CoC regions are responsible for planning across a range of services including outreach, emergency, transitional, and permanent housing. They conduct the annual count of homeless people and document shelter and housing bed use. They also coordinate data entry on homeless programs using HMIS.

Co-occurring   This term refers to two or more risk factors, like mental illness and disability status, that one homeless person experiences at the same time. Also called "co-morbidity," risk factors are used to prioritize people for housing based on mortality risk.

Criminalization   Criminalization refers to laws and practices that target homeless people. The National Law Center on Homelessness and Poverty documents forms of criminalization that violate homeless people's constitutional rights. Common forms of criminalization include sweeps of homeless encampments, citations for sleeping and camping, and panhandling.

Emergency shelter Emergency shelters are facilities that offer temporary access to a bed and may offer basic amenities including showers and meals. They are often bare-bones, congregate living spaces that require adherence to rules and requirements. Many are closed during the day or, in some areas, open only during the coldest months of the year.

Homeless Management Information System (HMIS) This is a database tool, first introduced in 2004, to allow providers to track service use over time, not merely in a one-time snapshot count. HMIS compares service use across programs and communities, allowing for greater detail than the PIT count.

Housing Choice Voucher Program (Section 8) This HUD program is administered through public housing agencies and allows homeless people, as well as those who are elderly or disabled, to rent in the private market. They typically pay about 30 percent of their income for a rental unit.

Housing First This is an approach to homelessness that advocates for housing as a first step toward ending homelessness. In this sense, it reverses the usual, step-wise progression from outreach to emergency shelter, to transitional, and eventually permanent housing. This approach originated with the Pathways to Housing Program in New York City. This program emphasizes the need for ongoing supportive services along with safe and stable long-term housing.

Housing inventory count (HIC) Data from the HIC is used in the annual AHAR to provide a count of the number of homeless beds in a CoC region. The five possible types of housing included in this inventory are emergency shelter, transitional housing, rapid rehousing, safe haven, and permanent supportive housing.

NIMBY "Not in my backyard." This acronym symbolizes how many residents feel when homeless shelters want to locate in their neighborhoods. The sentiment of NIMBYism has been strong enough to relegate shelters and service facilities to marginal city areas, far from other services.

Permanent supportive housing (PSH) This form of housing offers low-barrier assistance to individuals with disabilities. PSH offers rental assistance and ongoing, voluntary support services to address physical as well as mental health and other issues.

Personal Responsibility and Work Opportunity Act (PRWORA) This act was signed into law in 1996. It replaced AFDC with TANF, imposed stringent work requirements, and shortened the duration of assistance. PRWORA symbolized a change in welfare policy aimed at reducing spending and making employment an eligibility requirement.

Point-in-time (PIT) count The PIT count happens annually, during the last week of January. Every CoC region receiving federal support provides a count of the number of homeless people. Those in shelters are counted annually, and those who are unsheltered are counted every other year. Although some jurisdictions elect to perform annual unsheltered counts.

Single rent occupancy (SRO) SROs are typically large buildings that operate as hotels, charging minimum rates for low-income renters. Although they provide affordable housing, SROs are also susceptible to gentrification and are often the first to be redeveloped for economic gain.

Temporary Assistance for Needy Families (TANF) With the passage of PRWORA, TANF replaced AFDC. TANF imposed increased work requirements and shorter time limits for receiving assistance. TANF is administered to states through a fixed-amount block grant designed to limit federal welfare spending.

Transitional housing (TSH) Transitional housing, or transitional supportive housing, is a midway point between emergency and permanent supportive housing. It is typically for homeless people who are able to work or who contribute a portion of their income for housing. It can be part of an existing shelter facility or housed separately.

Note: Page numbers in *italics* refers to figures and page numbers in **bold** refers to tables.

About the Author

Michele Wakin is a professor of sociology and faculty director of the Center for Urban Poverty. She received a master's degree in education from Boston University and a master's degree in sociology from the University of California, where she earned her PhD in 2005. Her research interests include homelessness and poverty, inequality, and urban and community studies. Dr. Wakin has published in the journals *American Behavioral Scientist*, *City & Community*, and the *Journal of Workplace Rights*. She has published two books on homelessness, *Otherwise Homeless: Vehicle Living and the Culture of Homelessness*, in 2014, and *Hobo Jungle: A Homeless Community in Paradise*, in 2020. She was the recipient of the Ernest A. Lynton Citation for Distinguished Engaged Scholarship for Early Career Faculty, and her research has been funded by the U.S. department of Housing and Urban Development, the Centers for Disease Control and Prevention, the Institute for Labor and Employment, and the American Sociological Association.